A LIGHT
IN
DARK TIMES

MAXINE GREENE
AND THE UNFINISHED CONVERSATION

A LIGHT IN DARK TIMES

MAXINE GREENE
AND THE UNFINISHED CONVERSATION

EDITED BY

William Ayers and Janet L. Miller

TEACHERS
COLLEGE
PRESS

Teachers College, Columbia University
New York and London

For Maxine

---

*The photo montage on pp. 132–133 was created at the
Museum of Education at the University of South Carolina
by Lyn B. Rose under the direction of Craig Kridel, curator.*

Published by Teachers College Press, 1234 Amsterdam Avenue, New York, NY 10027

Library of Congress Cataloging-in-Publication Data

A light in dark times : Maxine Green and the unfinished
    conversation / edited by William Ayers and Janet L. Miller.
        p.   cm.
    Includes bibliographical references and index.
      ISBN 0-8077-3721-6 (cloth : alk. paper). — ISBN 0-8077-3720-8
(pbk. : alk. paper)
        1. Greene, Maxine.   2. Education—Philosophy.   3. Education—
Social aspects—United States.   4. Educational change.   I. Greene,
Maxine.   II. Ayers, William. 1944–   .   III. Miller, Janet L., 1945–   .

    LB885.G682T43   1997
    370'.1—dc21   97-38316

ISBN 0-8077-3720-8 (paper)
ISBN 0-8077-3721-6 (cloth)

Printed on acid-free paper

Manufactured in the United States of America

05   04   03   02   01   00   99   98   8   7   6   5   4   3   2   1

Contents

v

Publisher's Note

A painter I know, talking of art and the imagination, explains provocatively that in the process of making or knowing art, nothing remains of the imagination at all. In the end, you use it up and if you've used it well, what's left may be art. An active engagement with art leaves you breathless with its realness, consumed by its obdurateness, convinced of its inability to be any other way–ness. An encounter with Maxine Greene is much the same—there is a vividness that cannot be denied. Such encounter need not be personal: In her writing, her pull is equally strong, equally bright, equally gritty, equally unyielding. When she lends us her humanity and her intellect and refuses to give up either the poetry or the horror, we are richer and can be borrowed from in turn. The touch of Maxine Greene, softly urgent, moves us to act politically and humanly, spurs us to shun the light and reject the dark if together they cannot move us to act. Our imagination, fed by the glorious images she places before us, cannot be left in peace to enjoy simple beauty or simple justice—those "castles in the air." She implores us to mark the images and somehow, to resist. In the universe according to Maxine Greene, nothing is simple, nothing literal. We can only look over our shoulders and push onward in dark times.

In her writing and her speaking, when she reads a poem to us, describes a painting, a moment in dance or music or theater, we meet our own understanding and we are fully conscious. Her words rush one after another to make images of connections for us, ideas unconcealed for us, made real for us through her passionate, particular choices. We awake to the immediacy of her vision, the urgency of her message. No longer cynical, we can take new risks, tilt at windmills, separate out and listen to voices that were muffled before—we can become more human. When Maxine connects us to another's way of seeing, we feel powerful and compassionate and vulnerable all at once. We believe things can change and that somehow we can be a part of it. You cannot leave an encounter with Maxine Greene anesthetized—exhilarated, perhaps, or despairing, thrown off balance, always in the midst. . . .

I am neither colleague nor student of Maxine's in the usual sense. I am sometimes privileged to publish her words and in the course of that a friendship grew. Being here at TC, I could catch her—always breathless, just back from/just going to something interesting, something uncompleted, something requiring her presence and her passion. Yet sometimes a different kind of space opens and there comes a moment or two for coffee across the street. Ranging forward and back, among topics of rage and mind, we have never once failed to come around to our lived lives—to our children, our husbands, our families, our friends. And at the end, I am exhilarated or despairing, off balance, and always in the midst. . . .

Actions speak louder than words—unless you are a publisher. For a publisher, actions *are* words, and most of the time, that is a sobering thought. If you have had the good fortune to publish Maxine Greene, every now and then, the burden lifts and you can feel pleasure. By now, the exact origins of this book have been lost. Maxine is here, like the imagination, in the making and in relation to. Suffice it to say that planning went on for a very long time, the editors were sensitive to the concerns of their subject, and the publisher was too involved by half. Homage was not intended nor would it have been tolerated—canonization is not an option when you are in the process of becoming as Maxine Greene is. If an anti-icon exists, Maxine is its physical embodiment. And yet. . . .

To confront the power of her work and her ideas and to extend our own work shaped by that confrontation; to trace a trail so that others might search the ideas out for themselves; to turn them, flex them, and always keep the world in view—this seems a worthy purpose.

Carole Saltz

Preface

Maxine Greene described herself recently as "stumbling around with mostly questions, questions that continually arise, questions aching in my throat, questions leading to partial answers opening to other questions."

She was speaking at the art school at the University of Michigan, and it is fair to say that the students—tattooed and body-pierced with gaudy hair—were startled by this tiny woman with her huge vision, awed by her prodigious energy.

Maxine Greene invites us to "do philosophy," to struggle with ideas, with the arts, with the events of the world, with the daily newspapers and our idiosyncratic chance encounters—all in order to become more aware of ourselves and our world, more aware of our inter-subjective predicaments, and then, importantly, to act on our awarenesses. To act on what we find; to act, even with partial consciousness; to act, even with contingent understanding; to act, to be a participant in the world.

Maxine Greene invites diverse voices and unsettled questions, and she helps us to fight the vicious forms of relativism: cynicism, passivity, action-taming skepticism. She wants to change things.

She demands commitment and purposeful living, but she simultaneously fights the dogmas that ultimately distort and defeat those commitments. Maxine Greene is the preeminent American philosopher of education today. Her prolific outpouring of articles and books, her prodigious lecture schedule, and her ongoing teaching responsibilities have had an enormous impact on generations of teachers, researchers, academics, and school reform activists. Because her field is by nature boundary-crossing, and because her message is genre-blurring, she has unique influence in a range of worlds: arts and aesthetics, literature and literacy studies, cultural studies, school change and improvement, the teaching of literacy, teacher education, peace and social justice, women's studies, civil rights.

This book focuses on the issues and questions raised by Maxine Greene over several decades: social imagination, the place of activism, the importance of the arts, progressive school change, the role of culture, the meaning of freedom in the modern world. It is pointed toward the future, toward exploring these themes into the twenty-first century. While Maxine Greene's intellectual contribution and influence is touchstone, each author is identified and concerned with his or her ongoing works and projects, and this is the substance of each chapter. Each author takes off from Maxine Greene, a living, dynamic thinker and teacher, and moves forward. Each, in his or her own way, follows Maxine Greene's challenge to break through the frozen, the routine, the unexamined.

On the faculty at Teachers College, Columbia University, since 1966, Maxine Greene has taught courses in social philosophy, the philosophy and history of education, literature, writing, aesthetics, and education. She held the William F. Russell Chair in the Foundations of Education from 1975 to 1994 and is now Professor Emerita. As founder and director of the Center for Social Imagination, the Arts, and Education, she is currently working with schools and the arts community in New York and holds a monthly "educational salon" with city teachers in her home. Before coming to Teachers College, she taught at New York University, Montclair State College, and Brooklyn College. She has lectured widely at universities and educational associations here and abroad, was a Fulbright scholar briefly in New Zealand, and has participated in a number of European conferences on higher education. She is a past president of the Philosophy of Education Society, the American Educational Studies Association, and the American Educational Research Association. Her academic awards include a Delta Gamma Kappa Award for *Teacher as Stranger* as the "Educational Book of the Year" in 1974, two Phi Delta Kappa "Teacher of the Year" awards, the Teachers College Medal, honorary degrees from Hofstra University, Lehigh University, Indiana University, the University of Colorado, Bank Street College of Education, the University of Rochester, Nazareth College, the College of Misericordia, and McGill University. Her other books are: *Existential Encounters for Teachers, The Public School and the Private Vision, Landscapes of Learning, The Dialectic of Freedom,* and *Releasing the Imagination.* Maxine Greene continues to teach and write in interdisciplinary areas. She finds it impossible, apparently, to stop inviting students and colleagues to "do philosophy" in their own voices, to become more aware of their situations, to resist what they find unacceptable. She still hopes to create spaces where people will be willing to confront issues as they become visible in their consciousness and lived lives, to pose incisive questions, and to respond reflectively and actively to what they are able to disclose.

As she told us in a recent conversation: "When you have been around a long time and published enough, you can get installed on an unmerited pedestal. I try to avoid that, to keep saying I am still trying in these dreary days, that I do not know the answers, that I am still striving to pose the questions. And I am more and more convinced of the absolute necessity for encounters with the several arts from the range of cultures to keep imagination alive, to release young and old from confinement in single, closed rooms. . . . Asking, imagining, writing, teaching, I try with my companions, with my students, with live and wide-awake people . . . (in my own fashion) to awaken. Yes, I understand the absurdity; I know it does not matter under the blankness of the sky. But I have to resist meaninglessness along with objectness and cruelty and injustice. Otherwise, why live?"

Indeed, Maxine Greene is for many of us a light in dark times.

I

SEEING PAST EXPERIENCES
IN NEW WAYS

Looking back, I find myself seeing past experiences in new ways—and I realize what it means to say that I have lived one possible life among many—and that there are openings even today to untapped possibilities.

Maxine Greene
Releasing the Imagination

None of us can think of our own lives, can remember events and people and situations without some consideration of context, without some mention of social milieu, cultural forces, institutional life, historic moment. And as soon as we consider context, writ large, we are unable to retreat into a kind of privatism, or to withdraw from the world in ways that some versions of biographical self-exploration promote. Instead, we can periodically review our lives within contexts to which we must learn to attend in order to fight a plague, rebuild a school, tutor a child, or paint a canvas that makes a difference.

And so we look back, not just as a way of remembering our lives, but as an incentive for action. We remember our connections to particular individuals and places and events in order to see what still needs to be done, what still needs our attention as we move toward "untapped possibilities" for ourselves and others.

For a long while, Maxine Greene has been reminding us of the necessity for people to seek out their own human possibilities. Those possibilities exist only in relation and commitment to others and to taking action in an unjust and fragmented world:

I wish it were really easy to see consequences of our teaching. Sometimes five years later you get a letter. I had a funny experience on a bus; I got on a bus in New York and a man was getting off and he looked at me and said (this is a very common phrase), "Maxine Greene, my God. I had you." I thought, well, that's good, he remembered. He wasn't afraid to remember. I'm interested in the kind of reflection and remembering that involves making changes in a particular situation, not just an admiring of it, but an identification of deficiencies and lacks, and an effort to overcome those lacks. Dewey talked about thinking as the idea that knowledge involves participation in which the individual goes beyond, breaking through structures, trying to build new structures. Dewey always talked about the fact that it isn't simply experience, it is reflection on experience that enables individuals to understand that they must continue choosing themselves as they live. Experience itself is just one thing after another, and you try to pattern it by organizing and to make sense of it by reflecting, by turning back on yourself and reflecting on your own stream of experience. You ask yourself, "How does this world present itself to me? Against my own background, my own biography?" . . .

And so teaching is a question of trying to empower persons to change their own worlds in the light of their desires and their reflections, not to change it for them. The point of it all is for individuals to make sense of their own situations. Their social situations, their root situations have to feed back into their own sense making and their own actions. That's why it's so hard to know if you have any effect, really. If teachers come and tell me I saved their souls, I think I've failed. If a teacher comes and tells me, "You know, my kids got together and went to the principal's office and objected to the tracking that was going on," then I think, "Well, not too bad." (Miller, 1978)

REFERENCES

Miller, J. L. (1978, May). *An Interview with Maxine Greene*. Videotape. The Curriculum Collection, Museum of Education, University of South Carolina.

1

Doing Philosophy: Maxine Greene and the Pedagogy of Possibility

William Ayers

The venerable hall where John Dewey had lectured years before was filled to overflowing on that first fall evening, awaiting the start of Maxine Greene's introduction to philosophy class. The air was expectant; the antique room reeked of tradition and nostalgia. I was a new graduate student, and several people had told me to take this class, but I had never met Maxine Greene and had no idea what to expect. The topic was quaint, perhaps even decrepit—my expectations were decidedly low. And yet in the often familiar, sometimes odd collision of chance and choice, I found myself that first night only a couple of rows from the front—eye to eye with the podium—when Professor Greene arrived. I didn't know it then, of course, but it would become a seat I would seek out at every opportunity during my years at Teachers College and beyond.

Maxine Greene entered the room slowly, surrounded by animated students, weighted down with two shoulder bags brimming with papers and an overload of notes and books. I saw an already diminutive woman made tiny by the cargo accompanying her, and yet luminous somehow at the center of a crowd, the sudden, surprising eye of the storm. She moved steadily toward the podium, stopping often, speaking in turn to each student who sought advice for this, permission or a signature for that, and unloaded the chaos of paper and books, shuffling steadily through it, sorting, arranging, re-arranging, speaking all the while. By the time the last student had retreated to her seat—and without announcement or formal notice—class was underway. Like an intimate conversation with an old friend that is picked up, carried on, and then interrupted to be con-

An earlier version of this chapter was published in Kridel, C., Bullough, R. V., Jr., and Shaker, P. (1996), *Teachers and mentors*, pp. 117–126. New York: Garland.

tinued in the future, Maxine Greene's lecture was filled with spontaneity, intimacy, incompleteness, and forward motion.

"We were talking earlier—some of us—about what it might mean to *do* philosophy," she was saying, "as opposed to analyzing positions or searching exclusively for clarifying language. What might it mean to pose distinctive kinds of questions with respect to our own practice and our own lived situations, the kinds of questions that might make us more than 'accidental tourists,' more than clerks or bureaucrats or functionaries?"

Her way of speaking had lost nothing from a Brooklyn upbringing, and it was infused, moreover, with a lifetime encountering literature, existentialism, politics; her voice, husky from the ubiquitous cigarettes she then smoked, was filled, as well, with purpose and passion. Philosophy, she explained, had been understood in the classical mode to be a "love of wisdom" or the "queen of the sciences"; once philosophers broke with the notion that reason was tied inexorably to the "eyes of the mind"— and that Truth, Beauty, Goodness, and so on, could be apprehended by those wise enough or privileged enough to see through those eyes—philosophy began to be variously conceived. If it was any longer a "queen" at all, it was a queen whose crown had slipped considerably—it became a second-order discipline, one that did not possess its own ascertainable knowledge, one that was obligated to criticize, to question, to examine, to think about. William James had said that philosophy begins in wonder; Ludwig Wittgenstein associated it with resisting the "bewitchment of intelligence by means of language"; John Dewey with thinking about "what the known demands" in terms of attitude and action. Others thought about "doctrines ignorantly entertained," about "thinking about our own thinking," about the "identification of options and alternatives." Isaiah Berlin had spoken of philosophers "asking queer questions," not to be confused with ordinary factual questions or questions to be settled by logical argument or mathematical inquiry.

"Where is the nearest school?" Maxine Greene asked. "And how do state regulations affect that school? Does the curriculum include both physics and chemistry? Such questions, obviously, are variously answerable—like questions in the social sciences and even the natural sciences. But they are not the queer questions Berlin had in mind. Contrast them, then, with these: How are we to understand freedom? How are we to understand fairness, and how can it be reconciled with individual rights? How can we justify a commitment to critical reflection, aesthetic awareness, open-ended growth, or intercultural understanding to a public preoccupied with the need to focus on skills and proficiencies alone? Or more specifically, is it fair that my child be bussed to another neighborhood to go to school? Is it possible for the child of fundamentalists, say, to study Darwinian evolution in school and still accede to the creationist position? These are the types of questions that arouse the philosopher."

No philosopher myself, I was nonetheless aroused, as if startled from a dream by a flash of lightning. Professor Greene was challenging the popular notions of philosophy as a credo ("my philosophy is") or a high-sounding irrelevance ("that's just philosophy") or a condition of resignation ("I was philosophical about it"). She told us that when she had begun graduate school and had told her mother that she was studying philosophy, her mother had given her a long, cold look, full of disdain, and responded, "All right, Maxine, *say* something in philosophy."

But much more than discussing philosophy, she was challenging her students (and, I felt, me, personally) to join her in "doing philosophy": becoming more intentional and aware; confronting issues as they emerged in our own consciousness and our lives; interrogating our situations carefully and responding thoughtfully to what we uncovered and discovered. I thought of Amilcar Cabral's admonition to African revolutionaries: "Tell no lies; claim no easy victories." And I remembered Paul Potter's advice to young radicals in the early sixties: "Live your life so as not to make a mockery of your values." I was captivated.

"Doing philosophy" with Maxine Greene could be—had to be—both exhausting and exhilarating. Keeping up was the first challenge: She is a person on whom nothing is lost, an intensely observant person, vigorous as well as open in pursuing what is there to be seen. She sees largely what narrower minds miss, and sees particularity in vivid, nuanced detail. She is a voracious and acquisitive reader—and she reads, beyond philosophy, literature, science, the arts, politics, poetry, educational research, essays on feminism, and more—and the sources of her thinking include all of that as well as films and music and paintings and conversations and chance encounters and dance and political rallies. She somehow maintains the capacity to access a huge amount of what she has encountered, and she seems to draw infinitely upon it, inventing new connections, surprising ways of seeing, remarkable ways of being and acting. In one class session, we talked of the role of the arts in human consciousness and the ways in which "only beings who can think about the ways they are determined can free themselves." References were made that evening to Alice Walker, *Billy Budd,* Sartre and Dewey, Hannah Arendt, Isaac Asimov, Nat Hentoff, the murder of Leon Klinghoffer (who has a name) and the countless Palestinians in the bombed-out refugee camps (who remain nameless), "Breaker Morant," *A Room of One's Own,* and the cab driver who had told Maxine earlier that day that he hated the Cloisters because "it's up on that hill."

The explosion of the rocket ship carrying the teacher into space focused class another evening on the American infatuation with technology—"technicism" Maxine called it—and the degradation of science in the twentieth century through its marriage to technology, and on *Shoah* and Hiroshima and Lao-tse and Marguerite Duras and Albert Camus. "The problems we face," she said, "are not really technical—they are moral, they are ethical. A reliance on technical solutions leaves us still gasping, still empty."

At the very least students were given access to an active mind, inquiring openly and in full view. Because she harvested her teaching from her own lived experience, it always had an improvisational feel to it—fresh and vital and inventive, yes, but also firmly rooted in a coherent ground of core beliefs and large purposes. We could see imagination at work, and questioning that knew no limits, and dialectics. And students were invited, if they chose, to join in, to open themselves in dialogue and pursuit. "The purpose of this course is to shock ourselves into new awarenesses of what we take for granted and often do not see," she announced in her course outline. "It is to try to empower individuals to clarify and ground their own beliefs about the projects they have chosen for themselves to the end of creating themselves as thoughtful, articulate, critical, and humane practitioners in a profoundly uncertain world." When I hear people today talking about "high expectations for learners," and watch that, too, degenerate into a slogan, I think of Maxine Greene's expectations of us as a standard to strive toward, and of "shocking ourselves into new awarenesses" as a goal.

"My field of study is lived situations," she said one night, and that notion hit like a thunderbolt. She was gleefully blurring genres—philosophy, anthropology, literature, psychology, science, the arts—knocking down barriers, insisting on her right (and ours) to use everything—any discipline, any curriculum, any encounter—as nourishment, as a source to pose our own questions, confront our own problems, challenge our own fates. "I was proposing an arts project to a local school council last week," she said. "The council voted to spend their money on metal detectors instead. I was inadequate to explain the importance of the arts. On the other hand, what do I know of guns and knives and the importance of metal detectors? Maybe they're right."

"We are free and fated, fated and free," she often said, quoting Hannah Arendt, one of her teachers years before. "We are conditioned, entangled, thrust into a world not of our choosing, but also free to understand what is happening to us, to interpret, to envision possibilities, to act against all the 'determinisms,' to repair the deficiencies we find. We cannot choose to live in a non-nuclear world, for example, but we can, indeed, we must choose who to be in light of the threat of nuclear annihilation. Like Dewey, we can look at the world as if it could be otherwise, and then act on our own freedom." She told us, for example, about her feelings of horror as homelessness overwhelmed the city. One cold night, taking pity on a man she often saw sleeping across from her apartment, she steeled herself and invited him in for dinner. "What do you want from me, lady?" he snapped. "I ain't going nowhere with you." She admitted a sense of relief.

These were some of the riveting themes of her teaching (and her life). There are others:

- People are "condemned to meaning"—sentenced to create meaningful lives in the face of disorder and inhumanity, to read our lived worlds and to name ourselves in "our dreadful freedom."
- We can, with John Dewey, conceive of "mind as a verb rather than a noun," and can thereby open to the possibility of attentiveness, engagement, and action.
- Encounters with the arts can provide powerful opportunities for confronting the blandness of life and imagining a different world, a more humane social order.
- Freedom is neither an endowment nor a commodity nor an icon; freedom is not the Statue of Liberty, the flag, or any little fetish. Freedom can be thought of as a refusal of the fixed, a reaching for possibility, an engagement with obstacles and barriers and a resistant world, an achievement to be sought in a web of relationships, an intersubjective reality.
- To be human is to be involved in a quest, a fundamental life project that is situated and undertaken as a refusal to accede to the given.
- Teaching, too, involves a sense of the possible, of seeing alternatives, of opening new landscapes.
- The opposite of "moral" in our lives is not "immoral," but is, more typically, "indifferent," "thoughtless," or "careless."

None of this, for her, was put forth in class as simple, self-evident, or settled. She was not easily satisfied with principles or commandments or laws, even (or especially) her own. She demonstrated again and again a resistance to fad, to convention, to dogma of any kind. She chastised and prodded herself for our benefit, insisting on our right, indeed our responsibility to choose: "But still, I can't help myself, I wish you would choose Mozart and not rap." Pausing she added, "But maybe rap is better than Kohlberg in raising sharp moral issues."

Criticized by a student for assigning Marx, whose ignorance and insensitivity to issues of race and gender were righteously exposed, she replied, "I think you're quite right, but, then, I don't go to Marx to learn about racism or sexism." Challenged by a group of students to cancel class for the Jewish holidays, she steadfastly refused: "I don't celebrate religious holidays, but, of course, I recognize the importance of this to you." She typed her notes from class that evening and scheduled another class for any who wanted. And on another evening, when some students pushed the chairs and desks into a large circle as an emblem of equality and open discussion, she entered with a look of mild disdain, took her assigned seat, and said, "I don't think any of you signed up for this class to hear from each person equally. I certainly want access to your needs and desires, but I am not enslaved by them. I want to welcome your responsiveness, too, but let's not make a fetish of chairs in a circle."

"Some of us look with optimism at America becoming great again," she said one night. "We feel pious, patriotic, competent, and taken with the possibility of upward mobility. Others look with dread at a militaristic resurgence, at American power tied to indifference and decreasing public participation, American wealth amidst vast poverty." She challenged students to think of how their consciousness of the world plays on the way each of us looks at our own roles and responsibilities: "I must challenge mostly the muffled view, the way routines and methodical systems allow a life of habit and not choice."

The challenge, as always, was to choose in the muddy complexity of living a life without benefit of any entirely adequate road maps, or any court of last resort. Maxine Greene is a person of strong opinion and point of view and action, who can simultaneously question almost everything and use almost anything as a source of her questioning. She can act on behalf of her values and still hold even her own beliefs as, if not entirely contingent, at least worth another look. She can work hard and speak eloquently on behalf of women's rights, for example, or peace, or the environment—calling her an "anti-imperialist," an "environmentalist," or even a "feminist" feels somewhat false, a superficial reduction in her case. She is somehow beyond the labels, even the "good" ones, and perhaps in that there is an abiding lesson for all of us: "My field of study is lived situations"; "my goal is to challenge the taken-for-granted, the frozen and the bound and the restricted." When a group of curriculum "reconceptualists" attempted, she feared, to make her a kind of guru, she stopped going to meetings—I was reminded of Bob Moses, a civil rights leader in the South, changing his name when people insisted on him becoming a modern-day savior. When the "critical pedagogy" people embraced her, she continued interrogating and challenging all the pedantic posturing, all the certainty and settledness of the new dogmas. Running into an old friend at a Paulo Freire conference years ago—

someone making a name for himself as a neo-Marxist educator—I was asked, "You study with Maxine Greene; she's somewhat quaint, soft in her thinking, isn't she?" That he has moved from Marxism to "cultural liberation" is somehow not surprising. As for Maxine Greene, she embodies relationship, connectedness, attentiveness, aliveness to possibility, engagement with complexities—her own life project of citizen philosopher, activist, teacher. "Teacher can be posited as a goal, something to reach for," she said. "If ever I've arrived, I'm dead." This is what she seeks, imagines, holds as a possibility.

I was fortunate—I began teaching at the age of twenty in 1965 in a project linked closely with the civil rights movement. Our models were citizenship schools and freedom schools springing up all over the South, teach-ins just beginning in the large universities, and Myles Horton's Highlander Folk School. I absorbed the idea early that the hope for freedom and the practice of education could be linked, that teaching could be a powerful and natural key to social change. Because I first discovered and invented my teaching in upheaval it has remained, for me, an adventure full of struggle and quest, part of something larger, something far beyond itself. Teaching as pacification, teaching as the transmission of some certified, sanctified stuff, teaching as classification or invasion—this is what we were working against. What we sought was teaching as dialogue, teaching as resistance, teaching as action toward freedom.

And so when I was swept away from the classroom to a direct and dangerous confrontation with war and the state during those turbulent times, I experienced an unexpected coherence. Returning to a more formal teaching situation years later, I stepped into something close and familiar. No doubt, in teaching as in politics I could accede to an easy certainty, but for me teaching is (or can be) in important ways like fighting for justice, for peace, for freedom.

I expected no affirmation for any of this when I returned to graduate school at Teachers College, Columbia University, at the age of forty. Frankly, I was going for a credential alone: I would take only the minimum requirements; I would learn the language of the anointed; and I would move on, untouched. I expected no particular challenge, no substantial nurturance, no serious demand. But here I was wrong, for something dazzling—burning, bright, nourishing, and insistent—stood in my way.

I was by no means Maxine Greene's best student. I was no star in her universe. At one point, I angled for a job as her teaching assistant, offering to read papers or exams for her. She was a little aghast: "Students want my reactions to their writing, not yours." Another time, she responded to a paper I had submitted: "The first part is . . . illuminating as an instance of existential choice. . . . The second is, well, O.K. It uses a metaphor I think is questionable . . . and, it is a romanticized view. . . . I have to think of teachers and learners as situated, entangled, determined, engaged." This second part was soon published to wide critical praise. For me, Maxine Greene's luke-warm response and serious challenge to that praise remains the truest reading.

Maxine Greene has a boundless generosity—a willingness to share her time, her energy, her mind (especially her mind) with thousands of current and former students. Her table is always set for visitors, and whenever one arrives, that visitor is welcomed and embraced. Maxine knows people as well as events and can see to the heart of a friend as well as an issue. Her constant humility, sometimes glaring when set against her accomplishment, is a living example of inner security, wisdom, and maturity. She declines calling attention to herself, celebrating instead the accomplishments and possibilities she sees in others. She knows herself and knows her mission.

Every encounter with Maxine—her latest article, a book re-read, a lecture recalled, a card in the mail, a phone call, or a conversation over coffee—remains for me a sweet and perfect moment of support and challenge, of surprise and reunion. It is an opportunity to notice more of what there is to notice, to see more, to think more deeply, to *do* philosophy. I leave wanting to read more, to stay wide awake more, to resist the numbing effects of habit and convention, to consider the possibilities. Recently we talked on the phone, and she asked, "What do you make of the world?" We talked a long time. "I find in Europe cause for real despair. . . . But maybe at least in the children I can still see some hope," she said. Now I want to do more, to care for children more, to embrace people more, to dance more, to fight the power more, to move beyond where I am now. I feel spaces opening up before me; I feel called upon to pay closer attention; and I feel challenged to act on what I now see and understand. What more could any student ask of his teacher than that?

2

Philosopher of/for Freedom

Wendy Kohli

STRUCTURING THIS NARRATIVE:
A PROBLEM OF REPRESENTATION

I feel obliged to announce, up front, my partisanship toward Maxine Greene: What follows is not a dispassionate piece, an objective assessment of Greene's philosophical work. Emboldened by David Halperin's (1995) recent book, *Saint-Foucault: Towards a Gay Hagiography*,[1] I decided to risk the disapproval of my peers—and perhaps even of Maxine—and write what could be construed as an hagiography, that is, an essay that "venerates, idealizes, or even idolizes."[2] I do this because I believe that Maxine Greene is, simultaneously, one of the most influential and undervalued philosophers of education in this century. I also do it as an act of resistance against the typical way academics, particularly philosophers, criticize each other's work. I am not interested in setting my sights on the flaws in her arguments or in looking for inconsistencies in her positions over time. Instead, by engaging her writing on its own terms, I hope to convey some of the powerfully varied ways Maxine Greene has influenced education. To do otherwise would be to act in bad faith.

As I write this, piles—literally—of Greene's articles, addresses, and books surround me, engulf me, comfort me. Deciding how to summarize, synthesize, even organize her life-work is no small task. Do I move linearly, chronologically through her material, trying to capture the "essence" of her work in each decade? Or do I move in and out, recursively, stretching my gaze around themes that return over and over? How do I create the space for her voice(s) to come through, yet not lose mine in the process?

Reflecting her chosen philosophical grounding in existentialist phenomenology, with its emphasis on the problem of 'becoming,' Maxine Greene makes it difficult to fix a category on/around her or her work; she is continually encountering/constructing new realities and identities for herself. Anticipating postmodernity before it was *au courant,* she, just as her work, remains unfinished, incomplete, partial. So, what

11

might be the best way to represent Maxine Greene's place in philosophy of education?

Originally, I imagined a weaving. The sturdy warp, constituted by the persistent themes of freedom, justice, community, democracy, and imagination, meets the colorful woof threads spun out of the multiple realities from/to which she speaks: the realities of educators, artists, women, children, people of color, poets, activists, and policymakers. On second thought, I realized that this weaving might have to take the shape of a three-dimensional tapestry, a form open to improvisation, to complexity, to singularity. This would better express the passage of time and allow for the reenvisioning of themes, *over time,* in different contexts. For example, although Maxine Greene has written and spoken for more than three decades about freedom, *the context* in which she speaks and writes is inextricably linked to the meaning she gives to the concept. She continually asserts the *situatedness* of her thinking, of her being. Unlike many philosophers who write about abstract, disembedded, disembodied, unchanging, "essential" notions of freedom, Maxine invigorates hers with the flesh and blood of the lived-world in which she is engaged.

The situatedness of Maxine's thought, however, is not confined to or defined by the role of "objective observer" of education or society at any particular historical moment. It also envelopes *her own* subjectivities, her own multiple and often contradictory identities that have shaped and continue to shape her take on the world, and its take on her. I think especially of her own subject-positions of woman: daughter, mother, teacher, urban activist, and Jewish intellectual. These are infused with her rich political, literary, and artistic sensibilities. And they are given emotional texture by the particular "walls" that she has met and transcended,[3] walls internal to her and those put before her by others. Maybe these walls could serve as the loom for the tapestry, the frame through and from which her creations are made?

I doubt, however, if any one of these devices can represent adequately the work of this formidable writer/orator/teacher/philosopher and her complex way(s) of being-in-the-world. Certainly a straightforward flat-matrix weave is insufficient, too static. But even a fluid, multidimensional tapestry may not be enough. Perhaps what is required is what Donna Haraway introduces as the "imagery of the cyborg," a technology that, among other things, "suggests a way out of the maze of dualisms in which we have explained our bodies and tools to ourselves . . . and is a dream . . . of a powerful infidel heteroglossia" (1991, p. 181). It is Greene's commitment to such a heteroglossia that makes her work so rich, yet challenging to represent in its richness. I embrace this 'crisis of representation' as my limit-situation—that, and the constraints on length imposed by a volume this size.

THE PROFESSIONALIZATION OF
PHILOSOPHY OF EDUCATION

It is common knowledge for those who have followed Maxine's career that her initial connection with philosophy of education was a gendered accident; in her words it was "total chance."[4] I'm not sure that "total chance" is an accurate account of what happened; certainly personal decision and structural/cultural factors played a significant role in setting her course. But what is clear is that she did not start out as a young girl on a straight path to hold the William F. Russell Chair in the Foundations of Education at Teachers College. Just as Maxine situates her knowledge in lived-experience, I, too, shall situate her connection with philosophy of education to her own biography, particularly her identity as a woman.

Greene's formative involvement in philosophy of education at New York University in the late forties and early fifties coincided with the professionalization of philosophy of education as a field (Giarelli & Chambliss, 1991). According to Giarelli and Chambliss:

> Largely because of the enormous influence of Dewey, many philosophers of education in the first half of this century resisted the impulses to specialization and professionalization occurring in general philosophy. At the same time, however, the importance of philosophy of education naturally resulting from Dewey's influence made the development of professional training programs in philosophy of education unstoppable. Already by the 1930's and early 1940's, the second and third generations of people trained by Dewey and his followers at Teachers College were taking positions at outposts of higher education across the country and developing a professional conception of philosophy of education. The public schools were growing and teacher education programs needed faculty in philosophy of education. (p. 266)

They needed Maxine. As she tells it, she was "discovered" by one of these Deweyites, George Axtelle, who took her to lunch one day and encouraged her to go on for a Ph.D. She agreed. Soon she was teaching a huge (two hundred students) summer school course in Philosophy of Education, using the notes from the course she herself had just finished taking!

As a part-time instructor at NYU, Maxine was "hungry to teach anything," and learned as she went, teaching all kinds of "field courses" for teachers in the New York and Connecticut suburbs. When she got her degree in 1955, Axtelle moved on from NYU, leaving Maxine to fend for herself with a dean, "an awful guy," who thought she was "too literary." This, by the way, would not be the last time this criticism was made of her as a philosopher.

Seeking sanctuary in the English Department, she taught courses in "values and education" to survive. She also tried to get a job elsewhere in philosophy of education, but "there was nothing, especially for women at that time." Discouraged, Maxine toyed with going back to school to "get an honest Ph.D.," in philosophy.[5] Early on in her schooling, she got the idea that if any part of your degree was in education, "no liberal arts college would look at you—you weren't considered a real philosopher." So for a time, she thought she *wanted* to be "a *real* philosopher, a *real* scholar, not an education person."

These feelings, of course, did not result simply from her personal prejudices or proclivities. The field of philosophy of education as a whole struggled with its "intellectual self-image" (Giarelli & Chambliss, 1991, p. 267). There were deep differences over what counted as philosophy of education and what its distinctive contribution was to be. Tensions arose, especially for those who sought legitimacy through direct identification with the "parent discipline," philosophy. As Giarelli and Chambliss note:

> By the 1930's and continuing into the 1940's and 1950's, one way of relating philosophy and education was dominant in the professional literature. . . . Philosophy is the parent discipline, and education is to be nurtured by the wisdom of the parent. . . . On this view, the activities of education are derived from those of philosophy. (p. 267)

The Philosophy of Education Society (PES) was founded in 1941 to bring legitimacy to the field by "going professional" (p. 272). This involved identifying "philosophers of education as a distinct professional class marked by specialized training" (p. 268), a specialized training Maxine doubted she had. By the late 1950s and early 1960s, the period when Maxine Greene was entering the academic world as a philosopher of education, the primary source of philosophic legitimation came from the Anglo-American analytic tradition. This way of "doing philosophy" terrified Maxine; "it was so scary, the analytic time." According to her, she was "*so* scared at PES" that when she had to give a paper, she would "get all dizzy and almost faint." Friendly colleagues even offered to read her papers for her, although she never let them.

In addition to the hegemony of linguistic and logical analysis in PES, which did not provide a hospitable environment for a literary existential phenomenologist like Maxine, she had to face an almost all-male organization. Mary Leach, in an illuminating feminist reading of the society, found that "in 1961, for example, there was a lone female listed on the program, though a formidable one—Maxine Greene" (1991, p. 287). Things did not improve much until the late 1970s or early 1980s. Even then, it remained a predominantly male enterprise to present at PES, regardless of the ratio of males to females on the program, since the discursive practices that shaped the meetings were decidedly masculinist.

With things a bit unfriendly at NYU, in 1956 Maxine secured a full-time teaching position at Montclair State Teachers College—in English. It was through teaching a "mega-course" on world literature that she *learned* about literature; prior to this assignment, she had no "formal training in English, maybe one course, once." But the pressures of commuting, of a new baby son, on top of on-the-job training in literature were just too much. Not only was Maxine teaching "out of her field," she was also self-taught. This manifested itself in a lack of confidence and vulnerability to the judgments of those (men) who were constructed as "real" philosophers of education, those with *bona fide* training in philosophy and the blessing of the parent. After one year, she went back reluctantly to NYU as a part-time instructor for a few years before being appointed in 1962 to a tenure-track line at Brooklyn College teaching Foundations of Education.

"DOING PHILOSOPHY OF EDUCATION"

By the mid 1960s, Maxine had established herself as a formidable writer in academic and other public venues, including *Saturday Review* and *Mademoiselle,* and had moved from Brooklyn College to Teachers College. In retrospect, her arrival at Teachers College was nothing less than bittersweet. Although Lawrence Cremin, then chair of the Department of Philosophy and Social Sciences, wanted her on the faculty, she was forced to come in through the backdoor as editor of *Teachers College Record.* Hindsight suggests apparent sexist resistance to her appointment within the department; they had yet to ever hire a woman. It was only after first teaching for several years in the English Department that she was finally "allowed in" and given a proper appointment in Philosophy of Education. But Maxine's superb record as a teacher and scholar was uncontestable, leading decisively to her appointment to the Russell Chair in 1975.

Though an enigma to many, if not most, of her fellow philosophers in the Philosophy of Education Society, Maxine was elected to serve as its president in 1967. Her presidential address, "Morals, Ideology, and the Schools: A Foray Into the Politics of Education," took some brave shots at her language-focused peers. For example, she says:

> Now it is entirely evident that consideration of the social and political dimensions of education has not (with some notable exceptions)

interested most educational philosophers in recent years. Various as our orientations are, most of us seem to have agreed (tacitly or explicitly) on the necessity to turn our attention to the teacher's speech and action in the classroom, leaving to the behavioral scientists events in the public realm "out there." (1967b, p. 145)

Ever one to connect her "public" and "private" selves, she offers an indictment of her audience when she remarks,

As citizens, we may have served as consultants or participants; we may have raised our voices in debate; we may even have demonstrated and carried picket signs. *As philosophers, however,* [emphasis added] we have concentrated on the verbal moves characterizing learning situations, the implications of epistemological theories for curriculum-making, the structure of educational arguments, the contextual meanings of education concepts, the typical uses of educational terms. (1967b, p. 145)

In other words, they had not "done philosophy" as she would have it done; they had maintained the dichotomy and distance between their public and private worlds, keeping philosophy out of politics.[6]

Philosophy as a noun is transformed into a verb in the Greene lexicon. For her, the philosophical *act* requires one "to take the risk of thinking about what he is doing . . . to become progressively more self-conscious about the choices he makes and the commitments he defines . . . and to examine critically the principles underlying what he thinks and what he says" (Greene, 1973, preface).

Greene's approach to philosophy of education has made philosophical thinking possible for many different kinds of people; for her, it is not a domain reserved for the professional academic. Even as she confronted her own self-doubts about her status as a "real philosopher," she was able to blur those boundaries for others and invite them in. Teachers and administrators at all levels of the educational system have been transformed by her work, both written and oral. Greene breathes life into the educational cliche, 'connecting theory to practice.' Although complex and often overpopulated with references to other authors (Jacobs, 1991), Greene's writing invites the particular reader she has in mind—often a teacher—to adopt the stance of "someone who is involved and responsible, someone who looks out on the educational landscape from inside a specifiable 'life form'" (Greene, 1973, preface). There is inherent respect for the reader. Greene presumes practitioners can, of course, read philosophy and think philosophically.

For Greene, philosophy is not a dead body of knowledge, a static thing; it is an ever-evolving search for meaning and freedom; it is an opportunity to confront the world critically in order to change it; it is acting, choosing, deciding to live in-the-world, to experience the lived reality of one's existence. To do philosophy in this way is, echoing Jean Paul Sartre, Greene's "life project."

Her effort to make meaning out of the world in which she has been "thrown," is what resonates with so many educators. By speaking *from her own place* in the world, she is able to speak convincingly to them about *their* lived realities, *their* search for meaning, *their* need to make sense of *their* worlds and to change them. She offers openings, not orders, possibilities, not prescriptions.

PERSISTENT THEMES AND COMMITMENTS: GREENE AS PHILOSOPHER OF FREEDOM

Freedom is just one of several themes that have shaped the corpus of Greene's work over the past thirty years, themes that have been addressed with different audiences for different purposes, yet retain a certain consistency. Maxine's interpretations of freedom, justice, community, democracy, and imagination always reflect the changing historical, economic, social, cultural, and political situations in which they are embedded. They also mirror transformations in philosophy, as well as in social, political, and literary theory. In her work, Maxine struggles with the inevitable tensions between modernity and postmodernity, particularly as she takes note of difference, of 'otherness,' and yet speaks to the continued need for common connections among us. Being as prolific as she is, it is impossible to select one primary focus of Maxine's work. Her search for a multicultural democracy with people living justly in community is certainly reflected in decades of writing and speaking. But underlying this search is a necessary, even fundamental, commitment to and expression of freedom.

In an earlier essay (1989), I review Greene's work in relation to the problem of freedom, suggesting that as a result of her commitment to critical Marxism and existentialism, she insists "upon the agency of individuals and the possibility for freedom that comes through choosing and acting in the world as one recognizes and confronts the reality posed by external conditions" (p. 99). But this choosing and acting does not come without cost. As Greene cautioned us in one of her earliest works, *Existential Encounters for Teachers,* written in 1967, "Confronting his own freedom, his own need to choose, he is bound to suffer from disquietude" (p. 4).

And anguish. In her classic 1973 philosophy of education text, *Teacher as Stranger,* Maxine asserts that "anguish is the way freedom reveals itself. It is the expression of the nagging desire for completion—without any guarantee that the completion sought will be valuable when it is achieved" (p. 279). But this should not be a deterrent to action. Quite the contrary, for it is in this "dreadful freedom [that] the individual decides" (p. 279).

Emphasizing the connection between education and freedom, Greene reinforces the themes of decision and choosing. In her *Inaugural Lecture as William F. Russell Professor* in 1975, she says: "My concern is what can be done by means of education to enable people to transcend their private terrors and act together to give freedom a concrete existence in their lives. . . . My interest is not so much in freedom *from* or negative freedom as it is in the deliberate creation of the kinds of conditions in which people can be themselves" (p. 4). For Greene, acting, choosing, and deciding are what make a person free: "The person choosing breaks the chain of causes and effects, of probabilities, in which he normally feels himself to be entangled. He breaks it in part by asking 'Why?' by perceiving the habitual itself to be an obstacle to his growing, his pursuit of meaning, his interpreting and naming his world" (p. 7). Freedom, Greene says, "is the freedom to decide what sort of person you ought to be" (1973, p. 284).

EDUCATION FOR FREEDOM:
MAXINE GREENE'S GIFT TO US

Education can play an important role in helping people decide their own paths. In fact, for Maxine these "connections between education and freedom" are so important that she says they are, "perhaps, the main theme of my life" (1988, p. xii). Through her unique way of doing philosophy, Maxine has inspired countless generations to "decide who we ought to be."

Saying she "does" philosophy of education, however, cannot quite express the depth and breadth of her influence on educators, artists, and others who read widely across and between disciplines. Nor does it represent adequately the aesthetic quality of her work as she draws on popular culture, art, literature, poetry, and film. At the same time, this essay proceeds from the premise that she is, first and foremost, a philosopher of education. That she has, through her own volition, forced that category to include her own rendering of what it means to be one, of what it means to "decide" who we are as philosophers of education and not let others decide for us.

It is through this rendering that Maxine has made the field more hospitable for many of us who draw on continental philosophy, the arts, literature, feminism, and discourses of the 'other' to do our work. Perhaps this is one of her finest, most powerful contributions: the openings she has created for others, particularly other women, even if it has often been at her own expense.[7] Her own ambivalence toward philosophy of education, manifested in her multidisciplinary writings, may be, paradoxically, the most certain of her creations. This ambivalence does not paralyze; if anything, it allows her to see multiple realities, to choose to act with passion, to know that there are always other voices to be heard. No one says this better than she:

> Thought, the pursuit of meanings, freedom and concern: there is no final summing up the themes of what counts as Philosophy of Education. Passion should infuse all these: the passion of sensed possibility and, yes, the passion of poetry and the several arts. Thinking of ourselves as subjects reaching out to others and attending to the shapes and sounds of things, we may resist the anaesthetic in our lives and the drawing back to anchorage. We have to know about our lives, clarify our situations if we are to understand the world from our shared standpoints, our standpoints as philosophers of education ready to commit ourselves to small transformations as we heed the stories, the multiplex stories, as cautiously as we transform. (1995, p. 21)

Certainly there is evidence of Maxine's resistance to the "anaesthetic" in the multiple ways she has transformed the educational world, as she has jarred us to "wide-awakeness." From young children in arts programs in New York City, down to policymakers in Washington, across the country to countless teacher educators, teachers, school administrators, and curriculum workers, we all have been moved by her generosity, her imagination, her eloquence. Maxine's unique gift of the word, both oral and written, brings philosophy to life for her diverse audiences. One would be hard pressed to find anyone who calls themselves a philosopher of education who has touched as many people as Maxine Greene has in her fruitful, passionate, unfinished, life.

NOTES

1. Halperin's (1995) "uncompromising and impassioned defense" of Michel Foucault's work inspired me to be unabashedly proud of Maxine Greene's place in education. Although not currently under attack the way Foucault has been in recent years, Greene has faced her share of demeaning sexist treatment and marginalization, particularly in the early years of her professional life.

2. See *Webster's New Collegiate Dictionary.*

3. She introduces this concept in her 1988 book, *The Dialectic of Freedom,* when describing the internal and external barriers individuals must overcome in claiming their freedom.

4. From a personal interview with me on August 16, 1993. Most of the direct quotes in this paper are from this interview, although versions of her story have been told in other contexts as well.

5. Luckily for her, she thinks now, a Columbia University philosophy professor advised her to forget about that idea and "just write." Although grateful that she did not invest in another degree, it still gnaws at her that she "did not have a very good education." This self-doubt is exploitable in an insecure field like philosophy of education, especially for us women who, *as women,* often doubt our ability and legitimacy in any case.

6. Or so they thought. Many of us would question the possibility for any kind of 'objective' or 'disinterested' knowledge, science or philosophy.

7. Maxine's decision to draw on continental philosophy, the arts, and literature was often met with skepticism, even disdain, by many of her (male) peers who, steeped in a more Anglo-analytic tradition, thought her work "unintelligible" and certainly "un-philosophical."

REFERENCES

Giarelli, J. M., & Chambliss, J. J. (1991). The foundation of professionalism: Fifty years of the Philosophy of Education Society in retrospect. *Educational Theory, 41*(3), 265–274.

Greene, M. (1967a). *Existential encounters for teachers.* New York: Random House.

Greene, M. (1967b). Morals, ideology and the schools: A foray into the politics of education. *Proceedings of the twenty-third annual meeting of the Philosophy of Education Society.* Edwardsville, IL: Southern Illinois University.

Greene, M. (1973). *Teacher as stranger: Educational philosophy for the modern age.* Belmont, CA: Wadsworth.

Greene, M. (1975). *Education, freedom and possibility: Inaugural lecture as William F. Russell Professor.* New York: Teachers College, Columbia University.

Greene, M. (1988). *The dialectic of freedom.* New York: Teachers College Press.

Greene, M. (1995). What counts as philosophy of education? in W. Kohli (Ed.), *Critical conversations in philosophy of education* (pp. 3–23). New York: Routledge, Chapman, & Hall.

Halperin, D. (1995). *Saint-Foucault: Towards a gay hagiography.* New York: Oxford University Press.

Haraway, D. J. (1991). *Simians, cyborgs, and women: The reinvention of nature.* New York: Routledge, Chapman, & Hall.

Jacobs, M. E. (1991). *Diary of an ambivalent daughter: A feminist re-visioning of Maxine Greene's discursive landscapes.* Unpublished doctoral dissertation, University of Maryland, College Park.

Kohli, W. (1989). Education and freedom in the American experience: Critical imagination as pedagogy. *Harvard Educational Review, 59*(1), 98–107.

Kohli, W. (Ed.). (1995). *Critical conversations in philosophy of education.* New York: Routledge, Chapman, & Hall.

Leach, M. (1991). Mothers of in(ter)vention: Women's writing in philosophy of education. *Educational Theory, 41*(3), 287–300.

3

Dinner With Maxine

Mark Weiss, Candy Systra, and Sheila Slater

We all have different versions of how Maxine first came to meet with us at Bronx Regional High School in the South Bronx in 1988. We remember her stepping out of the cab on Reverend Polite Avenue with her long skirt, wide-brimmed hat, and a shopping bag nearly overflowing with articles, reprints, magazines, the newspaper, and books. We remember sitting in on her classes (and Maxine sitting in on some of ours), going out to dinner, and attending conferences together. Best of all, we remember the conversations. Maxine calls them "conversations that echo from somewhere else, some deep place." The following text is such a conversation—one with many openings, reflecting themes we continue to explore together—academia and practice, friendship, community, social justice, art and politics, creativity, and narrative, and it still goes on. . . .

• • •

MAXINE: The point I want to make has to do with narratives. To me, a good narrative, a real authentic narrative, is really an effort to dig down and shape what you find in your life, in your history. Not just babble it or write it down for catharsis, but give it a shape so it will be understood by somebody else. That's like good communication. What's important is what in each of us is seeking expression, and what's different about us is what we have at hand to give it expression. I think what we try to do with kids is to help them with that expression. With you all I felt humble in a way. You're all good teachers, you're in such a hard place. Teachers College is such an armchair compared with the school where you worked. The setting, everything about it, the street outside. I was full of admiration that you were there with such spirit and such love for kids and respect for each other.

I don't see that in academe. In academe, I see competition and, still, white man elitism. I remember when Gaynor McCown, another teacher at your school, talked about the time a student was arrested

22

for murder, and she showed a letter he wrote. He said, "I don't want my family to think I'm a murderer." He used a false name. I just remember Gaynor's feeling about that. I just couldn't get over that because that kind of access, concern, legitimacy you do not see, at least I do not see, in higher education.

SHEILA: One of the reasons we felt and feel so drawn to you is that there is a certain acknowledgment, a recognition by somebody, *you,* coming from academe, who sees the importance of all of this, and of those of us who are doing it.

MARK: When we talk about our teaching with you, it raises the level or it does something to whatever it is we're talking about. I'm not sure that we believed about ourselves all that you saw in us, but we lived up to some of the things. Your presence caused us to reflect on our teaching. It makes it more important; it connects it with a body of philosophy that I don't know, but you do.

SHEILA: Our discussions, these stories and your references to writers, to different philosophical points of view that you know very well, Maxine, show each of us that the road is not just one way. And it is in a way what we do with our students. It's what you do with teachers and students you're working with. You're listening to them; you're listening to what they say.

MAXINE: I hate to quote Hannah Arendt, but I always do. She says, when people get together as who they are and not what they are, an "in-between" opens between them. There are worldly relationships and over that there is the delicate web of human relationships.

• • •

MAXINE: I fell into this kind of work so randomly. I wanted to be a writer, and I was a political activist. After World War II, it was a little difficult to be an authentic activist. I thought I could incorporate somehow some of my ideas into teaching. I always suffered a kind of guilt, you know. It was a very peculiar feeling. First of all, people like me didn't become professors. Being Jewish, I found it weird being a professor. I also suffered guilt, a middle-class guilt mixed up with female guilt at acting like a big-shot male professor, wearing shoes that weren't mine. So the gift you gave me by accepting me was very important.

I wouldn't underestimate randomness in people's lives. It has a dramatic and a romantic appeal, and we are, all of us, like it or not, intellectuals, because we love ideas and puzzles and causes and wonderings and things like that. I think maybe in teacher education we don't make enough of that.

The funny thing is, I wanted to be a writer. Sometimes you wonder if what you first wanted stamped you. But I am sure now I couldn't have been a writer. And I probably would have been terribly disappointed. I did write two and a half unsuccessful novels. When I read someone like Raymond Carver, I know I couldn't do what he did. Or I read *The English Patient,* which I loved so much; and I think, that's the life, that's what I would have been happy to be able to do, to be a poet. I started out when I got out of college. It was my revenge on my American history major and the bad teaching I suffered. I wrote a very "subversive" novel in American history. It was about a folk singer I made up during the American Revolution who tacked his songs to trees, and then it was about the pre-Jeffersonian period, the Alien and Sedition Acts under which people were sent to jail for their sympathies with the French Revolution. They had these Democratic societies, sometimes secret. I was nineteen. I went to Philadelphia, and I got these penciled minutes for the Democratic Society meetings and didn't even know I was doing research. So I wrote a seven hundred page novel.

SHEILA: What did you do with it?

MAXINE: A friend of mine knew a literary agent. By then I was married, but my old Spanish Civil War friend used to come to the library and see me writing. The agent sent it to Little, Brown in New York and they sent it to Little, Brown in Boston. They thought it was too left-wing or something. I was so young; I didn't understand. It hurt to have something rejected, so I put it away. I don't think it was really good in any case. The second one was about a mulatto woman, a pianist, and this time I did all the research on the WPA Arts Project. Then Duell, Sloan, and Pierce asked me to rewrite it in the first person. I didn't know how to write about sex or anything like that; again, I failed. I started a third one years later. This was about a daughter of someone like John Dewey, who had maybe yes or maybe no squealed on somebody to the Un-American Activities Committee. She is looking in a quarry at the start, wondering if her father committed suicide. My own father committed suicide almost right after I wrote that, and it scared the living hell out of me. I never again wrote any kind of fiction. Then I was remarried and all that. My husband said, "Why don't you go back to school? At least you know you were good at school." When my little Linda had trouble adjusting to her new school, I thought, well, I'll take her back to her old school every day and I'll go to school myself. I wrote to every university asking where I could be a special student. All I needed was that it had to be between ten and two so Linda could be back at her Brooklyn school.

SHEILA: How old was she?

MAXINE: She was seven, and I'd been divorced. I always tell people, it's lucky it wasn't a physics class meeting from ten to two; it was philosophy and history of education at NYU, eight points, twice a week, three professors. I fell into it that way. But the funny thing is, that isn't what I wanted. I wanted it once I got in. You want the little success that comes next. I became the assistant in the class the next term. When I took my certification exam at NYU with five hundred people from all over the university, they said only 20% passed. When I took that exam, I was so sure I flunked that I wouldn't even register the next fall. It shows you that I didn't think I belonged. I haven't even bought a cap and gown, after all these years. I have always rented because I never thought . . . I never even had a card printed. You know how people have cards; I don't have a card because I never thought I would last.

I went to the New School when I was nineteen, and discovered I had enough honors points to leave Barnard. Nobody said, "Stay. Go to graduate school," or anything. I eloped, moved from my family's home, wanted to write. I was working with the American Labor Party and went to the New School part-time. I had these old German social democrats as teachers. I wrote a paper on collective security. Remember that? It was one of the icon phrases, "collective security." The United States would join the Soviets and others, I suppose it meant, in a common front.

MARK: When was that?

MAXINE: 1939 or '40, I think, at the end of the Spanish Civil War. When Barcelona fell, I thought I would commit suicide, that it meant the death of all our hopes because the Fascists had won in Spain. The New School people dismissed me, would not give me credit for my paper. They said I wasn't scholarly, was too radical. That is how I know what they were then. They were the ones, after all, who allowed the Nazis in and then they got kicked out.

SHEILA: I didn't know that. That's interesting.

MAXINE: I forgot their names; but I know various people have written about them. It seemed strange because the school was founded by such magnificent people—Alice Johnson, a Midwestern progressive (whom I once interviewed); John Dewey; Horace Kallen, one of the first pluralists among that group, who really believed in diversity.

SHEILA: I've never heard some of these stories before.

MAXINE: I'd like to tell it. It may be too old.

SHEILA: We talk about oral histories, and this is what we are doing in some sense. And I think it's just as valuable for us as it is for our students.

MAXINE: That's true. I don't know if this belongs here or not. My father had a factory when I was young. I became so ashamed about it, really ashamed. It was on 23rd Street and 4th Avenue in Brooklyn. Generations of Italian families worked for him, we were told.

MARK: Why were you ashamed? Where did the other values come from?

MAXINE: I try to remember now. He was paternalistic to his workers and, of course, hated unions. When I was at Barnard, I guess I met some radical people who confirmed what I was thinking. Among the high moments of my life was the time the SS *Bremen* came in from Germany, and many young people marched to the harbor, where some climbed the mast to try to pull down the Nazi flag. I wanted desperately to do that, but I could not climb. Not long after, probably with the same people, I was picketing some stores on Fulton Street in Brooklyn because they would not hire Black cashiers— and that was in Bedford-Stuyvesant.

SHEILA: You must have met so many interesting people.

MAXINE: I did, and I was arrested for picketing. Then I joined something called the Workers' Alliance, which specialized in taking furniture back after evictions. On one occasion, I saw something I never forgot in my life. It helped make me feel guilty and still makes me feel guilty. I saw a kid with a rat bite on his lip. I never forgot that.

  The next thing that happened, I was pregnant and we were having a meeting at this Workers' Alliance thing, and a man came up with a pail and threw lye in the chairman's eyes, blinding him. There was a kind of continuum, I guess.

  When I was a junior, my father let me go to Europe with a classmate. He gave me a list of tasks to perform for his business that I did not understand. On the boat, I met some men going to fight in Spain with the Abraham Lincoln Brigade, and I wanted to go to Spain. Obviously, I couldn't, but eventually I got to Paris and found a job with the Loyalist Embassy. It was the year of Guernica, and of a World's Fair. I met people I thought were noble people—Constancia de la Mora, Louis Aragon; and I cabled my father that I did not want to go home. He said I had to go home and finish college. Once back here, I began lecturing on Spain, and that was when I learned to lecture.

SHEILA: When I went to China in 1957, I didn't want to come back either. When we returned, we went around lecturing to different schools, showing slides. . . . I had been at a World Youth Festival in Moscow, and the Chinese delegation invited Americans to go to China and forty-two of us went for six weeks, and when we returned our passports were confiscated. I had no passport for years.

* * * *

SHEILA: Maxine, I've thought a lot about your lectures about aesthetics and the role of aesthetics, the role of art and creativity in my own life and how rewarding it is for me personally. I have seen the effects of art experiences with many students of mine who are nonreaders-nonwriters and yet who have great feelings about self-expression and creativity and artistic expression. When people individually have high degrees of self-expression, that's when the community functions at the highest level. I really believe it's the community that decides on the values, and that individual expression should be one of the values. I'm thinking about how I don't view it in terms of individual against community. I think in this system of education, the way you get individual expression is to have a sense of community.

MAXINE: That was Dewey's idea.

SHEILA (*laughing*): I knew I must have read it somewhere.

MAXINE: Is there a sort of invisible community that you feel part of? I think it's true in my world, because I think that you imagine people with high values and a certain way of teaching and doing literature. How do you identify yourself with respect to the context when you're living in a gruesome society? How do you think about what you do?

SHEILA: And how do you build a sense of community that moves in a more positive direction.

CANDY: It's so hard for our students to develop a sense of community. We value community so much, and we are trying to do things to foster community. But we can't do it only in a microcosm. There's a community outside, too, right? Sometimes the community that exists out there has a very negative impact for very real and very true reasons. Students ask, "What does a high school diploma get you? What does hard work get you?"

MARK: Now you're dealing with the issue of hope.

MAXINE: I like Dewey's idea of a community in the making. Not that there *is* a community, but community in the making: through dialogue, through doing things together, through shared concern, identifying something that is shared that can move you to some kind of action. Every time you say "community," it suggests there are all these concentric communities and you want your kids to make at least one. I have a feeling if you were to make a community within the big circle of a Martin Luther King ceremony, it would have to be made in terms of this generation's Martin Luther King, which is different from ours. The other thing I was wondering, when we talk about community, does that allow for very small local things like coming together to walk the little ones across the project yard, or to see to it that somebody has lunch? I think you make community by doing those little things. I think all we can think of now is local things, and hoping that (I don't know, you know much better)— you keep hoping that the outrage the children feel might be directed to something they can repair. They can't repair very much, but even the outrage they experience when the house is empty in the afternoon is sort of connected. Here's another example. A student of mine wrote a paper. She said her sister was in the riots in Los Angeles teaching in a school there. Two of the kids in her class were killed by crossfire. She said there was something positive about the fact that the children kept calling the teacher, even found out where she lived and came to her house. She felt it was a positive thing, that they came to her for protection, a white teacher. I suppose those are little moments when something happens.

SHEILA: I don't think you ever know the value of these moments, these experiences that the kids have and that we have, how they're going to re-emerge in people's lives, how they're going to be incorporated. Most of my students come from other countries, and they've recently arrived within the last few years. There's an enormous lack of trust about this country, this city, and the schools, and white teachers. I think for kids to experience something that you build together, and to know that it's possible, means that you know it *can* happen. The fact that you experience it means you can then assess why it does happen in certain situations and why it doesn't happen in others.

MARK: But you know it can happen in your classroom and they know that it can happen in your classroom.

CANDY: Are you saying that what you try to do in your classroom, as much as anything else, is establish this? Are you thinking consciously of collective, of community? This little group working together is a goal of yours?

SHEILA: In my classroom, we work very individually because of the nature of the task, but yes, I have a consciousness of developing a sense of community.

MAXINE: Is it common subject matter?

SHEILA: Well, that's interesting. It can be that. It can be a discussion about a particular topic. It's also the way we all interrelate in the classroom with one another—the responsibilities that we all have in order to live together.

CANDY: So, can I tell one short story? I was in a math class at a jail on Riker's Island. It was Peter Masongo's class. He's such a good teacher! Everyone was looking at math word problems. The idea today was not to solve the problem, but to answer the question, "What information is included in the problem that is unnecessary?" The first problem Masongo put on the board was, "Joe makes $8.50 an hour. He has $500 in his savings account. If he works a forty-hour week for seven weeks, how much money does he make on the job?" Well, first of all, a bunch of people got very upset because how much he has in his bank account is private information and should not be revealed. They didn't want to get to anything else because this conversation had to happen first. We found out a whole lot of stuff. Also, there was somebody who couldn't do the math but he could read the problem. The guy next to him didn't speak any English but was pretty good in math. So one of them was reading and translating into Spanish, the other was helping him, and Masongo was sitting there saying, "Gee, I have nothing to do."

SHEILA: He has such a great sense of community.

CANDY: So the class as a whole was doing this problem. I was off in a corner trying to teach subtraction. "If this is 1995 and you're twenty-nine years old, let's see if we can figure out through math the year you were born," which of course he already knows. It's all happening at the same time. It is a community, even though we're doing individual things, and—

SHEILA: Well, in a community of people helping one another, it doesn't matter whether they're doing it in one form as individuals or all together.

MARK: But the major thing of teaching is being okay not to know something, for everybody. It's okay not to know.

SHEILA: Yes, but people don't always believe that.

MARK: If that happens, if it's okay for the teacher not to know, then it's okay for the student not to know.

SHEILA: The student has to believe that whoever is saying that means it.

MARK: But that goes back to a connection with Maxine, which is that it's okay not to really know some philosopher. Not to know him personally, the way she does.

* * * *

MAXINE: I saw the president of the college today because a colleague and I went in to argue for the hiring of another philosophy teacher. My colleague and I had different ideas. My colleague thinks that a philosopher should be an intellectual center who keeps Teachers College in touch with the aims of a graduate school. I said I thought that a philosopher at Teachers College should really have something to do with the philosophically complex issues, say, of professional development schools and teacher education. Does that make sense to you, or does that just justify my own life?

CANDY: Why does it have to be either/or?

MAXINE: Well it doesn't really, except that the really academic philosophers don't see it that way. They think to do philosophy, to keep Teachers College's head above the murky waters of practice, is to read Heidegger, to focus on the classics and the canon. I'm interested in metaphor and its many implications for practice and thought. Also, I am interested in the role of theory and the connections between philosophy and literature, and I keep thinking about the meanings of all this for public schools and their present day populations. I believe a good teacher is the kind who can get fascinated by many sorts of ideas even though she won't have much chance to teach Habermas. It is odd, though, to determine what is relevant, what really matters in the world of ideas. Before now, in social philosophy, I taught Marx, the neo-Marxists, the existentialists, the critical theorists, Foucault. This time I used a large number of essays on liberalism, on issues of freedom and equality, on the public and the public space. We read Don DeLillo's *White Noise* and Camus's *The Plague*. And I decided to end with a book on Camus, Arendt, and the idea of rebellion. It's not the usual neo-Marxist thing I did, but people do get fascinated with Arendt. So you say, what's the use of that if they're going to go wherever it is and teach New York City's high school students?

CANDY: But you don't believe that.

MAXINE: No, I believe a good teacher should have a tough time learning, should not be given soupy stuff, should be introduced to ideas and struggle with them. Really, I was trying to say to the president that the concerns of teachers are as profound as any philosopher's concerns could be. They have to do with good and bad, with freedom, equality, and justice and all these things. Don't they?

MARK: Well, there's so much lack of content in teacher education. It's so often solely about methodology.

SHEILA: It depends on where it is. When I did my master's in Adult and Community Education at City College, I felt that there was a lot of struggle in the department about what the content of the courses should be and that they should be related to real issues.

CANDY: On the other hand, part of what upsets me so much in high school classrooms right now is that it seems like the content somehow comes from God. There's not an urgency to be creative, to be thinking actively, to be making what Maxine was calling those possibilities. I worry about that. What exists is a variation on the theme of the right answer.

MAXINE: Oh really, still the canonical thing?

MARK: I would like to get back to the issue you were raising about a philosophy professor, and philosophy, and how it informs the teacher who is practicing in the classroom, and the relationship among the four of us. In Paulo Freire's new book, *Pedagogy of Hope,* he talks about this exercise that he did where he says to a group of peasants, "You ask me a question that I can't answer, then I'll ask you a question you can't answer." They go through ten things. And the peasants have ten questions he can't answer about agriculture, and he has ten questions they can't answer about philosophy.

MAXINE: That's exactly the point I was going to make; I think that's very good. Very good. You talk about story and narrative; we each have our story. We have the language in which to express it. If you do away with that position of power, all there are are different stories.

But Paulo goes beyond that. After that dialogue with the peasants, one of them asks, "How come the doctor knows all those things?" "Because his father was rich and sent him to college." And then Paulo goes on to say that you have to teach them more than how to oil the wheel. There's a language of power that people have to know. To me the delicate issue with schools is how you affirm the richness of people's original stories and at the same time make them want to go beyond. That's my idea of imagination. How can you make them want more? I mind some teachers romanticizing the stories so much, and some of the stories would be so much better if the language was richer, if they knew a little more, if they could make metaphors. Teachers sometimes forget that the students, too, need to be empowered: to say better, to say more clearly, more richly what they have to say. It's not just the language of power that you have to know in order to make it in this society, and Paulo says that. But I really do believe that people like us, if you read poetry and novels and so on, begin to talk less literally and have more flexible use of language.

I was listening to NPR to the poet Mark Strand, whose work I love, who did a book on Edward Hopper, the painter. Strand was saying that everyone in Hopper's paintings is thinking about something. It's not just that they're lonely, they're thinking about something. His use of words opened up the Hopper painting of the woman in the window in my mind. It wasn't that they were big words, it was the arrangement of words and the metaphor and the simplicity. I thought, if we could all talk like that, if teachers could do that, what kids would see.

CANDY: Yes, his use of words opens the possibilities. Art acts as a model. Now that I know Mark Strand can do that with Edward Hopper, maybe I could decide that I could do that with something else. And why is that seen as the province of the arts? Why can't we open that to studying history? Why can't we create the moment of indecision? Instead of studying what the encyclopedia says, if you really had to do the research yourself, if you really had your own historical questions and you had to face the indecision or the complexity, wouldn't that open up history for you?

MAXINE: I keep giving an example of how teaching the Civil War could be changed by the movie *Glory*. It's very moving, but according to one of my students, these guys are sacrificed, there's no point to it, and it's a male military ideal that's used. I knew that, but I didn't know it as much until that student said it. The other funny part was that I thought I never knew there was a black battalion. I thought I never knew, but Robert Lowell has a collection called *For the Union Dead,* and the poem "For the Union Dead" is about a monument in the Boston Commons, and it's a monument to Drew Scott, that young colonel from the movie. It describes the whole thing. I read it and dropped it out of my mind until I saw the movie, and that was as interesting as anything else.

SHEILA: You know, it's funny, I showed *Glory* to my class two months ago. Some of the kids said, that's crazy to volunteer knowing you'd be killed. Then we ended up talking about what it meant for these black soldiers to be fighting for an end to slavery.

MAXINE: It was a wonderful issue to raise. Moving around from perspective to perspective, using language can enrich kids if they say better what they meant to say, as long as you respect what they want to say. They have to feel the dignity of being listened to.

MARK: The building is such a delicate process. You say, "I respect you; we trust each other," and they have a voice.

MAXINE: That's what I'm getting at.

4

In the Presence of Others

Karen Ernst, Maureen Miletta, and Kathleen Reilly

One of Maxine's favorite philosophers, Hannah Arendt, said, "For excellence, the presence of others is always required." Maxine believes this and is extraordinarily generous with her time. For five years, our writing group has reflected her interest in collaboration as a way to take the stuff of our lives and experiences as teachers and reshape them. For the most part, Karen concentrated on her dissertation, taking us through the phases of interpreting data about the connection between art and writing, and really preparing the basis of her now published book, *Picturing Learning* (Heinemann, Portsmouth, NH, 1994). Maureen was teaching at Hofstra University and pulling together the threads of her experience developing an innovative multiage classroom; she has just finished her book, *A Multiage Classroon: Choice and Possibility* (Heinemann, 1996). Kathleen was just beginning her work as a teacher researcher by applying for National Council of Teachers of English (NCTE) grants and trying to synthesize and make sense of her data. Her studies are published in "Teacher Research and the Clearing House." Maxine was doing at least twenty or more different kinds of writing. Sometimes she would read a preface she wrote for someone else's book, or she might have just delivered a paper in Iowa about aesthetic education; she could have a draft of a piece about French feminist writers for *Harvard Educational Review,* or she could have an idea floating around that she just whipped into five or six pages.

We certainly were from diverse backgrounds and in different places when we came together, but each of us left with something uniquely centered on our work. Maxine was interested in our projects, always seemed to have a nugget of current information that informed our writing and encouraged us to keep at it. Her energy is staggering. Her strength lies in her openness to other worlds, in her intense curiosity about the way other lives are lived, and in her commitment to the belief that it is in community that change flourishes. Our afternoons with Maxine affected each of us profoundly, as you will read here, and we share a deep respect and affection for our dear friend.

* * *

KAREN

I drew six-year-old Jessica as she got up from the rug to approach a painting, another student's copy of van Gogh's *Starry Night.* I noticed the contrast between her tiny, hot pink "Snoopy" sweatshirt and the boldness of her response to the painting. Pointing to the picture, she moved her hand in a circle as she spoke. I recorded Jessica's words: "I notice the swirls in the trees. I notice how she put her own colors in the picture because she probably didn't like the colors he chose. I like all the details." Drawing this event into my research journal helped me focus on Jessica and remember the importance of my job as a teacher to help my students notice their world, to respond to art and literature, to express themselves in many ways, and to know how to learn independently. As I recorded Jessica's words I made the connection to Maxine Greene. Her questions and ideas permeate my classroom experiences. Jessica and all of my students have a distant teacher in Maxine Greene.

She was my mentor, a member of my dissertation committee, and she propelled my thinking, heightened my understanding of what I do as a teacher, and continues to push me to provide experiences in my classroom that open the world of imagination and art to my students. It was from reading Maxine's words and listening to her speak at Lincoln Center that I began developing an understanding for a philosophy of education that made sense to me. It was from that experience along with teaching that led me to pursue a doctorate. Sitting next to her in our writing group, I thought that she remained larger than life.

Line and word is the way I record experiences in my journal. At each group meeting, I drew Maxine as she listened to our stories and laughed at our anecdotes about the classrooms where we taught. I used my journal at these meetings to draw her, to help me focus on her and capture her words as they seemed to tumble from her mind. "Imagination is the capacity to open spaces. Art can contribute to the drive for the men and women who change the world." I also drew her to calm and center myself, knowing that it would be my turn to read, to unveil the chapters of my dissertation, and then be suspended by her questions (see Figure 4.1).

Figure 4-1.

"I am interested in how you disclose. You are making sense of the world by using line. Drawing is unconcealing," she said. Her responses would fall on my ears in rapid succession. She would at once help me to know what I had taken for granted, connect it to theories and philosophies of others, and then challenge me. "There is that whole problem of image and words. This is only an approximation. How is art a form of knowledge?" I learned not to try to answer her questions but only to write them into my journal. At every meeting her response would send me to more reading, more thinking, writing, and realization.

Each time I read, she challenged me to be aware of my selection of words. Maxine loves words and plays with the subtleties between them. "What does meaning mean? Should we use understanding instead of meaning?" "What do you mean by powerful ownership? What is the opposite of powerful?" "That is not the title you want. Let's look for another." Hers was the philosophy supporting my work, while at the same time she participated in its creation. She taught me to consider the art of my teaching and the craft of the languages—drawing and words—I used to tell the story of my experience. She elevated my experience as a teacher to a picture that seemed larger than I had imagined, then she challenged me to look at its expression in the smallest detail.

She would point out what meaning was there and then question the idea. "This is a story. Is it a celebration? There is great danger in this being a personal journey." Her questions kept me in a constant state of tension, and I now know that it is the tensions in my own classroom that propel me to question, change, and make learning better for all of my students. "Aren't you showing you have broken down the barriers [between art and writing]?" "Emphasize how independent they become in your classroom." Her questions helped me consider what I should show in my narrative. My heightened awareness made me see my students and classroom in a new way and has helped me understand the value of my work with young children.

"Is it the same for all children? How does it feed into the culture?" she challenged. I could never be satisfied with the microcosm of my own classroom. She urged me to look larger, to question how my work could touch others and how what I was showing would challenge the children to look in new ways. She cautioned me every step of the way. "Watch out when you refer to art as meaning that which children do. They are not fully developed artists." "How does image get translated into poetry?" "What is the relationship between freedom and structure." "Show that the arts are not elitist." Maxine urged me to stroke the canvas of my work with wide, bold strokes, then work at the details with a tiny brush, and to always step back and question and change.

My mind would feel the pressure of her wide and deep knowledge, but she was there listening, laughing, supporting, looking for a better word, and moving me in new directions and to new understandings. I wrote in the margin of my journal, "It is a compliment," on the day she said, "I've never read anything that makes it possible." Was she referring to the Jessicas who march up to the picture and respond with an authority beyond what I would expect of a six year old?

"Dewey," she said, "talks of making connections in experience. For me, it has to reach beyond the appearances." Most days in my classroom as students share their paintings, write about the meaning inside their pictures, or respond to my questions about imagination, art, and learning, I feel a connection to Maxine. I look for ways that art can be central to learning, and in my days of off-balance I look for new possibilities. I push myself to go beyond appearances, to go beyond a celebration, and now urge other teachers to do the same. When six-year-old Jessica stood before that painting that day, moving her hands and her words with feeling and care, I knew Maxine was present. Maxine helps me make learning possible in my own classroom.

MAUREEN

Maxine walked to her class on the philosophy of John Dewey, struggling to balance books and papers. She dumped everything down on the table at the front of the classroom and announced to the sixty or seventy assembled students that she was terribly nervous. She always was, she said, at the beginning of a semester. She hadn't slept well, and her stomach felt "queasy." Every teacher in the room knew just what she meant. I fell in love right then and there.

Maxine's openness is more than symbolic. She gives herself completely to her students and invites them to follow her example. What is most appealing about Maxine is the combination of hubris and insecurity that she embodies, which captures the essence of what it means to be a teacher. On the one hand, we dare to engage in the reconstruction of schooling, but we also suffer the consequence of feeling that whatever we do will never be good enough or wise enough or sufficiently significant. Meeting with her in our writing group is cerebral, but I always experience the same mixture of confidence and uncertainty every time we meet. I am particularly aware of it when I have to read something I have written. Kathleen and Karen and I know ourselves to be capable, competent writers, but we often put out a disclaimer before we share our pieces. Maxine does the same thing. She will shyly pull a manuscript from her black bag, muttering, "I'm not sure if this works," and then she'll read her magical, metaphorical prose, and we'll be transported and inspired and amazed.

Maxine can make the most unintelligent questions sound brilliant. "I hear you saying," she'll begin. Or, "I think you mean," and then she'll rephrase the question referring to the most recently published novel, or last night's television drama, or the morning *Times*. She makes the same transformations for us in our writing group. She listens intently for nuance and asks questions that cut to deepest meanings—sometimes hidden even from the author. She supports us, but also points us to new paths and possibilities. I remember working on a piece about children's picture books and Maxine's supportive but insistent questioning of its relevance to diverse student groups. I worked in a suburban setting, and Maxine was there to remind me that I needed to pay more attention to city schools and their problems.

Maxine was once asked what she thought were the characteristics of a good teacher, and I keep remembering that, when she listed a few, she included a "tolerance for ambiguity." Perhaps the greatest gift she has given us in our writing group is the awareness of the ambiguous nature of teaching and an understanding that when our timidity is battling our aggression, we are ourselves becoming more attuned to subtlety, to profundity, and to possibility at the same time that we are struggling to make sense of our experience.

Though others may seek conformity and certainty, Maxine asks those hard questions with elusive answers that cause confusion and sometimes pain. But she always opens windows and, as our afternoons end, she sends us off to discover new ways to look at the familiar.

KATHLEEN

Whenever I hear myself say that I have been in a writing group with Maxine for several years, I have to quickly add that she certainly doesn't get any help from me . . . when Maxine reaches into her bag and casually pulls out a work-in-progress, it's usually in need of very little editing . . . maybe just a patch here and there, but never anything major. So, if I do talk about being in a writing group with her, it is mostly "to edify, to explain" in J. D. Salinger's words. She is such a city mouse, and when we meet at my house, she travels an hour and a half north to the Connecticut woods and the river that runs parallel. At a June meeting in 1991, she pulled into the driveway with Maureen, and stepped out with her signature black straw hat pulled down around her face the way I like to think Edna St. Vincent Millay wore hers. As she walked through the gate, she tossed off the question, "Will there be croquet?"

It was at this session that spread through a long afternoon in my sunroom that I just made notes about the way she asks questions. She told me later on that day, "I'm so full of questions that I can't answer." That was her response to my struggles with my research questions. I thought that I was colliding with myself . . . too many questions . . . data enough to drown in. . . . I was moaning about being loaded with questions and impatient for answers. Maxine nodded with complicity . . . she has the most natural way of easing you into her intellectual jet stream, as if you belonged. "Questions gather in me and sizzle," she continued, "I think too fluidly; I was obsessed with the imaginary when I was younger, . . . not so sure I've changed that much." Here was a typical Maxine response giving me permission to wander, to grope with my barrel of questions about my students and their writing . . . she never said that I should shape my approach in a different way. Rather, she instantly recognized that I was stuck with my own musings, and in a heartbeat, she added . . . "You really should celebrate your embeddedness, Kathleen." Hmm . . . should I do that? . . . that would be some trick, I thought . . . but the afternoon wore on after lunch, and I found some change occurring. Rather than fight for definition and refinement in my research, I would just proceed even though I was weighed down by it.

I read my journal, describing the way Anne Berthoff's *Dialectic Notebooks* were helping my students audit their own meaning when they read and wrote about the literature we studied. Maxine, Karen, and Maureen listened to my discoveries, frustrations, wonderings . . . with all of the student papers and notebooks to look at, make sense of, write about, I felt that there was no way out of this that would mean anything to anyone else . . . but, Maxine again, said the right words: "I could never break with my involvement," she remarked . . . and there was another gift . . . I was involved in the way that every teacher should be . . . up to my ears in change . . . and Karen, Maureen, and Maxine brought me to that fact face to face . . . it simply had not occurred to me that I was a factor in this research . . . I preferred, I see now, to be a spectator, too . . . . but, that would never do . . . not with this group.

Maxine's presence always lightened and deepened our sessions together . . . she is very witty, loves to laugh, and does it spontaneously . . . ideas amuse her, perplex her, seduce her . . . and it is all there on her face when she is listening to one of us, responding, questioning. Her questions can be killers, more global, and far reaching than we want at times . . . in a discussion about the way that journals work in my classroom, she posed "Is there a pedagogy of journals?" Eek, I thought, of course there is, isn't there? . . . or at least, there should be, I realized. The summer afternoon continued with the four of us taking turns reading, writing notes, responding . . . I remember that I was still stuck in my own thick descriptions of research, and I suggested to Maxine that I was thinking too abstractly, perhaps . . . what do you think? "A metaphor brings the severed parts together . . ." she added . . . and she was right, of course.

Maxine knows instinctively about the balance of the abstract and concrete . . . she taught me that teacher research is a way to change, and I learned, too, in our meetings together, that change has already happened before you know it. The process involves grappling, considering possibilities, and it was in our group that I learned to write the story of the changes I made as a teacher. It was during our sessions that I came to recognize my own epistemology, what it is to know something, to admit that meaning is contextual. Learning to connect what I know with what I experience was the critical piece that initiated the changes in my classroom. Writing and thinking together brought me to Maxine's theory that qualitative research was an aesthetic activity, that seeing the subtle gradations of change in my classroom were "framed moments," in her words, points of reference frozen in the context of the classroom.

I think Maxine has convinced us that all of the "psychic risks" that surface during our writing group are the grist for a life lived fully. Many of those touched by Maxine will agree that she is the most informed, current, on-the-cutting-edge woman they know . . . she's seen every movie, play, museum show, and her connections to literature boggle my mind! After an afternoon of listening to Maxine make allusions to so many and varied works, I remarked that I felt as if I hadn't read anything. Typically, Maxine answered, "Oh, I know what you mean . . . so do I!"

So, I have taken the cues from Maxine: I have learned to think more fluidly than ever, to wallow in my data, to pile up questions until I feel stuffed, to trust my instincts, to value the entire process. Writing with Maxine, Maureen, and Karen has been liberating, inspiring, energizing. Often I think we have lost all focus, that we should have an agenda to follow . . . but it never will happen that way.

II

A COMMUNITY
IN THE MAKING

All depends upon a breaking free, a leap, and then a question. I would like to claim that this is how learning happens and that the educative task is to create situations in which the young are moved to begin to ask, in all the tones of voice there are, "Why?" . . . I place the release of imagination with which I am so deeply concerned in context in a variety of ways while discussing an emergent curriculum, the moral life, and justice in the public space. Because so many of us are newcomers and strangers to one another, I particularly emphasize pluralism and heterogeneity, what is now often called multiculturalism. I choose to do so in connection with the arts and with a community always in the making—the community that may someday be called a democracy.

Maxine Greene
Releasing the Imagination

In a recent conversation, Maxine Greene drew our attention again to issues of freedom, imagination, democracy, and the making of community:

I want young people . . . to identify themselves by means of significant projects. . . . It seems important, as I have said too often, that the projects are most meaningful when they involve others, when they touch on others' lives. Care may be important; but more important in my life has been the feeling of connectedness in marches or campaigns or deliberate efforts to make something better—to plant, to build, to stop the killing, to cherish the young. There is, as most of us know, a special joy in being part of a movement directed to something in the distance, something that shines and beckons and is not yet. Hannah Arendt once wrote about the French poet and resistance fighter,

René Char. After the Second World War ended in France, he wrote about
the sadness of going back to the "opaqueness of private life" from the freely
chosen Resistance experience. Leaving that behind, he said, "we lost our treasure." The treasure was being face to face with others in a struggle for liberation. They had all chosen in their freedom to take part; and they were
together without masks or pretenses, as *who* each one felt herself or himself to be. . . . Maurice Merleau-Ponty wrote of unexpected moments when
people feel their identity with other suppressed groups they never knew, and
how, acting in the experience of that mutual recognition, they opened a space
where they could be free. I suppose that is an ideal possibility. It is an image
of a journey we hope to take with others. . . . I choose to live the life of someone capable of indignation at undeserved suffering and silence and exclusion,
someone who refuses to feel a righteousness of indignation. An effort must
be made to change what is wrong, what seems so deeply, desperately unjust.
And oddly, I know that the real joy in life stems from the feeling of incom-
pletion, of not having found the way. So, like so many others, I reach out for
roles to play, for personalities to come in touch with, for an abundance of
desire. I do not want to end up in isolation, even in the midst of things; I never
want to become accustomed to a dry little life. And I realize fully that to live
otherwise is up to me.

In teaching, I suppose I want to communicate that. I feel successful if
I can make it possible for students to come upon ways of being they have
not thought of before. Part of that demands an activation of imagination; part,
a refusal to screen the self off from the world. None of us is separate and
autonomous; none of us can possibly be an "island" in John Donne's sense.
We are, like or not, part of a "main" our imagination can bring into being.
(Ayers, 1995, p. 323)

So much of the bewildering ennui of modern life is built upon our isolation
from one another. We blame ourselves. After all, we are said to be free, we
are told that we are a nation of communities, we see all around us the rigging
and the decorations of democracy.

There is a deep sense of alienation, of powerlessness, of a loss of any
normal human agency, and an accompanying language of victimization and
determinism. Overwhelmingly, there is a sense of immutability, of permanence.
Crime, crummy schools—these are simply *there*, God-given and unchange-
able. An attitude of alienation, abandonment, and atomization descends and
permeates our relationships. Most of us can remember a time *before* homelessness was a major social problem—all of us remember a time when we did-
n't see children begging on the streets. Now homelessness is another "given"—
we have become accustomed to one more unacceptable dimension of life.

The enduring loneliness is propelled in some measure by the official insistence that democracy is a text already written—it is the flag; it is the vote. Never
mind the Tweedledee-Tweedledum sameness of the Republicrats; never mind

the millions of dollars required to hold office; never mind the alienation of most people from meaningful public life. Our democracy is good; your problems are personal.

To think of democracy as participatory, to think of people actually making the decisions that affect our lives, is to notice that while we experience our problems as personal—we can't find adequate child care, perhaps, or our child is not learning as she should in school, or the options for our aging parents are inadequate—they are, indeed, social. It is to move from me to us, from loneliness to society. It is to move in a different direction.

REFERENCE

Ayers, W. (1995). Interview with Maxine Greene. *Qualitative Studies in Education,* *8*(4), 319–328.

5

On Becoming American: An Exploratory Essay

Sonia Nieto

What does it mean to be an American? This is in some ways the quintessential American dilemma, yet it has not historically invited a deep or sustained critical analysis. In spite of repeated attempts to answer the question throughout the successive generations of both newcomers and old-timers that have characterized the building of our nation, either easy speculation or pat answers have been the usual result. Why is this? For one, there is in place an unstated assumption of what it means to be an American; for another, questioning the assumed definition seems almost heretical because a number of troubling contradictions challenge the taken-for-granted definition. Yet for many, it is a deeply troubling issue that, it seems to me, is at the root of much of the continuing disunity in our country.

The question of becoming an American is one that has haunted me for many years, but until recently I have not focused on it in any deliberate or conscious way. My intense fascination with this question is motivated by my own background: Even though I was born in this country and have spent my entire life here, even though I was formed and educated and lead a productive professional life in the United States, when I am asked the inevitable question, "What are you?" I always answer "Puerto Rican." Why is it that for me being an American seems inherently to conflict with being a Puerto Rican? Ironically, I myself recognize that I am in some ways undeniably American; that is, my experiences, tastes, and even values immediately define me to most onlookers as "American," albeit with a deep connection to my Puerto Rican heritage. Several years ago, I was jarred when speaking with an island-born Puerto Rican who commented that he could tell at first glance that I was born and raised in the United States simply by looking at my body language! Here I was, convinced that I was as Puerto Rican as any Puerto Rican, that I had *"la mancha del plátano"* (the stain of the plantain) firmly imprinted on my face and body, and yet he saw my American roots through it all.

I must also admit that the unprecedented opportunities I have been given in the United States have made it possible for me to far transcend what my possibilities might have been had I not been raised and educated here. Although it is true that these opportunities are not held out to the majority of Puerto Ricans, among many others, and that our society has a long way to go before fulfilling its ideals of equal access and opportunity for all, it is nevertheless true that the fact that the ideals exist *at all* has made a dramatic difference in the lives of many people. My life as a fairly successful academic, teacher, and writer would probably have been impossible if I had been raised on the island in the working-class family with little formal education from which I came. Yet I resist being defined as American, and this is troubling for me because on some deep level I understand that I deserve the right to claim this identity if I mean to work to change what it means.

I am not alone in the quandary concerning my identity. I have met a great many people over the years who have similar feelings. Many of us who are what can be called "bicultural" (not necessarily because we have chosen to be so, but because of our circumstances) have faced the same dilemma (Darder, 1991). Is one an American by the mere fact of being born here? Can one be born elsewhere and still be an American? How many generations does it take? Do we belong here or there, in neither place, or in both? Does being an American have to erase or diminish automatically our accents, our values, our hues and textures? Where does our language, which sometimes is unacceptable both in our communities of origin and in the larger society, fit in? Do we have to "trade in" our identity, much as we would an old car, to acquire the shiny new image of American? How can we reconcile the sometimes dramatically differing value systems, languages, expectations of appropriate behavior, and the contradictory activities that take place in our everyday lives?

The question of identity is reverberating with more meaning and currency than ever as we approach the year 2000. Our nation is becoming more diverse and also more divided along lines of race, ethnicity, language use, social class, and other differences, although it can be argued that this division is not due necessarily to our growing diversity but rather to our inability to deal with it. Addressing issues that arise as a result of increased diversity demands both insight and care rather than arrogance and simplistic notions of unity. It is my purpose in this exploratory essay to reflect on the question of what it means to be, or as I have stated it in the title of this chapter, to *become* American, not only as it might be answered in a personal way for me, but also how as a society we might think about it.

DICHOTOMIES AS ANSWERS

In my own life, I had often come across a simple answer to the question of being an American: One is either an American or one is not. Simplistic *either/or* formulations are commonplace in our society, and problems such as these generally get answered in terms of dichotomies. Maxine Greene's work has provided me with both insight and hope in trying to answer the question of becoming American, so I begin this essay by referring to her thoughts on dichotomies. Rather than considering *community* and *pluralism* as necessarily or deterministically irreconcilable, she has instead challenged the respective boundaries and rigid parameters of both of these concepts. For example, she has written, "I want to break through, whenever possible, the persisting either/ors. There is, after all, a dialectical relation marking every human situation. The relation between subject and object, individual and environment, living consciousness and phenomenal world. This relation exists between two different, apparently opposite poles; but it presupposes a mediation between them" (1988, p. 8).

The traditional boundaries of fixed identities became clear to me when I was doing research in preparation for my first book several years ago (Nieto, 1992). Extensive interviews with ten academically successful students from a variety of cultural backgrounds revealed to me the familiar image of my own persistent dilemmas with identity. This was somewhat surprising because these young people were about three decades younger than I, but the same kinds of challenges were apparent in their lives as had been in mine when I was growing up in Brooklyn in the 1940s and '50s. I thought that surely by now this issue would be resolved one way or another; what I found instead was that the students were in the tumultuous midst of developing their identities in an ever-changing and even more complex world than was mine. Yet the students, unlike me, were also tentatively challenging the assumption that one must sacrifice culture and identity to become an American.

Although we had not asked these young people to lay claim to an exclusive identity, many of them chose to do so and often they defined themselves as either American or as a member of their national origin group. Underlying this choice seemed to be a recognition that our society demanded complete allegiance in return for the privilege of becoming an American. These young people were not always willing to pay the price. Take, for instance, Manuel, a young Cape Verdean man of nineteen who was the youngest of eleven children and the first to graduate from high school, an accomplishment that he must have known might not have been possible had he and his family remained in Cape Verde.

Yet in his eyes, the price in loss of identity that is frequently paid for the privilege of an education, success, and "fitting in" may be simply too high. Manuel stated the problem in this way: "That's something that a lot of kids do when they come to America. They change their names. Say you're Carlos, they say, 'I'm Carl.' They wanna be American; they're not Cape Verdean. . . . That's wrong. They're fooling themselves. . . . I identify myself as Cape Verdean. I'm Cape Verdean. I cannot be an American because I'm not an American. That's it" (Nieto, 1992, p. 176).

James, a Lebanese Christian (Maronite), faced a similar dilemma. Although by all outward appearances James was "American" in tastes, habits, and future goals, he too felt the pressure of difference. Born and raised in the United States, he had learned from his parents to cherish the Arabic language he spoke, the religion he practiced, and the culture they still maintained. This was not easy, however, in a school where he was a member of a minority so invisible that it did not even make the school cookbook, the international fair, or the foreign-language-month celebration, the few indications of the school's response to a growing multicultural student body. What other students knew about his background was thus mired in a web of superstitions and stereotypes. Try as he might to dismiss these as unimportant, it was clear that they had an impact on him: "Some people call me, you know, 'cause I'm Lebanese, so people say, 'Look out for the terrorist! Don't mess with him or he'll blow up your house!' or some stuff like that. But they're just joking around, though. . . . I don't think anybody's serious, 'cause I wouldn't blow up anybody's house—and they know that. . . . I don't care. It doesn't matter what people say. . . . I just want everybody to know that, you know, it's not true" (Nieto, 1992, p. 134).

Nevertheless, rather than hide behind the identity "American," which he could certainly claim and which might prove far easier to negotiate, this is what James said about who he is: "First thing I'd say is I'm Lebanese. . . . I'm just proud to be Lebanese. If somebody asked me, 'What are you?' . . . everybody else would answer, 'I'm American,' but I'd say, 'I'm Lebanese' and I feel proud of it" (p. 136). Further reflecting on this complicated issue of identity, James used the example of his idol, the biking star Greg LeMond, as a critique of forced assimilation: "Even though somebody might have the last name like LeMond or something, he's considered American. But you know, LeMond is a French name, so his culture must be French. His background is French. But, you know, they're considered Americans. But I'd like to be considered Lebanese" (p. 136).

One of the youngest students to be interviewed, thirteen-year-old Yolanda, who self-identified as Mexican, also talked about the saliency of her background. Although aware of the low status of Mexicans in the

general population and of the conflict that might lead other young people to either hide, change, or erase their identity, she stated, "I feel proud
of myself. I see some other kids that they say, like they'd say they're
Colombian or something. They try to make themselves look cool in front
of everybody. . . . I don't feel bad like if they say, 'Ooh, she's Mexican' or
anything. . . . For me, it's good. For other people, some other guys and
girls, don't think it's nice, it's like, 'Oh, man, I should've been born here
instead of being over there.' Not me, it's O.K. for me being born over
there 'cause I feel proud of myself. I feel proud of my culture" (p. 184).

In this research, one of the most consistent, although unexpected, outcomes was the striking combination of *pride* and *shame* that these young
people felt about their culture. That is, the great pride they felt was not
sustained without great conflict, hesitation, and contradiction. For these
young people, pride in culture was neither uniform nor easy. Upon closer
reflection, this was an understandable response: After all, a positive sense
of cultural identity flies in the face of the assimilation model held out as
the prize for sacrificing ethnicity, language, and even family loyalties.
But the internal conflicts that resulted were also quite apparent.

Sometimes the conflict and pain are too great and, rather than attempt
to somehow reconcile cultural differences, the choice may be made to
become an American on traditional terms. The alienation from family and
culture as chronicled by Richard Rodriguez in *Hunger of Memory* is a case
in point. In the following reflection from his book, Rodriguez speaks
with tremendous nostalgia about losing his native language, but also with
absolute certainty about the folly of providing such programs as bilingual education as a bridge or buffer for children to learn to fit into what
he called the "public world" of school and society:

> Without question, it would have pleased me to hear my teachers
> address me in Spanish when I entered the classroom. I would have felt
> much less afraid. I would have trusted them and responded with ease.
> But I would have delayed—for how long postponed?—having to learn
> the language of public society. I would have evaded—and for how long
> could I have afforded the delay?—learning the great lesson of school,
> that I had a public identity. . . . I continued to mumble. I resisted the
> teacher's demands. (Did I somehow suspect that once I learned the
> public language my pleasing family life would be changed?). (1982,
> pp. 19–20)

Nowhere can a more poignant reminder of the wholesale acceptance of
the "either/ors" to which Maxine Greene refers be found. Rodriguez's
dilemma, that is, was predicated on a difficult choice: either lose your
"private language" to become a public person, with all the benefits it

entails; or retain your "private language" and forfeit a public identity. Rather than *English plus Spanish,* the formulation was *English or Spanish.* The result, in Rodriguez's formulation, was learning English and accomplishing a high level of academic achievement. However, as we see from his autobiography, this kind of "success" is often accompanied by tormented musings on what might have been lost in the process. The idea that one can be *both* successful *and* maintain one's cultural and linguistic identity is not part of this formula.

An alternative approach, also in the "either/or" paradigm, is to resist assimilation and instead maintain one's native language and culture. This approach operates on a continuum, ranging from retaining an idealized and pure image of the native culture, to a more pragmatic approach where learning the second language and becoming more or less familiar with the host culture is the outcome. The more extreme form of this cultural maintenance, that is, complete isolation and rigid nationalism, in the short run provides a shield against assimilation and can be seen as a healthy response to the violent stripping away of identity that is characteristic of what it has meant to become an American. In the long run, however, it is unworkable and unrealistic in today's complex and interdependent world. In speaking about the more extreme forms of Afrocentrism, it is what Cornel West has called "a gallant yet misguided attempt," (1993, p. 4) because to believe that any culture will remain intact and static when placed on new ground is hopelessly romantic at best. Culture, writes Thomas Bender, "is not an emblem of achievement to be worn; it is a resource to be used. It is not fixed and permanent. Cultures change as they are used as resources for addressing new experiences that history presents to us" (1992, p. 13). Thus, culture is dialectical, responding with inventive new creations to both the positive and negative influences of transplanted migrations and immigrations.

In the end, a static cultural maintenance is both implausible and exclusionary and this realization may help explain my impatience with "cultural purists." In some gatherings of Latinos, for instance, there is sometimes a fervent insistence that only Spanish be spoken (almost the flip side of the "English-Only" insistence, but without its institutionalized and hegemonic power). Ironically, this kind of purism may in the process alienate further those second-, third-, and even fourth-generation Latinos who happen not to speak Spanish. Or my anger when Spanish-speaking elitist intellectuals, for example, disdainful in their rejection of U.S.-based artists, state unequivocally that Latino literature can be *only* that literature written in Spanish. For them, English, Spanish and English, Spanglish, or any of the other creative combinations used by U.S.-based artists, are simply out of the question because they represent a corruption of what it means to be a Latino. These kinds of definitions, whether of Latino or of American, fall back on simplistic notions of culture as static and fixed and are thus flawed and untrue to reality. That is, they fail to acknowledge that culture must be mediated in human interactions. Rather than a bounded box of artifacts and values, culture is more like an amoebae that changes shape with every move. Either/or dichotomies are unsatisfactory in either case.

CHALLENGING THE "EITHER/ORS"

If one is to eschew either/or positions, that is, if one cannot either wholly maintain native culture, nor accept assimilation as inevitable, what is to be done? The young people who we interviewed for my study offered a range of possibilities, although in most cases culture was still perceived as immutable. Some of them, although feeling quite proud of their culture, of their ability to function effectively in at least two worlds, and of their bilingualism, also learned to feel ashamed of their culture and of those who represented it. Sometimes, it was clear they blamed their parents or others in the community for perceived failures, and they absolved the school of any wrongdoing. For others, the conflict was too great and led, among other things, to reaching the conclusion that one could not be both American and Cape Verdean (as in the case of Manuel); that "Puerto Ricans are way badder than Whites" (as in the case of Marisol, a Puerto Rican girl who nevertheless loudly proclaimed her pride at being Puerto Rican); or that their culture should not necessarily be important in the school, although it is in the home (as in the case of James, whose culture was so invisible in his school).

The pressures of assimilation proved too great for Vinh, who talked at length about what was apparently a depression he had suffered: "I've been here for three years, but the first two years I didn't learn anything. I got sick, mental. I got mental. Because when I came to the United States, I missed my [parents], my family and my friends, and my Vietnam. . . . I am a very sad person. Sometimes, I just want to be alone to think about myself. . . . Before I got mental, okay, I feel very good about myself, like I am smart. . . . But after I got mental, I don't get any enjoyment. . . . I'm not smart anymore" (Nieto, 1992, p. 146).

The choices made by most of the young people were based on hard-learned lessons concerning the price of cultural assimilation. Forced to make a choice, they were generally making it in favor of their heritage. This decision can also be problematic because, although a courageous stance in light of the negative messages of ethnicity and culture that they hear and see daily, it may limit their possibilities. That is, in choosing *not* to be American, they may have also decided that they are not deserving or entitled to help shape and change their society. Making the choice to have no attachment, they may feel also that they have no rights or responsibilities.

Needless to say, questions of race, colonial status, and social class (in sum, issues of power or powerlessness) are at the very heart of the conflicts I have described. In particular, the weight of a history of white supremacy and racist ideology, unacknowledged but unmistakable in their impact, are a continuing legacy in our notions of who is most likely to be defined as American. Most Europeans, even relatively new immigrants, can be accommodated into the cultural mainstream almost immediately because of their white skin privilege, their status as more or less "voluntary immigrants," and also often because of their middle-class or professional backgrounds. Although they may face the pain and alienation of all new immigrants, they, and certainly their children and grandchildren, rarely have to contend with even making a choice; it is made for them. They almost immediately become "American," fitting into the mainstream of race and class that has been defined as such. Asians and Latinos, and ironically even American Indians, on the other hand, may have been on this soil for many generations but are still asked the inevitable "Where are you from?" reserved for outsiders. Their faces or accents are constant and unmistakable reminders of their roots in Africa, Asia, Latin America, and even Indigenous America, and this question once again belies our society's claim to accept all people on an equal basis.

BECOMING AMERICAN: A NEW PROPOSITION

Departing from either/or formulations, some new directions are being proposed, both by theorists who think about marginalized ethnicities and cultures, and by those who live these realities every day. What if we were to insist that everyone needed to *become American,* rather than begin with the premise that they need to *be American,* so that all of us, including those from the dominant cultural group, found it necessary to renegotiate identity on a continuous basis, to be formed and reformed every day?

This new formulation would lead to Maxine Greene's "passions of pluralism," where the newly conceived "great community" of which she speaks might become a true possibility (Greene, 1993). Community, of course, without the informed consent of its constituents becomes simply an imposed and bureaucratic identity, and those who have not had a hand in constructing it chafe under its definition. This is what has happened with so many of us who resist the label "American" because we have had no hand in determining what it means. Redefining American means not reconstituting it as much as searching into what is already there, recapturing the living and breathing cultures so apparent in our cities and towns, and in our schools and homes. Creating "the expanding community," in the words of Maxine Greene, requires this kind of search: "Something life-affirming in diversity must be discovered and rediscovered, as what is held in common becomes always more many-faceted—open and inclusive, drawn to untapped possibility" (1993, p. 17).

The insistence on the untapped possibility of pluralism is where the redefinition of becoming American must begin. But a redefinition that ossifies a new canon is not what is called for. Examples of a new, monolithic multicultural canon are apparent in programs of "pablum multiculturalism" defined in an "everybody is beautiful, let's celebrate diversity" way, or multiculturalism as an uncontested, unconflicted, smooth road to upward mobility that refuses to tackle the difficult realities of structural inequality.

As Maxine Greene reminds us, diversity must be problematized, studied, and understood as a dialectic rather than simply "celebrated." This means rejecting the "sunny-side-up diversity" that attempts to paper over important differences. A more critical multiculturalism is based on *agency,* that is, the power and the ability to create culture. Being cultural beings implies that we are also cultural creators and negotiators and cultural critics, struggling to develop identities that retain important insights and values while also challenging the limitations that both our native and adopted cultures may impose on us.

Creating a new culture also does not mean inserting ethnic tidbits into an already existing culture, thus replicating what James Banks has called the "contributions approach" (1991) to American culture and history that is the favorite of too many programs in multicultural education. All cultures exist in relation to one another, and that is what a process of renegotiation needs to consider. In terms of learning a new language, for instance, this might mean injecting it into the old and creating something new, and this complex process is described by Eva Hoffman in this way: "Each language modifies the other, crossbreeds with it, fertilizes it. Each language make the other relative. Like everybody, I am the sum of my languages—the language of my family and childhood, and education and friendship, and love, and the larger, changing world—though perhaps I tend to be more aware than most of the fractures between them, and of the building blocks" (1989, p. 273). More aggressively, Gloria Anzaldúa speaks of the "borderlands" inhabited by Chicanos and the crucial role that language plays in this creation:

For a people who are neither Spanish nor live in a country in which Spanish is the first language; for a people who live in a country in which English is the reigning tongue but who are not Anglo; for a people who cannot entirely identify with either standard (formal, Castilian) Spanish nor standard English, what recourse is left to them but to create their own language? A language which they can connect their identity to, one capable of communicating the realities and values true to themselves—a language with terms that are neither *español ni inglés,* but both. We speak a patois, a forked tongue, a variation of two languages. (1987, p. 55)

Language is an important symbol of cultural identity, and the stubborn resistance to accepting wholesale a language of imposition is evident in the research of Juan Flores, John Attinasi, and Pedro Pedraza on the language use and attitudes of residents of El Barrio, a Puerto Rican community in New York City:

By virtual consensus, Puerto Ricans want to maintain Spanish. This is true even for young people who admit to not knowing much Spanish. The feeling is that Spanish should be audible and visible wherever Puerto Rican culture exists, an attitude that connects to both observed language use and the postulated life cycle of language competence. . . . Puerto Ricans also want to learn English; for most, a person who is more fluent in English than in Spanish is neither a paradox nor an anomaly, much less a case of deliberate or unwitting cultural betrayal. These findings reveal that both linguistic and cultural identity are changing in response to economic and social transformations, and that interpenetrating bilingualism is the idiom in which these cultural changes are expressed. (1993, p. 167)

The process of re-creation must concern and involve all of us, but young people who feel marginalized are particularly important in the creation of a new culture. In a new conception of American, native cultures do not simply disappear, as schools or society might expect or want them to. Rather, aspects of them are retained, modified, and reinserted into different contexts to become valid and workable. But the process of creating a new culture is generally neither conscious nor planned. It is instead the inevitable conclusion of cultures co-existing in uneasy, conflicted, but also rewarding ways. Neither assimilation nor cultural purity is the result. Hip hop, break dancing, and any number of new music forms are good examples of this process, as are the English/Spanish/"Spanglish" poetry of urban Latinos and the redefined murals of the inner city. By changing the complexion, attitudes, behaviors, and values of society, we can all experience the comfort of the known as well as the pain and dislocation of the unknown.

The process of *becoming American* is not merely an academic exercise, but must connect to schools in fundamental ways. Students and teachers need to learn how to construct curricula that affirm all students while also challenging the idea of fixed or idealized identities. They need to search for new sources of knowledge to create a shifting canon that includes all students and communities. And they also need to develop the "great community" to which Maxine Greene refers, not in a mechanical or unproblematic way, but through constant negotiation and renegotiation.

LIVING WITH CONFLICTED DEFINITIONS

I am left then with the question with which I began this essay: What does it mean to become American? In the case of Puerto Ricans, the example closest to my heart, it remains a riveting and defining question. I close with a reflection on the Puerto Rican experience, not just because of my own self-interest, but also because it may help enlighten others for whom the questions of belonging, identity, and fitting in are so central. Roberto Márquez discusses these concerns in an elegant essay on the experiences, dilemmas, and challenges of Puerto Ricans in the United States:

> What emerges from all this is the biculturally and binationally problematic, inventive, intrinsically challenging nature of this "new" Puerto Rican who, in a very important sense, is in fact no longer an (im)migrant at all, but is also, unmistakably, the historical product and extension of the "old" Puerto Rican (im)migrant and clings as fiercely to his island roots. No less an inveterate commuter, this Puerto Rican's *place* is now both *here* and *there* and, invariably, neither *here* nor *there.* Between *one* and *the other,* it is no longer the termination points or patrolled borders but the syncretic results of constantly moving between and beyond them that becomes central; it is the oscillating intensity of being both fixed and in constant motion that nourishes a creatively defiant endurance and dynamic vitality. (1995, p. 114)

This reflection on what it means to become American, mired as it is in both contradictions and complexities, will not make it any simpler to answer the other inevitable question I am asked when meeting someone for the first time: "Where are you from?" they may ask (sometimes a substitute for "What are you?"). I usually pause for a long second before answering with my own series of questions, "Do you mean where was I born? Or what is my ethnic background? How do I identify? Or where do I live?" All these are possible answers, but it would be much easier to answer, without hesitation, "I am an American." But because "American" does not yet include me in any significant way, I am not able to do this. I cannot even yet say, "I am a Puerto Rican-American" because I cannot bring myself to live as a hyphenated person. And I particularly refuse to be included when those who, with an arrogance so complete that they are not even aware of their own ignorance, attempt to include me under taken-for-granted definitions into the "club" on their terms (at the conclusion of an unresolved conversation about differences, they may say, winking broadly at me, "After all, we're all Americans, aren't we?").

I hope that, if not for my children, at least for my grandchildren the answer will be a less conflicted one. But I hope that it will not come too easily either. If being an American means that they must leave behind or forget their own multiple identities, they will have lost something precious in the answer. For my daughters, the answer is already even more difficult in some ways than it has been for me. My older daughter, half Puerto Rican and half Spanish, and with a deep sense of her Latino heritage, also has to think before answering. For my younger daughter, adopted, with a Puerto Rican, Canadian European, and American Indian heritage, it is even more problematic given current definitions. And for my little granddaughter, who is all that and also African American, I can only hope that being American develops to mean all of this and more.

As long as there are newcomers, as long as there are those who refuse to be included in a definition that denies them both their individual and group identities, the question of becoming American will be with us. The challenge for us as a society is to make room for all of them. Maxine Greene refers to these people when she says, "There are always strangers, people with their own cultural memories, with voices aching to be heard" (1988, p. 87). Perhaps by making room for these cultural memories, these achings to be heard, our society as a whole can begin constructing a new definition of becoming American.

REFERENCES

Anzaldúa, G. (1987). *Borderlands/La* Frontera:*The new mestiza.* San Francisco: Aunt Lute Books.

Banks, J. (1991). *Teaching strategies for ethnic studies* (5th ed.), Boston: Allyn & Bacon.

Bender, T. (1992). Negotiating public culture: Inclusion and synthesis in American history. *Liberal Education, 78*(2), 10–15.

Darder, A. (1991). *Culture and power in the classroom: A critical foundation for bicultural education.* New York: Bergin & Garvey.

Flores, J., Attinasi, J., and Pedraza, P. (1993). La Carreta made a U-turn: Puerto Rican language and culture in the United States. In J. Flores (Ed.), *Divided borders: Essays on Puerto Rican identity.* Houston, TX: Arte Público Press, pp. 157–181.

Greene, M. (1988). *The dialectic of freedom.* New York: Teachers College Press.

Greene, M. (1993). The passions of pluralism: Multiculturalism and the expanding community. *Educational Researcher, 22*(1), 13–18.

Hoffman, E. (1989). *Lost in translation: A life in a new language.* New York: E. P. Dutton.

Márquez, R. (1995). Sojourners, settlers, castaways and creators: A recollection of Puerto Rico past and Puerto Ricans present. *The Massachusetts Review, XXXVI*(1), 94–118.

Nieto, S. (1992). *Affirming diversity: The sociopolitical context of multicultural education* (1st ed.) White Plains, NY: Longman Publishing Group.

Rodriguez, R. (1982). *Hunger of memory: The education of Richard Rodriguez.* Boston: David R. Godine.

West, C. (1993). *Race matters.* Boston: Beacon Press.

6

Maxine Greene and the Incompleted Project

Herbert Kohl

Once upon a time there was two men who were always fighting so one day a wise man came along and said fighting will never get you anywhere they didn't pay him no attention and they got in quarrels over and over again. So one day they went to church and the preacher said you should not fight and they got mad and knock the preacher out. Moral: Can't find no ending.

Franklin
Sixth-grade student, Harlem, New York

In a recent conversation with Maxine Greene, she referred to her life as an incompleted project. We had been talking about Jean Paul Sartre, who is one of my heroes and someone whose work she knows and has studied with a passion. Passion and Maxine go together. There is no one else I know whose life and work so embodies intellectual passion and the practice of love.

The practice of love requires an understanding of incompleted projects. Incompleteness is as important and positive an idea as its opposite, completeness, though it is hardly ever considered that way. The idea of completion is a positive value in school and society. You're supposed to finish what you begin, carry through something to its end, do an exhibition of what you learned that summarizes and completes your learning. If you don't complete a book you start, or finish a hobby project, or get all your credits in school, or turn in all of your assignments, there's something wrong with you. You are irresponsible, lazy, and unreliable.

I have learned how to complete things but must admit that the most interesting things I've ever tried to do have never been finished. Some have been put on hold; others have been abandoned. And a few are still in my mind, floating about, still interesting in some ways and yet not compelling enough or clear enough to be brought to the surface and completed.

58

My first encounter with incompleteness was with Kurt Gödel's theorem; my second with the works of Jean Paul Sartre. Gödel's theorem is one of the most important mathematical and intellectual achievements that I have ever encountered. Simply put, it states that every mathematical system that is adequate to account for the theorems of arithmetic is essentially and irreparably incomplete in the sense that there will be an infinite number of well-formed statements in that system that are neither provable nor disprovable.

One way to visualize this is to imagine having a box of infinite size full of all the statements that can legitimately be made in the system. Gödel's theorem states that no matter how you try to sort out the statements into two groups—into those which can be derived from the axioms or those whose negatives can be proved—an infinite number of statements will remain in the box.

Gödel proved once and for all the impossibility of Leibnitz's idea of creating a universal calculus, a computer that could turn out all and only mathematical truths. No such technique or machine can ever theoretically be created. The best one can do is develop techniques or create computers that pull out a subset of the whole of mathematical truths.

The acceptance of this limitation on the possibility of system building—instead of having a limiting effect on the development of computers—had the positive effect of focusing mathematicians and logicians on defining useful subsets of theorems that could in fact be predictably generated, either through imaginative proof or computing techniques. The search for a universal computer inhibited the development of actual computers; once Gödel's theorem was accepted, more specific problems were defined and solved.

For me Gödel's theorem became a metaphor for the essential incompletability of human institutions and dreams. It made me acutely conscious of the potential limits of system building. It pointed out that a thorough understanding of complex systems, whether cultural, social, or political, might not be possible. This provided me, on the one hand, with a healthy humility when it came to analyzing history or trying to predict the effects of current practices. On the other hand, it gave me a sense that the consequences of attempts at societal change are not as predictable or controllable as people in power would like them to be. The limitations imposed by completeness metaphorically represent the limits of control and the possibility of small people making large changes. It indicates the space for the convergence of authentic action and the accidents of space and time.

As I've implied above, extending Gödel's theorem into the metaphoric domain, while useful for thinking through problems, is not grounds for the development of social theory. Maxine Greene, I'm sure, would understand; she understands that metaphor is a tool for the social imagination. One of the centers of Maxine's life and work (and they are not distinguishable), whether it is in kindergarten or graduate school, is the development of a sensitive and compassionate social imagination. This is another way of saying that Maxine is a practical dreamer, a radical utopian, a person who, while understanding current social, economic, and political realities, has a vision of a more decent way of organizing human life and society.

This vision, being both artistic and utopian, is not limited by arguments that cite "the way the world is" or "human nature." For Maxine, human nature is made, not fixed, and the vision of a decent world serves to extend people's notion of the possible. Not surprisingly, Maxine has studied Sartre and has thought deeply and fully about his work. But my sense of Maxine as having profound affinity with Sartrean thinking comes from a more personal source. It is from Sartre that I first understood the idea of an incompleted project.

In 1959, when I was living in Paris pretending I was a writer, the life of French intellectuals fascinated me. At the time, Jean Paul Sartre, Albert Camus, Simone de Beauvoir, Maurice Merleau-Ponty, and others were engaged in passionate arguments over their positions on the war in Algeria. They were arguing and writing about ways of reconciling individual freedom with socialism and Marxism and at the same time they were engaging in the social and economic struggles of their society. This was new for me. Harvard philosophers were engaged in arguments over fine points of language and logic and tended to be liberal and conservative but never radical or seriously engaged. No serious questioning of capitalism ever arose in class or in conversation. Paris was liberating to me and in a funny way brought me closer to the Bronx, where I grew up listening to my grandparents and their friends argue socialism all the time.

Sartre was a particular favorite of mine. He wrote plays and novels, produced philosophical tomes, and was a public figure as well. I remember sitting in my tiny apartment on the Rue Git Le Coeur reading the first three volumes of his planned tetralogy, The Road to Freedom, and realizing that there never would be a fourth volume. He had left everything in the lives of his characters irresolvable and had the courage to leave the three volumes an ambitious, interesting, incompleted project. That was not Sartre's only incompleted project. His biography of Flaubert never was finished. Nor was The Critique of Dialectical Reason. Sartre reached deeper than most people and took his projects as far as his imagination and understanding allowed him. He reached high and far and often failed. Yet from him, I learned the dignity of an incompleted grand human project and the pride that can come from a life as an activist intellectual and artist, and in a modest way I have used insights into how he lived and worked as guides for my own life and work.

Maxine Greene is a kindred spirit who spends her life as an activist intellectual and writer reaching to the largest, most compassionate and militant view of a decent future. She, too, is honored by her incompleted projects. Some people shy away from incompleteness and make their dreams and projects small. Others gamble on winning and walking away from things. But Maxine, true existential dreamer, embraces the incompleted projected that is her life. She dreams big, and the dream stays alive because she honors it despite its Gödelian essential incompletability. She wants the perfect kindergarten and the perfect world, perfect in that everyone is challenged, loved, and full of compassion, and she steps in that direction. In that, Maxine is our finest teacher and I am delighted and honored to be one of her friends and comrades.

7

What Role for the Arts?

Leon Botstein

Maxine Greene, in a courageous way, stood alone for many years, fighting for a tradition in progressive education through periods in which the word "progressive" had become synonymous with something quaint, or even bad and evil; it became a code word for sloppiness or for an absence of standards. In many ways, she has taken the tradition of John Dewey and kept the faith without making it seem hopelessly old fashioned. Of her many contributions I want to focus on the challenge she has set out: to make the arts not a marginal part of how we deal with children and young people, but an integral part of their lives and their minds. This work benefits not only the arts as such, but also education in its fullest sense, for she has sought to integrate the arts into how we teach children and adults. This emphasis on the arts continues a powerful tradition of progressive educational philosophy, but in a new spirit that attempts to fight a much-simplified notion of what it means to teach and what it means to learn. That simplified notion of education is adhered to by the neo-conservative movement today, and by political forces in all times that are, in the final analysis, antidemocratic.

Can the arts play a role in improving the quality of education that we offer to our young people? It's a simple question—not complicated—and it assumes that the education we are now offering students is not adequate. Indeed it is true that education today is inadequate. And the education of our teachers is likewise inadequate. Can the arts play a role in improving the quality of education that we offer to teachers as well as to our young people?

The answer cannot be fashioned in the traditional way, which would be to say: Once upon a time, there were good schools where teachers taught and students learned something. The task we face now in this country is radically different from the task that existed in the twenties, thir-

Revised from a speech delivered November 1995 at the Conference on Social Imagination, the Arts, and Education at Teachers College, New York.

ties, and forties. The basic issue of access and the question of who goes to school are so radically different today that it is quite pointless to talk about the past in nostalgic comparisons. In fact, one of the worst things we can do to today's children is ruminate about a long-lost, wonderful past. Nothing is more depressing for children than to talk about their present as if it were nothing more than a pale reflection of a glorious past. I wouldn't sit still behind a desk or any electronic contraption in the name of education under such premises, yet almost every adult faced with a child appears to be instantly filled with nostalgia for some ship that has already left the harbor.

I would prefer to frame the problems we face in a much more simple way. I don't want to recapture a mystified past. My own schooling wasn't great, and I would wish on my children considerably better than I received. I don't have to criticize the past nor praise it. I have to look at what is happening here, now, and reflect on how we might make things better.

It is significant that after the Second World War many leading intellectuals and leaders decided it would be important to integrate American pragmatic philosophy and the thinking of John Dewey into a new German educational system to help shape a democratic Germany. Dewey's philosophy, it was hoped, would provide a way to help educate people for democracy, to develop an educational system congruent with democratic participation. The essence of Dewey's project was correctly identified. He thought of education as a means of inspiring people to develop and improve autonomously in a democracy. Still, it doesn't pay to merely hang on to ideas of the past even when we like those ideas.

But it does pay to ask the same questions: What kind of system will fit a vision of what citizens need to do in a democratic society today, and how might we work together to make that happen? There is a certain irony about the quality of the political debate in the United States today. It has reached its lowest point when the people going to the polls have had the most education; there is an inverse relation between the quality of political discourse and the number of degrees and years of college credit held by Americans. The political debate was better when fewer people had access to school. Now obviously this is a provocative claim that could be taken apart as overstated. But there is a core of fundamental and disturbing truth. We would have assumed that with the broadening of education the quality of political debate would improve. Today, the name-calling, inarticulate ugliness, and hypercritical obsession with private lives are incongruous with the efforts of education.

The question remains for the educators of the future, what role for the arts? Do the arts have some peculiar way of opening up for a child,

or for any of us, the integral sense of his or her importance and uniqueness in a free society? Can the arts develop the motivation to use mental capacities broadly? There is, perhaps, something inherently liberating, inspiring, quite individualistic, and at the same time broadening about
contact and association with the arts. In the thirties, the kind of ham-radio
tinkering that was encouraged was associated with teaching science and
was viewed as encouraging cognitive independence. "Explore like Edison,"
we taught. Teaching the arts might create new things as well: a motivation to learn, a sense of the importance of making things, of doing something we can call learning, a sense of expressive individualism, which
is in contrast to the kind of group solidarity that we identify with ethnicity and nationality, or those linked to religious sectarian organizations.
Integrate arts into the curriculum, and you can actively help individuals
become people who think of themselves as having some worth, who retain
a sense of individuality, and who might resist conceiving of themselves
as mirroring an essentialist group identity. They will learn that the arts
are highly subjective, that it is less important that you achieve professional status in the arts than that you encounter them, discover dimensions in the world and yourself through them, enjoy them, and that
somebody else takes pleasure from what you do.

Now I want to be ardently critical of the issue as I've posed it. What
is the place of the arts in a democratic society? What is their role? And
second, what's really the realistic motivation toward improving the schools
and in what direction? And third, can we possibly get the arts to play a
role?

In this country there is an enormous fear of the arts, which takes
many forms. People fear the arts and artists because they seem to have
some competitive role with religion. Why do we worry about
Mapplethorpe? Why do we worry about what happens in the name of
the arts? Why is there a lingering interest in censorship? The arts are
considered in some way critical of moral standards; they are iconoclastic, and, regardless of content, they compete for the souls of the public.
In that sense, the cliched image of Allen Ginsberg can be compared to that
of David Koresh. The notion that there is something inherently seduc-
tive in artistic expression, in the sense of the opposition between sexuality and morality, creates a suspicion of the arts as related in part to unbridled sensuality—the same suspicion that is evident in the tale of Moses
coming down and looking at the golden calf. This country was founded
with a great deal of religious fervor despite deism. Remember that all
theater was banned in the 1780s and '90s in Philadelphia. In fact, in many
areas of the United States, all forms of artistic expression were banned
as somehow at odds with puritan faith, discipline, and the love of God.

I think that one cannot help but confront the residual and diverse religious reactions to the arts in relationship to the question of how those might function in education. The "competition," those invested in religion, fear the artist-as-charismatic-figure that we have otherwise celebrated historically.

Today, America is sometimes construed exclusively as a marketplace. It is amazing and more than a little ironic that people who represent constituencies that consume the work of Madonna, MTV, dramatizations on film of gore, destruction, violence, beheading, dismemberment, and rape—which make fortunes in Hollywood—simultaneously worry about nudes in art. The hypocrisies are enormous. But Americans believe that if the marketplace wishes something, it must be satisfied. The marketplace logic, then, overrides the moral concern. However, if one sets the popular culture question aside when talking about the arts and about the responsibilities and duties of our schools, there is still a specific heightened concern about the influence of the arts. The first fear is that they compete for the soul in ways that are morally dangerous. The second is that the arts are irrelevant: Children need mathematics; even schools are failing at math, but there it is. The arts, then, are viewed as irrational and therefore inherently marginal and critical. The idea that somebody is telling you something that is incomprehensible—that modern music is beautiful, that abstract art is beautiful, that subjective use of language is beautiful, that Jackson Pollock's art is the same as the Mona Lisa— becomes hard to convey. If we could explain art as central or understandable to the majority of people, maybe it would be more convincing. For example, art and science are compatible. But artists will soon create something at odds with conventional taste. Many people will look at a Norman Rockwell painting and say, "Well that's art!" Art is good, if only decorative and alternative in a kind of toothless way. As a policy, that would be a nightmare. That is after all the kind of art the Nazi regime loved. Governments know how to use art, which is why we have poets at inaugurations, why we have military music—the rulers in all times have known art is indeed powerful. Soldiers in uniform and a big military band, and bagpipe, and trumpeting harmonies—you can't help but respond with some stirring of hatred, solidarity, or fear in your soul. And in fact, anybody who denies that is obviously not being candid.

Despite such practicalities, the arts are made often to be intentionally impractical. The number of people who agree that arts are in some way useful are indeed few. Microsoft wasn't built on arts education, and it is not clear that the future of employment is contingent on the arts, even though art tourism is significant. Now, of course, such arguments can be made, and are. But more often one hears that the arts are fundamentally elitist. The truth is that we're caught in a difficult contradiction. On the one hand, those of us who are involved in the arts fear the classic critique of the arts in capitalism, that they are merely objects of consumerism. It's not that I think Steven Spielberg's dramatization of the Holocaust was bad. It was fine. But it isn't comparable to a historical document and it isn't comparable to the literature of Primo Levi. It simply isn't. Despite its virtue, a feature film is necessarily part of a money-making, entertainment agenda. In a sense, that is the overwhelming agenda. It's a kind of very successful entertainment. But there's usually something more to art, which is why the marketplace—profit and loss—cannot be the only yardstick of success.

We have legitimate questions about art in the United States. Whose art? Who judges what is art? We need to challenge the limits of the aristocratic traditions of taste in art—what the Medicis collected or what Esterhazy supported or what the European, upper-middle class played and paid for in the later nineteenth century. That obviously isn't all of art. There's also the idea that this sense of art is not a democratic experience. It is often implied that most people can't appreciate art, or won't appreciate it, or don't appreciate it. Educators often put themselves in the position of preaching to the masses, a project, by the way, that totally failed in the old Soviet Empire. There, they took high art, poured money into it, made tickets for concerts cheap, and supported an "official art." Now, the whole, huge, wonderful theater tradition and musical organizations of the old FDK and Poland are in ruins. This is so because high art was associated by a new generation with the old regime; therefore rebellious young Germans fell in love with American rock music and video popular culture. And the high art that the Communists wanted to make the "possession of the people" totally failed because they propagated high art in a context of total unfreedom and total censorship. The project of making art part of the American popular experience and educational experience cannot avoid this yet unresolved dilemma of the aristocratic and monarchical traditions of high-art patronage, or the notion that the judgment of what is art is not the province of mere popularity. We don't vote on what constitutes good art. And in fact, the historian of art would point out that often art that is rebellious, aggressive, difficult, and hard to digest can later become beloved. Someone threw some canvas out yesterday that someone today might pay a million dollars for. In a democracy, art is about protecting extreme dissent, the dissent of the marginal individual to whom nobody wants to listen. Even, or especially, dissent that seems outrageous, irrelevant, and incomprehensible.

These are some of the challenges that come from Maxine Greene's work. The point is not to make better painters, better poets, and better musicians, but to integrate what we identify to be unique in the artistic experience with the experiences of young people in schools. What is the significance of doing so? First of all, art creates a language. It is not that the arts are another kind of language—I don't believe that. I don't believe that music is another language, or that poetry has a kind of emotional cognitive spirit that is divorced from language. Language ends up being at the center of artistic activity. When we hear music that has no words, our response to it can be visceral, but at some point it's translated into language. Language comes into play, and how we talk about the art is part of the challenge of teaching, seeing, and learning. What the products of the aesthetic imagination do is create realities in our social experience about which we ultimately have to talk. And they create, in a way, diversionary experiences that open up the range of how we talk to one another. What the arts do is create something that does not already exist, that is not predictable or entirely rational, which forces us to talk to ourselves and to other people in new ways. So in a classroom full of racial, gender, class, ideological, and economic strife, hostility, suspicion, and everything else, the arts create something that forces some conversation that cannot be totally reduced into the preexisting labels and categories of expected discourse. It's irrelevant whether the art under discussion is good or bad in some kind of museum sense. Its existence demands response in a way that circumvents the habitual, destructive ways in which we now converse.

The arts permit a reconciliation with the irreconcilable. It suggests the legitimacy of the individualist and challenges group identity. This is the premise of art: I am unique. I have a name. My name is X. Perhaps somebody else has my name, too. But nobody has my fingerprints, and nobody has my DNA sequence. But this "uniqueness" is often left to languish. I'm unique in being my parents' child, but my parents divorce so often that the traditional uniqueness of family is washed away. I'm married or have quasi-married relationships with enough people in sequence that there is no uniqueness in intimacy. In that fact lies the fraud of the cliches of romantic seduction. We rehearse them so many times that their power is washed away. And we act so blandly that our lives sound like soap operas, which is why we like soap operas. Television only underscores the irony that life imitates art of the wrong kind.

Yet "I think I want to be an individual" is still the rhetoric out there, particularly in our schools. How do we make the rhetoric work? The arts can allow us to do it. My daughter Abigail came home from elementary school years ago, where she was involved in a Thanksgiving turkey activity. She had a note from her teacher saying that she was too willful. She painted a purple and chartreuse turkey. And she drew outside the lines.

I admired her dissent. She was a bit upset, and I said, "Trust yourself and not the teacher. She's wrong. That's the lesson here." My point is that it is possible for all to create something unique in the making of art. And our arts advocates can facilitate that.

Opera troupes traveled all over the United States in the 1820s and 1830s. At the opera house in New Orleans, there was an integrated audience, segregated to be sure (black audience in the balcony, and a white audience of all classes on the main floor) but black and white were under one roof for a white event. I'm not suggesting this as an ideal, but it represents an important example of how art creates new ways for a public to gather together. And through such public contact, people may begin to know one another. The arts have the potential for reconciling individualism with a new sense of community, not in a hokey way but in a concrete way, allowing people to construct a community, a sensibility prior to verbal communication.

In a cognitive manner, the making of art does do something new. It does not build a passive consumer, but an active creator. Real time, the time of a speech, the time of my biological rhythms, the time of my day at work—those conceptions of time can be expanded by sensibilities of time that are generated by different experiences within the arts and not within the usual frameworks of everyday life. Painting, seeing a movie, listening to music, all expand and alter our perceptions of time. What one remembers, what one thinks about, and what one perceives are expanded dramatically by exposure and experimentation in forms of activity that we identify as the arts.

Finally, the arts permit a conversation that links strangeness and sameness over time. Duke Ellington didn't consider Beethoven a dead white man. If someone told him that idea, he would have been astonished. The arts are about creating the ability to migrate beyond the historical and contingent reflexes, to redeem some kind of conversation that is normative about what is common and among us all. DNA, which is different for everybody, is ultimately also based in a uniformity; that is the paradox of commonality in humanity, because it contains the seeds of individuality.

The most important thing is to get children and young people to do art, to make art. But to do that, one has to be honest about it—that it is not simply about art for art's sake. Aestheticism is not necessary. Art always has a political and moral agenda. There is no art that is free from interpretation as an act within society. Even if art is designed merely to entertain, that in itself is a decision. Look at what constitutes "only entertainment." Whom are you entertaining and within what context are you entertaining? By defining entertainment a certain way, you want something that now exists in the world to remain undisturbed and even affirmed by entertainment. Remember the Serrano piece that has been so hotly debated, "Piss Christ"? It seems that, for some, religion is really about wanting to make an exclusive claim on imagery. Art might not be religious at all, but that is part of its provocation and its potential. We also have to be very careful about encouraging our own "official" art like the Thanksgiving turkey and relegating the arts only to a boosterism role.

We have to assert carefully but clearly the relationship of art to the issues of ethics. We must do that because in the late twentieth century one has to confront the ultimate historical paradox of our age. Twentieth century efforts to put the arts into education were used against moral education. Remember, the Nazis were great collectors and conservers of art. The paradox of the twentieth century is that the killers, and the brutal individuals who did the greatest harm, also knew the difference between Picasso and Rubens. And they whistled great music and recited by heart Goethe and Shakespeare. As Adorno put it, "Is poetry possible after the Holocaust?" And that remains an unanswered question. Did art successfully retard evil? Did the creation of an aesthetic sensibility successfully block the committing of egregious evil? No. That fact, however, does not make the aesthetic enterprise a powerless or illegitimate one.

Free and uncensored art creates tension in society. What is important about Mapplethorpe's work is that it exists. Even if you hate it, it reminds us of the price and sins of freedom. And the act of making it and showing it is itself an ethical good. And the creation of "rules of civilization" that permit art to happen is also the ethically desirable objective. That is the lesson of the Salman Rushdie case. It isn't that his book is good or bad. It's not even whether the book is blasphemous; let's even accept that, to some, it is blasphemous. But the society that permits it to exist, to be subject to criticism and praise, is in fact a society that has potentially more of an ethical future than one that does not. And therefore, it is the creation of things that defy easy reading that also permit the most freedom. The message is often not clear or easily understood. Just as art creates language, it cannot always be reduced to language. Sometimes it is anybody's guess what a poem or painting is about. Even if the image before us shows something horrible to us—pissing on the altar of Christ—the dialectical power of art may in fact become a clarion call to Christians to return to their faith. To teach the arts, you have to be convinced that art and its controversies have some relationship to improving a free and democratic world. And, especially in our pluralistic society, where diversity is something we must find ways to developed and cherish, art can create tolerance and a sense of ultimate but not vacuous universalism.

Perhaps the most important thing that plagues American education is hopelessness and lack of motivation. Our adult malaise and pessimism filter down to our young people. Why do art? Why be curious? Why gain these skills? If you can't be Midori, or Madonna, or Katharine Hepburn,why try? Fame and stardom can't be the only goal. Yet, ironically, the arts are the greatest key in developing motivation and fighting boredom for all. The sense of boredom, the sense of emptiness, the sense of disenfranchisement, the sense of hopelessness are easily combated by the activities associated with the arts. The arts generate a place we can define for ourselves. They distill our sense of beauty and tell the truth. They are critical and divergent and allow us to express ourselves. For every teacher in every field—English, history, mathematics, chemistry—the aesthetic sensibility, the sense of courage, invention, and individualism central to the arts, is crucial. The separation of art from these other fields of education is wrong. Newton and the great scientists were great artists. Einstein was a great artist. Edison was a great artist. The sense of what makes art—discipline, concentration, invention, action, the over-reaching of one's own instincts—is common to all of them. Given the absence of real confidence in the political future, our sense of historical pessimism, and our reflexive hopelessness about our society, the arts can reach and build a sense of individual hope, which then can be translated in the classroom into a sense of public possibility. This is what Maxine Greene's work opens us to. That is why our work as educators should follow in her footsteps.

8

Social Responsibility and Imagination: Lessons and Letters

Sandra Hollingsworth

Maxine Greene is a teacher. She is a visionary in the field of education who wears her responsibility as a scholar, not as a function of codified principles and duty and privilege—but as a "project" of life and imagination. Maxine is also a mother of a daughter who died too young, a feminist philosopher who was long denied official entry into the field of philosophy because she captures meaning through art, a dedicated faculty member for over forty years because—as she says—she "flunked retirement." Maxine's complex and changing identities have positioned her as a mentor and friend to many artists and teachers and scholars—including me.

I've learned from Maxine Greene about the dialectical relationship between social responsibility and imagination. I want to write what I've learned about nurturing their development in academic settings through explorations of biography, freedom, and life's "project." I'll attempt to create a tapestry of classroom vignettes and research communities, drawing from Maxine's work as it has influenced mine, from our life stories, and (with her permission) from the letters we've written to each other across the years.

IDENTITY

The first lesson I applied in my own classroom had to do with the importance of understanding biography in the interpretation of current experience. Maxine graduated from Barnard College, Columbia University, in 1938. In 1995, she was presented the Willystine Goodsell Award of the

71

American Educational Research Association. In her invited address—titled "The Shudders of Identity"—she spoke of her early experiences as a wife and mother, which shaped her philosophy:

> [After graduating from Barnard,] I eloped almost immediately with a poor physician and found myself answering his phone, doing routine tests, things I knew nothing of, and vaguely wondering where the aura was, the aura promised for marrying a "nice doctor." In spare hours, I wrote two unsuccessful novels, worked for various causes, went home again to mother when my husband went overseas to serve in the war. When he was away, I decided it was a good time to apply to medical school, took pre-med courses in preparation, and ended up with such a bad and lengthy pneumonia, I missed too much to make up. So I performed peripheral war services, worked in a factory, tried to do justice to my young daughter at the same time, carried a briefcase whenever I went out to lunch, even if I were not going to the library to write, so that I would be identified as somebody other than housekeeper, mother, as if identity was made by another person's look.
>
> I was not really conscious of discrimination against women, exclusion, infantilization, and the rest until I went to graduate school some seven years after Barnard, after being divorced, remarried, and, after a while, having another child. My apologies for distracting obligations to my children are still audible to me. I was totally ashamed when I had to say one was sick, or the sitter had not come, or that one kept crying when it got dark and I did not appear. Yet I was not able to attribute that to anything but my own stupidity, my own poor management, my own weaknesses. It never occurred to me to ask my husband to share child care, nor to challenge the department or the college to do something about the responsibilities that differentiated men and women. For all my trying to be "wonderful" on my own, whatever identity I was forging as wife-mother-student-activist was contingent on patriarchy, and I did not, could not recognize it.
>
> I began to come awake little by little, when it became apparent that I was not being offered several jobs after getting my Ph.D., even though I had already published more than fellow students, more than other contemporary Ph.D.s. My sponsor, who claimed to feel as if he were my father when my father died, offered an instructorship to a young man who had not finished his dissertation because, after all, I had someone to take care of me and he did not. I began to see, although just a little. The fields of philosophy and philosophy of education at the time were dominated by the analytic gods of British philosophy, the linguists, the positivists and their preoccupations with verifiability, conceptual clarity, specters of meaninglessness, distancing, and rigor. . . . The words used for me had to do with "soft cognition," or "too literary," or "subjectivist." Clearly, they helped those who used them to sustain the oppositions that helped them construct their cognitive worlds.

The clean, dichotomous, mechanistic views of the world that influenced education in the late 1940s when Maxine began her work at New York University were simply not part of her experience. Her life story helped me understand why she has embraced an existential philosophy and continues to challenge the psychological and positivist paradigms that have constrained our field, limiting opportunities for women, African Americans, and poor people, and why she has vigorously argued for alternative visions of schooling and educational research. In "Teaching: The Question of Personal Reality," she taught me that we must take time in our education courses for teachers to come to know themselves and their own stories:

> Looking back, recapturing their stories, teachers can recover their own standpoints on the social world. . . . Making an effort to interpret the texts of their life stories, listening to others' stories in whatever "web of relationships" they find themselves, they may be able to multiply the perspectives through which they look upon the realities of teaching; they may be able to choose themselves anew in the light of an expanded interest, an enriched sense of reality. (Greene, 1979, p. 33)

THE TRANSFORMATIVE PEDAGOGY
OF CONVERSATION

Professionally, I changed the way I taught and conducted research to include more conversation that created space for biographical examinations of how and why we interpret the world as we do. One of the conclusions of a study titled "Learning to Teach Through Collaborative Conversation" was that our learning community worked because we "valued our biographical differences"—or how our lives had led us to interpret teaching and learning differently.

> As we talked together, we began to understand not only our common concerns, but how our different life experiences, similar goals and values as teachers, and particular teaching settings informed our current perspectives. . . . The implications of this understanding for teachers' work with increasingly diverse student populations was powerful. (Hollingsworth, 1992, p. 386)

Personally, I began a long-term examination into why I interpret the world as I do. Maxine's stories of her life through her letters were helpful in that process.

March 7, 1995

Sam dear:
    . . . Yes, I have been caught in networks since I was a child—family networks, then and now. Political networks, a radicalism made of obligations and guilts. (It was rumored that I picketed my father's factory when I was a teen-ager. I didn't but the union guys did talk to me. They knew my predilections because I had picketed and was picketing the stores on Fulton Street in Brooklyn . . . because the stores in that all Black neighborhood would not hire Black cashiers. . . .) We weren't rich, but we were up and down, and I felt guilty about it all the time. Even in one of the down times when I was working in Altman's shipping room and carrying little packages around the city. I needed more and more suffering to exorcise my privilege, if that is what it was.

    It may be (but I am not sure) that the recognition of the holocaust by the safe American Jewish child and young woman added to the guilt and the desire to be heroic. My then husband (during the war) was a doctor who went overseas to England, then to Europe with Patton's army; and he was there at the liberation of Buchenwald. Maybe a half-awareness, a horror at all that, a stunned recognition of almost infinite darkness and cruelty made existential philosophy so meaningful to me—and optimistic explanations, sweet explanations as irrelevant as technicist and analytic ones. There has to be a shared realization of the "human" condition—and a scream on the part of women (every now and again) that the "human" includes them absolutely. . . .

    Maybe that is one reason I feel so much in search of a self in a world with so many doors. Again, the alternative is silence, an ebbing of meaning, a recognition of objective meaninglessness. I keep iterating: I have to keep identifying myself, choosing what it is to be a woman, a teacher, a grandmother, a mourner after a lost daughter (knowing how we would be fighting if she were still alive). What does it mean to be a friend? To be the wife of an old husband, with whom I can share a few news stories, a few jokes, but who does not hear well some of the time and is not interested in my kind of thing most of the time, but is still a good enough fellow to have around and to give a kind of structure to my life. Who am I with regard to the little grandson adopted in Bucharest, with his look of a Moldavian soldier, his occasional 4-year-old angers—"Find my beautiful soft blanky or I'll kill you"—interspersed with moments of unabashed passion. I look. I wonder about buried memories, about his poor mother who had to abandon him in a maternity hospital because she could not support the five babies she was forced to have. . . . Where is the essence to be found?

Maxine

FREEDOM

A teacher in search of his/her own freedom may be the only kind of teacher who can arouse young persons to go in search of their own.

Maxine Greene
The Dialectic of Freedom

The second lesson I took from Maxine into my classroom, my life, and now my work as an administrator is her unique concept of freedom. Unlike traditional notions of freedom "ordinarily associated with an individual stance; signifying self-dependence rather than relationship; self-regarding behavior rather than involvement with others" (Greene, 1988, p. 7); as well as escaping given structures and being left alone, Maxine helped me understand that freedom is the space to create something new in relationship. She wrote:

> Freedom shows itself or comes into being when individuals come together in a particular way, when they are authentically present to one another (without masks, pretenses, badges of office), when they have a project they can mutually pursue. When people lack attachments, when there is no possibility of coming together in a plurality or a community, when they have not tapped their imaginations, they may think of breaking free, but they will be unlikely to think of breaking through the structures of their world and creating something new. It does not matter whether those structures as everyday as constraining family rituals, as banal as bureaucratic supervisory systems, as shabby as segregation practices. There must be a coming together of those who choose themselves as affected and involved. There must be an opening of a space between them, what Hannah Arendt called an "in-between" (1958, p. 182), deeper and more significant than merely practical or worldly interests. (Greene, 1988, p. 17)

I found Maxine's interpretation of "freedom" to be transformative in the way I was taught to teach and conduct research on teachers' learning. It confirmed my suspicion of intellectual detachment, "objective methods," and generalized findings. To find validation for her perspective, Maxine taught me to go to the arts.

Here's an example of a report two teachers and I published in the Canadian journal *Curriculum Inquiry* in 1993. In stark contrast to a single-authored psychologically based piece published in the *American Educational Research Journal* in 1989, it is centered around images contained in Marge Piercy's poetry, which talks about "navigating" through life "by chart and chance and passion" (Piercy, 1987).

Through coming to see learning to teach as an on-going process in conversation with their peers, the freedom that Mary and Leslie gained
from this process of inquiring into their own learning not only increased
their children's academic success and sense of self-worth, but let the
teachers know that they had the knowledge to create and evaluate any
reading program they might choose to try. The sense of emancipation
that defining success for themselves gave them from curricular packages and text was important to their learning to teach. Leslie used that
freedom to rally support among her peers to challenge what they perceived to be other inequitable curricular policies. (Hollingsworth,
Dybdahl, & Minarik, 1993, p. 24)

LIFE'S "PROJECT"

The third lesson from Maxine that I've incorporated into my teaching, my
research, and my life is the notion of actively pursuing the "project" of
teaching for social responsibility as a possibility.

There came a time, finally, when we began thinking about teaching as
a way of spending our working lives. Like all other human beings, we
could not but "future," in some sense, think about what might be. As
Jean-Paul Sartre has written, our behavior is not only determined by our
relation "to the real and present factors which condition it", but by "a
certain object, still to come, which it is trying to bring into being." And
Sartre (1963 p. 91) went on to say, "This is what we call the project."
(Greene, 1979, p. 26)

Maxine Greene encouraged me to continue my attempts to develop critical consciousness in the classroom by writing to me about her own difficulty reading her life as a feminist:

I can't exactly remember becoming a feminist—only reacting to slights
along the way, believing the men who treated me as soft and darling and
willing to type all the membership cards, someone who had a baby
before anyone else and was always making excuses about absent sit-
ters and colds and nauseas—none of it relevant to real life. Trouble was,
having been reared with Daddy's view as The Right View, the view from
Nowhere, as it was, I figured they were right; and I had to be the best
male philosopher in a way—although the stubbornness in me (which
I did not associate with feminism) made me insist on the existential
view and the literary material and the contingency on perspective and
the frailty of the human being whoever she or he was.

My latest attempts to pursue my "project" by applying what I've learned from Maxine Greene about the dialectical relationship between social responsibility and imagination are continuing in new contexts. There are many new lessons to come.

REFERENCES

Arendt, H. (1958). *The human condition.* Chicago: University of Chicago Press.

Greene, M. (1979). Teaching: The question of personal reality. In A. Lieberman & L. Miller (Eds.), *Staff development: New demands, new realities, new perspectives* (pp. 23–25). New York: Teachers College Press.

Greene, M. (1988). *The dialectic of freedom.* New York: Teachers College Press.

Hollingsworth, S. (1989). Prior beliefs and cognitive change in learning to teach. *American Educational Research Journal, 26*(2), 160–189.

Hollingsworth, S. (1992). Learning to teach through collaborative conversation: A feminist approach. *American Educational Research Journal, 29*(2), 373–404.

Hollingsworth, S., Dybdahl, M., & Minarik, L. (1993). By chart and chance and passion: Learning to teach through relational knowing. *Curriculum Inquiry, 23*(1), 5–36.

Piercy, M. (1987). The perpetual migration. In *The moon is always female.* New York: Alfred A. Knopf, p. 115.

Sartre, J. P. (1963). *Search for a method.* New York: Alfred A. Knopf.

9

Education for Democracy

Linda Darling-Hammond

Education that nurtures the social imagination keeps our shared life alive, allowing a society to survive and to find its soul. Imagination is infused with freedom, and imagination is a theme that fuels Maxine Greene's work, and through her, the work of so many others of us. These are especially critical times for democratic education. Education that enables a more intense, disciplined, and expanding realization of meanings is education for democracy. Our society—and that of so many other democracies struggling to find and enable the best of the human spirit—needs the kind of unfettered education W.E.B. DuBois (1970) described in the darkening days of the early McCarthy era:

> Of all the civil rights for which the world has struggled and fought for 5000 years, the right to learn is undoubtedly the most fundamental. . . . The freedom to learn, curtailed even as it is today, has been bought by bitter sacrifice. And whatever we may think of the curtailment of other civil rights, we should fight to the last ditch to keep open the right to learn, the right to have examined in our schools not only what we believe, but what we do not believe; not only what our leaders say, but what the leaders of other groups and nations, and the leaders of other centuries have said. We must insist upon this to give our children the fairness of a start which will equip them with such an array of facts and such an attitude toward truth that they can have a real chance to judge what the world is and what its greater minds have thought it might be. (pp, 230–231)

We are entering an era in which all people must learn flexibly and effectively to survive and succeed in a fast-changing world. If we cannot accomplish this task at this moment in history, a deeply stratified society—one divided by access to knowledge and the opportunity to learn—will undo any chance for democratic life and government. These changes define a new mission for education and for teaching: one that requires schools not merely to "deliver instructional services" but to ensure that all students actually learn, and that requires teachers not merely to "cover the curriculum" but to enable diverse learners to construct their own knowledge and develop their talents in effective and powerful ways.

What are the critical issues that face us as we enter this new world and recommit ourselves to an education for social strength and democracy—one built upon equality, humanity, and freedom? I see three related issues as the challenges of our times: The first is the provision of educational opportunity—of access to knowledge—to all children on equal terms, so that they can contribute to and partake of democracy. The second is the reinvention of schools as humane and enlivening places that function as democratic communities of learners. The third is the development of a profession of teaching that will serve as the foundation for empowering education by ensuring that all teachers are prepared to teach in ways that are both learner-centered and learning-centered.

By learner-centered I mean teaching that responds to individual students' intelligence, talents, cultural and linguistic backgrounds, needs, and interests. This is teaching that is deeply informed by understandings of learners and learning. By learning-centered I mean teaching that is aimed at genuine understanding—that supports active, in-depth learning leading to powerful thinking and flexible, proficient performances. Teaching of this kind creates paths to freedom and empowerment for all students; it enables them to become full members in a democracy.

EDUCATION FOR DEMOCRACY:
RECOVERING OUR ROOTS

If equality, humanity, and freedom are the promise of democracy, then education is the promise-keeper. In the birthing of America, in the great debates over whether a people could create and sustain a truly democratic rule, Alexander Hamilton is said to have mounted this most powerful argument against popular democracy. "Thy people, sir," he told Thomas Jefferson, "are a beast." Thus challenged, Jefferson argued that "the people" could be enabled to govern responsibly through a system of public education that would develop an intelligent populace and a popular intelligence, thus enabling democratic decision-making and providing the best protection against tyranny.

Public education is central to the promise of American democracy in another way as well: It provides a vehicle for all citizens, regardless of wealth or circumstances of birth, to secure their inalienable rights to life, liberty, and the pursuit of happiness—"the good society and the good life" that Amy Gutman (1987, p. 14) describes. The ability of all citizens to aspire to the rights and benefits of this society enables them to create a community with shared purpose. As Maxine Greene notes: "Freedom is made possible only when people come together with some common notion of personal integrity . . . in a life consciously lived in common" (1984, p. 5). Thus, the individual good and the common good are inextricably intertwined.

In order to ensure a popular intelligence and an intelligent populace capable of democratic decision-making, schools must cultivate in all students the skills, knowledge, and understanding that both lead them to want to embrace the values undergirding our pluralistic democracy and arm them with a keen intelligence capable of free thought. Schools must provide an education that enables critical thinking *and* communal experience, so that citizens can intelligently debate competing ideas, weigh the individual and the common good, and make judgments that sustain democratic institutions and ideals.

The provision of such an education has always been a struggle, and it remains one today. At the turn of the last century, in the 1930s, and in the 1960s, progressives banded together to invent democratically run schools that enabled all students to experiment, think, and create, to find their voice, and to develop their social imagination. Many contemporary reforms were pursued in each of these eras: a "thinking" curriculum aimed at deep understanding; cooperative learning within communities of learners; interdisciplinary and multicultural curriculum; projects, portfolios, and other 'alternative assessments' that challenge students to integrate ideas and demonstrate their capabilities. Indeed, with the addition of a few computers, current scenarios for twentieth-century schools are virtually identical to the ideal offered by John Dewey in 1900.

Today, a growing number of schools are once again reinventing teaching and learning, roles and responsibilities, and relationships with parents and communities, so that they can help a greater range of students learn more powerfully and productively. These efforts, aimed at more child-centered teaching and more universal, high-quality education were undermined in each of the previous reform eras by underinvestment in teachers and in school capacity. Lawrence Cremin argued that "progressive education . . . demanded infinitely skilled teachers, and it failed because such teachers could not be recruited in sufficient numbers" (1965, p. 56). Because of this failure, in each of its iterations progressivism gave way to standardizing influences, in the efficiency movement of the 1920s, the teacher-proof curriculum reforms of the late 1950s, and the "back to the basics" movement of the 1970s and '80s. But these attempts at simplifying schooling also failed, leading to renewed criticisms of schools and attempts to restructure them.

Current efforts at democratic school reform are likely to last and spread only if they are built on a foundation of teaching knowledge and are sustained by a commitment to structural rather than merely symbolic change. This will mean reinventing school organizations so that they can be humane and socially productive, strengthening the capacity of teachers, and attending explicitly to the inequalities that threaten to undermine our society as well as our schools.

INEQUALITY AND ACCESS TO KNOWLEDGE

America's struggle in confronting issues of inequality is nowhere so apparent as in our tortuous efforts, waged for more than two centuries, to address the unequal access children have to an education for democracy. The fact that the U.S. school system is structured such that students routinely receive dramatically unequal learning opportunities based on their race and social status is simply not widely acknowledged. Despite widespread and stark disparities in school funding and radically different levels of educational quality available to students, the prevailing view is that if students do not achieve, it is both their fault and their sole burden to bear.

However, the costs of this inequality are increasingly high, for our society as a whole as well as for the individual young people placed at risk by their schools. For those who cannot find a productive place in an increasingly competitive economy, who cannot find a way to connect to and become a part of the community in which they live, personal tragedy translates into social tragedy. Growing rates of crime, incarceration, structural unemployment, homelessness, drug use, and social dysfunction increasingly victimize those trapped in a growing underclass, as well as all of those who pay—financially and socially—for its costs to the broader society. In many and growing ways, unequal access to education threatens the foundation of democracy.

This is not a new problem. Institutionally sanctioned discrimination in access to educational resources is older than the American nation itself. In his history of eighteenth-century colonial education, Lawrence Cremin wrote:

> For all of its openness, provincial America, like all societies, distributed its educational resources unevenly, and to some groups, particularly those Indians and Afro-Americans who were enslaved and even those who were not, it was for all intents and purposes closed. . . . For the slaves, there were few books, few libraries, [and] few schools. . . . The doors of wisdom were not only not open, they were shut tight and designed to remain that way. . . . [By] the end of the colonial period, there was a well-developed ideology of race inferiority to justify that situation and ensure that it would stand firm against all the heady rhetoric of the Revolution. (Cremin, 1961, pp. 411–412)

It is that ideology, developed to justify slavery and honed in the eugenics movement at the turn of the twentieth century, that has festered for decades, recently erupting in a new representation of pseudoscience, *The Bell Curve.* This resurgence of racialist thinking has been received with a remarkable presumption of credibility despite the fact that Herrnstein and Murray's (1994) work seems almost wholly ignorant of the last twenty years of research on cognition, intelligence, and performance, along with research on the effects of education on performance, and the inequalities in educational opportunity that exist and affect performance. Their analysis relies on tests that are not good measures of intelligence and then, in internal contradiction, they ignore research demonstrating the closing of the racial achievement gap in performance on exactly those measures. For example, on the Scholastic Aptitude Test, one of the measures Herrnstein and Murray incorrectly use as a measure of intelligence, the scores of African American students have climbed a total of 54 points since 1976, while those of white students have remained stable. This closing of the gap is directly related to school desegregation and efforts to equalize access to education that started to take root only twenty-five years ago. But these efforts are far from complete.

In a recent American Psychological Association *Monitor,* Howard Gruber, Curtis Branch, Jeanne Brooks-Gunn, John Broughton, Morton Deutsch, Maxine Greene, Herb Ginsberg, Deanna Kuhn, and Harry Passow issued a succinct and compelling rebuttal to *The Bell Curve.* They conclude:

> The only scientifically established race differences in this country are the pervasive discrimination against black and other minority groups and the widespread poverty, ill-health, and poor education that are faced by many in these . . . groups. The task facing American scientists is not to make excuses for the failures of our society, but to seek creative ways to rectify the social evils that afflict us. (1995)

From the time Southern states made it illegal to teach an enslaved person to read, throughout the nineteenth century and into the twentieth, African Americans have faced de facto and de jure exclusion from public schools throughout the nation, as have Native Americans and, frequently, Hispanic Americans and Asian Americans. In 1857, a group of African American leaders testified before a New York State investigating committee that the New York Board of Education spent $16 per white child for sites and school buildings, while the comparable figure per black child was one cent. David Tyack notes that while black students occupied school buildings described as "dark and cheerless" in neighborhoods "full of vice and filth," white students had access to schools that were "splendid, almost palatial edifices, with manifold comforts, conveniences, and elegancies" (1974, p. 119) These traditions continued with segregation and unequal funding of schools in nearly all of the South and much of the North, with white schools generally allocated five to ten times as much money as black schools, and with higher education institutions almost entirely closed to nonwhites until the 1960s.

Educational experiences for low-income students and students of color continue to be substantially separate and unequal. Nationally and in New York, almost two-thirds of "minority" students continue to attend schools that are predominantly minority, most of them located in central cities and funded at levels substantially below those of neighboring suburban districts. Not only do funding systems allocate fewer resources to poor urban districts than to their suburban neighbors, but schools with high concentrations of low-income and "minority" students receive fewer instructional resources than other schools within these districts. And tracking systems exacerbate these inequalities by segregating many low-income and "minority" students within schools, allocating still fewer educational opportunities to them at the classroom level with fewer and lower quality materials, less qualified and experienced teachers, and less access to high-quality curriculum.

Jonathan Kozol's 1991 *Savage Inequalities* describes the striking differences between public schools serving students of color in urban settings and their suburban counterparts, which typically spend twice as much per student for populations with many fewer special needs. *Savage Inequalities* is replete with familiar yet poignant stories: MacKenzie High School in Detroit where word-processing courses are taught without word processors because the school cannot afford them, P.S. 261 in New York City where recess is not possible because there is no playground, and East St. Louis Senior High School whose biology lab has no laboratory tables or usable dissecting kits. Meanwhile, children in neighboring suburban schools enjoy features like a twenty-seven-acre acre campus, an athletic program featuring golf, fencing, ice hockey, and lacrosse, and a computer hookup to Dow Jones to study stock transactions.

The students notice. As one New York City sixteen year old notes of his school, where holes in ceilings expose rusty pipes and water pours in on rainy days, in comparison with others:

> You can understand things better when you go among the wealthy. You look around you at their school, although it's impolite to do that, and you take a deep breath at the sight of all those beautiful surroundings. Then you come back home and see that these are things you do not have. You think of the difference. (1991, p. 104)

His classmate adds:

> People on the outside may think that we don't know what it is like for
> other students, but we *visit* other schools and we have eyes and we have
> brains. You cannot hide the differences. You see it and compare. (1991,
> p. 104)

The message is clearly conveyed: Some children are worth less than
others in the eyes of society.

The vast differences in curriculum opportunities across U.S. schools
are the single greatest source of differences in outcomes among students.
Studies over the last decade repeatedly find that student achievement increases
for underserved students when they are placed in environments with better resources, more challenging curriculum, and better teachers. Students
from different groups who take similar courses and have access to equally
rich curriculum and equally well-qualified teachers perform similarly.

However that kind of equal access is rare. As Robert Dreeben (1987)
found in a comparative study of first graders across seven Chicago schools
with the same kind and quality of teaching, African American and white
students had comparable reading achievement. However, the quality of
instruction received by African American students was, on average, much
lower than that received by white students, thus creating a racial gap in
achievement over time even for those who started out ahead of their white
counterparts in other schools.

Perhaps the most important differences in what happens to children at school depend on who their teachers are: what they understand
about children and about learning, what they are able to do to respond
to the very different approaches and experiences children bring with them
to the learning setting, what they care about and are committed to as teachers. What James Banks (1993) calls an "equity pedagogy"—one that makes
knowledge accessible to all students—requires teachers who are able to
connect the diverse experiences of their students to challenging curriculum
goals, and who can marry a deep understanding of students and their
learning to a wide array of strategies for bringing knowledge and critical
discourse to life.

Although recent studies confirm (Darling-Hammond, 1993) that
teacher expertise is one of the most important predictors of student achievement, the deprofessionalization of teaching in the United States means
that this resource is not available to all children. Because of short-sighted
licensing and hiring policies, unequal resources, and lack of attention to
teacher recruitment, the most vulnerable students are continually taught
by the least qualified teachers. At least 50,000 teachers annually are hired
without adequate preparation for their jobs, primarily to teach disadvan-

taged students in cities and poor rural schools. Many students are taught throughout their entire school careers by a parade of inexperienced, under-prepared, and unsupported novices, many of whom stay less than a year in the classroom, alternating with substitutes who also come and go.

In stark contrast to their students' needs, these teachers are least likely to have encountered knowledge about how children grow, learn, and develop, or about what to do to support their learning. Studies of underprepared teachers consistently find that they are less effective with students and that they have difficulty with curriculum development, classroom man-agement, student motivation, and teaching strategies. They tend to teach autocratically and to stress rote learning that is more easily controlled. They are less able to understand student learning styles and differences, to anticipate students' knowledge and potential difficulties, or to plan and redi-rect instruction to meet students' needs, and less likely to see it as their job to do so, often blaming the students if their teaching is not successful.

Unequal access to good teaching sacrifices human potential—the opportunity each person should have to find a place to shine, to value and be valued in society. Especially today, as the nation simultaneously catapults into a knowledge-based economy demanding high levels of understanding and skill from all of its citizens and incorporates the largest wave of immigration since the turn of the twentieth century, its success in embracing and enhancing the talents of all of its new and previously unincluded members will determine much of its future.

THE NEED FOR HUMANE AND EMPOWERING EDUCATION

As society increasingly requires the full range of human abilities poten-tially available to it, teaching that consciously develops the many dif-ferent capacities of individuals is ever more necessary. Whereas a cen-tury ago, the mass of citizens could be expected to spend their lives at unskilled labor in the factory or on the farm, today's society demands an ever-expanding array of wide-ranging skills and abilities. Howard Gardner's (1991) idea of "individually configured excellence" as a goal of schooling derives not only from an understanding that humans pos-sess multiple intelligences, but also from an understanding that it is in society's interest to better develop the diverse potentials of students.

Democratic life requires access to empowering forms of knowledge that enable creative life and thought, and access to a social dialogue that enables democratic communication and participation. Growing up a humane and decent people who can appreciate others and take satisfaction in doing things well requires schools that allow for humanity and decency, that cultivate appreciation, that create social community, and that support deep learning about things that matter to the people in them. For all the other purposes of schooling, education is a source of nurturance for the spirit, although it can be, and too often is, conducted in a way that deadens and demoralizes. Schooling, managed as a tedious and coercive activity, can create frustrations that must emerge sooner or later in self-deprecation or cruelty to others. However, where a real connection is made between students and teachers in the pursuit of meaningful accomplishments, the possibilities for developing life-long capacities for learning, doing, and relating to others are greatly expanded.

Unfortunately, the bureaucratic school was not created to meet these needs for intellectual development or for nurturing. The characteristics of today's schools were forged when the goal of education was not to educate all students well but to process a great many efficiently, selecting and supporting only a few for further educational pursuits. Although progressive educators like Dewey argued that the challenges of the dawning 20th century should be met by creating democratic schools where communities of learners would engage in meaningful work connected to real-life tasks, the prevailing model of school reform that instead took hold in the United States mimicked the then-popular factory assembly line managed by centralized bureaucracy.

Like manufacturing industries, modern schools were designed as highly specialized organizations—divided into grade levels and subject matter departments, separate tracks, programs, and auxiliary services—each managed separately and run by carefully specified procedures engineered to yield standard products: the students. For the masses of students, the goal was to instill rudimentary skills and the basic workplace socialization needed for early twentieth-century jobs that required following orders and conducting predetermined tasks neatly and punctually. As Frederick Taylor, the father of scientific management, made clear, most of these future workers would not be paid to think—and it was imperative that they not be encouraged to do so. As Taylor put it, "One type of man is needed to plan ahead and an entirely different type to execute the work" (1911, pp. 37–38). The rote learning needed for these early assembly-line objectives still predominates in today's schools, reinforced by mandated curriculum packages and texts focused on lower level cognitive skills, multiple-choice tests, and continuing underinvestment in teacher knowledge.

The system might work if students were car doors to be assembled. But they are not, and the results of treating them in this way are widespread disengagement and alienation. A mother who withdrew her child from the Detroit public schools in 1924 when this system was first implemented understood more than the efficiency experts who designed it. The mother wrote that the long lines of children marching from room to room "looked to me like nothing so much as the lines of uncompleted Ford cars in the factory, moving always on, with a screw put in or a burr tightened as they pass—standardized, mechanical, pitiful" (Carrajat, 1995).

Students perceive that the system is structured for not caring. A New York city dropout from a large, comprehensive high school described his experience this way,

> At one time school was important to me. I liked getting good grades and making my parents proud of me. [But in high school] I never felt part of the school. It didn't make no difference if I was there or not. The teachers just threw me aside, probably because I was Spanish. I felt like I was being ignored, like I wasn't important. (Carrajat, 1995)

A California high school student put it succinctly: "This place hurts my spirit." An administrator in the same school voiced the poignant dilemma of caring educators caught in the squeeze between mandates and children: "Yes, my spirit is hurt, too, when I have to do things I don't believe in" (Carrajat, 1995).

Education for democracy requires not only experiences that develop serious thinking, but also access to social understanding developed by actually participating in a democratic community and developing multiple perspectives. The factory-model school, with its enforcement of a single, official knowledge, its fragmentation, and its segregation of groups of students by track and social class encourages disengagement, silence, and separation where intense communication, inquiry, and connections are needed.

Schools must enact democracy. In *Democracy and Education,* Dewey (1916) noted that "a democracy is more than a form of government; it is primarily a mode of associated living" (p. 87). He stressed the importance of creating circumstances in which people share a growing number of interests and participate in a growing number of associations with other groups, noting that:

> In order to have a large number of values in common, all the members of the group must have an equitable opportunity to receive and to take from others. There must be a large variety of shared undertakings and experiences. Otherwise, the influences which educate some into masters educate others into slaves. And the experience of each party loses in meaning when the free interchange of varying modes of life experiences is arrested. (p. 84)

Finding what we have in common requires that we communicate from the vantage points of our separate, but increasingly related, interests.

Each of us has to find a way to express and locate our own experiences in the course of our education in order to connect with new knowledge and with the experiences of others. We also need a way to find and understand the experiences of others so that we can communicate with them in an educative manner. Thus, all of us need a multicultural education to be citizens together.

Far from encouraging separatism, communications about our diverse experiences help us educate each other and ourselves about the connections among our different associations. It is our commitment to communicate about and across our multiple perspectives that is the essence of a democracy and the glue that holds a democratic society together. A communication that is, in Dewey's words, "vitally social or vitally shared" (p. 84) is one that allows us at least partially to experience the perspectives of another, and by that connection to develop understanding and appreciation for that person's experience and understanding of the world.

These appreciations of other perspectives provide the foundation for a broader *shared* perspective that in turn allows us to form communities and societies. It may seem paradoxical, but it is only by acknowledging the reality and the legitimacy of diverse points of view that we can begin the work of forging a common point of view that takes account of the others. Such an education helps us avoid what Edmund W. Gordon et al. (1990) describe as "communicentric bias: the tendency to make one's own community the center of the universe and the conceptual frame that constrains thought" (p. 19).

The capacity to achieve associations beyond those of any narrow group—to live and learn heterogeneously together—is required for the development of democracy, for the expansion of knowledge, and for the search for truth. Just as inquiry about important problems must cross departmental boundaries, for the same reasons, such inquiry must also cross community and cultural boundaries. The basis of the very earliest universities was that they tried to bring together scholars from all over the known world. They sought to create ways to share diverse perspectives from various geographic areas, cultures, and disciplines as the basis for developing knowledge and finding truth. The same ideal of knowledge-building and truth-finding—of looking for powerful, shared ideas to arise from diverse understandings and experiences of the world—undergirds the concept of a democratic, multicultural education that encompasses the many views of its participants—that is, all of the views that must be accommodated in the common space that comprises social life.

Tracking and unresponsive forms of teaching subvert the purposes of schooling in a democracy by creating unequal classes of citizens, providing only one class with the skills and knowledge necessary for full participation in the society. This jeopardizes the foundations for democracy and prevents students from learning how to engage in the joint construction of community because they are kept separate and disengaged by the structures of schooling. As we reinvent education for the next century, we need schools that are structured for community and for caring as well as for critical thinking.

"Learner-centered" schools organize their work around students' needs for active, experiential, and culturally connected learning opportunities that build on students' experiences and support their individual talents and learning styles. Learning is organized around more complex and integrative tasks; students and teachers are grouped in ways that enable teachers to come to know the minds and hearts of their students well. Teachers work with groups of students for longer hours, over multiple years and across several curriculum areas, so that their work is less fragmented and disjointed. This enables a more integrated and holistic view of learners, and a more interdisciplinary and in-depth approach to learning. Alongside these curriculum changes are new forms of assessment that better capture the outcomes of more challenging work and the range of talents that students are developing, and that illustrate how children think and learn as well as what they can do.

Central Park East Secondary School, the Urban Academy, International High School, and the Satellite Academies in New York, as well as a growing number of schools nationally, provide vivid examples of learning communities that are grounded in democratic practice and culturally connected learning. Their students thrive and achieve in small schools that violate all of the norms for inequality and disengagement that are so often assumed to be inevitable. Following a common core curriculum with no tracking or pull-out classes, students participate in decision-making, engage in continuous social learning and debate, and meet the high standards embodied in a graduation requiring research papers, scientific experiments, essays and critiques, and oral defenses of their work. Most of these students come from low-income Latino and African American families and many are eligible for special education services. If they had attended most of the other schools in their neighborhoods, over half would have dropped out. Instead, over 90 percent of them graduate and go on to postsecondary education armed with an understanding of different viewpoints, capacities to see connections among different ideas and points of view, the ability to seek out and evaluate evidence on all sides of a question, to think critically and to communicate with others—in sum, to participate as a member of a democratic community.

Though virtually all students would benefit from this kind of education, the opportunity for this sort of schooling remains acutely restricted.

In many instances, the reason for the restriction is the scarcity of teachers who can teach in the fashion such schooling demands. Education that is empowering for students can occur only if a profession full of teachers are prepared for learner-centered and learning-centered practice.

The importance of transforming teaching is becoming ever more clear as schools are expected to find ways to support and connect with the needs of all learners. Responsive teaching cannot be produced through teacher-proof materials or regulated curriculum. To create bridges between common, challenging curriculum goals and individual learners' experiences and needs, teachers must be able to develop learning experiences that accommodate a variety of cognitive styles, with activities that broaden rather than reduce the range of possibilities for learning. If teachers are to engage in the pursuit of "individually configured excellence" for all students, they must be able to tap multiple intelligences and employ multiple pathways to learning. They must understand child development and pedagogy, as well as the structures of subject areas and a variety of alternatives for assessing learning. And they must have a base of knowledge for making decisions traditionally reserved for others in the educational hierarchy.

The implications for teacher education are many: Teachers will need to be prepared to teach for understanding with deeper knowledge of their disciplines, of interdisciplinary connections, and of inquiry-based learning. They will need to be prepared to address the substantial diversity in experiences that children bring with them to school—the wide range of languages, cultures, learning styles, talents, and intelligences that require in turn an equally rich and varied repertoire of teaching strategies. They will need to look at and listen to children through a lens informed by knowledge about how children learn and develop to understand what their students know and can do as well as how they think and how they learn.

ACCESS TO DEMOCRATIC COMMUNITY

Building humane schools and empowering teaching can enable us to achieve both excellence and equity, to develop the abilities of all children for the contributions they want to make and can make to a democratic community that is vitally social and vitally shared. Schools alone cannot transform the inequalities of our society. That is a collective responsibility that falls upon all public institutions (and many private ones), as well as the public will. But since schools are the first public institution that most individuals encounter in their society, and since they

encounter schooling first at the most tender moments in their development, schools have a special responsibility and a powerful opportunity
to teach for democracy—for both intellectual and social development.

Schools must do this not by preaching but by example. Because individuals will learn what to expect from society's institutions from this first
encounter, educators have a special responsibility to become capable of supporting multiple forms of excellence. For democracy to survive and flourish, those who have been silenced need to find their voices. Those who have
been marginalized need to seek, create, and find a myriad of possible
places for themselves in society. They must be able to find their dreams in
the American landscape if our nation is to enact the democratic dream.

REFERENCES

Banks, J. (1993). Multicultural education: Historical development, dimensions,
and practices. In L. Darling-Hammond (Ed.), *Review of research in education* (Vol. 19, pp. 3–49). Washington, DC: American Education Research
Association.

Carrajat, M. A. (1995). *Why do academically able Puerto Rican males drop out
of high school?* Doctoral dissertation, Teachers College, Columbia University.

Cremin, L. (1961). *The transformation of the school: Progressivism in American
Education, 1876–1957.* New York: Vintage Books.

Dewey, J. *Democracy and Education*

Dreeben, R. (1987). Closing the divide: What teachers and administrators can do
to help black students reach their reading potential. *American Educator,
11*(4), 28–35.

DuBois, W.E.B. (1970). Education and work. In P. S. Foner (Ed.), *W.E.B. DuBois
Speaks.* New York: Pathfinder.

Gardner, H. (1991). *The unschooled mind.* New York: Basic Books.

Gordon, E. W., Miller, F., & Rollock, D. (1990). Coping with communicentric
bias in knowledge production in the social sciences. *Educational Researcher,
19*(3), 14–19.

Greene, M. (1984). *Education, freedom, and possibility.* Inaugural lecture as William
F. Russell Professor in the Foundations of Education, Teachers College,
Columbia University, New York.

Gruber, H., Branch, C., Brooks-Gunn, J., Broughton, J., Deutsch, M., Greene, M.,
Ginsburg, A., Kuhn, D., Passon, H. (1995). *Monitor,* The American
Psychological Association, January 1995.

Herrnstein, R., and Murray, C. (1994). *The bell curve: Intelligence and class
structure in American life.* New York: Free Press.

Kozol, J. (1991). *Savage inequalities.* New York: Crown.

Taylor, F. W. (1911). *The principles of scientific management.* New York: Harper-
Collins.

Tyack, D. (1974). *The one best system.* Cambridge, MA: Harvard University.

III

LOOKING AT THINGS LARGE

My interpretations are provisional. . . . All we can do, I believe, is cultivate multiple ways of seeing and multiple dialogues in a world where nothing stays the same. All I can do is to try to provoke my readers to come together in making pathways through that world with their students, leaving thumbprints as they pass. Our 'fundamental anxiety,' one writer has said . . . is that we will pass through the world and leave no mark; that anxiety is what induces us to devise projects for ourselves, to live among our fellow beings and reach out to them, to interpret life from our situated standpoints, to try—over and over again—to begin. In a sense, I have written . . . to remedy that anxiety. It grants a usefulness to the disinterest of seeing things small at the same time that it opens to and validates the passion for seeing things close up and large. For this passion is the doorway for imagination; here is the possibility of looking at things as if they could be otherwise. This possibility, for me, is what restructuring might signify. Looking at things large is what might move us on to reform.

Maxine Greene
Releasing the Imagination

The very realization that we live in a world "where nothing stays the same" often provokes individuals to search for projects that will guarantee stability of identity and meaning. Often, those kinds of projects do not enable or encourage one to "reach out" to fellow beings. Instead, in the quest for certainty and for a place in a supposedly stable world that such projects aim to create, individuals retreat into isolated and separate spheres of activity and into predictable patterns of meaning-making. Even if those patterns of meaning-making entail what Carol Shields, in *The Stone Diaries* (1993), describes for her heroine Daisy Stone Goodwill as a "primary act of imagination," it is a form of imagination that is a "blend of distortion and omission":

> She understood that if she was going to hold on to her life at all, she would
> have to rescue it by a primary act of imagination, supplementing, modifying,
> summoning up the necessary connections, conjuring the pastoral or heroic or
> whatever . . . getting the details wrong occasionally, exaggerating or lying out-
> right, inventing letters or conversations of impossible gentility, or casting con-
> jecture in a pretty light. (pp. 76–77)

There is a difference, then, between forms of imagination that open us to the
possibilities of "looking at things as if they could be otherwise" and forms of
imagination that result in "truncated" versions of lives, actions, and meanings
that reinforce notions of stable and unified identities and worlds.

> If you were to ask . . . Daisy the story of her life she would purse her lips for
> a moment—that ruby-red efflorescence—and stutter out an edited hybrid ver-
> sion, handing it to you somewhat shyly, but without apology, without equiv-
> ocation that is: this is what happened, she would say from the unreachable
> recesses of her seventy-two years, and this is what happened next. (p. 283)

Such forms of imagination, although used in the service of people "obliged every
day to reinvent themselves" (p. 283), are not synonymous with Maxine Greene's
call for imagination as the touchstone for reform, as a way of breaking with what
is and moving toward what might be or should be. Maxine Greene urges us toward
forms of imagination that compel us to "look at things large" in order that we
might see beyond fixed versions of ourselves and others. She constantly reminds
us of the necessity of new beginnings, of the necessity of trying "over and over again
to begin." In those attempts, our interpretations of ourselves and our worlds are
provisional, given a "world where nothing stays the same." And yet, each day we
begin, not to finalize one version of life, but to look at things "as if they could be
otherwise" (Greene, 1995, p. 16) and to act with others to create such possibilities.
    Maxine Greene has been urging us toward such forms of imagination
and life-projects for a long while:

> I feel so strongly that I want to do something to counter the narcissism, the
> privatism, the self-involved kinds of activities which are undertaken out of
> despair. I know people laugh at me because I use jogging as an example, and
> I think jogging is a fantastic thing to do, but not if it becomes your new reli-
> gion. I know people who ran in the New York City marathon and who are
> living for the next marathon. Do you know how much time it takes to prepare
> for a marathon? There isn't much organizing you can do. You are not spend-
> ing much time in community. I really think it's because there is nothing else
> you can do to give yourself meaning—to test yourself. I think that we have
> to try to define possibilities of community work to give us the same sense
> of achievement in existential triumph that running twenty-six miles in New
> York City streets or Boston streets gives. . . .

Those same people in another time could spend all that time and energy and idealism working in a tutoring program or doing something in a freedom school or doing something to build a community theater. I think that's a part of what I have in mind. Of course, it's messier to do the community thing. You have to work with others and you have to worry about others' imperfections. And secondly, you can't be sure you will get that same kind of existential reward at the end, you know, "Now I can try anything." I remember in the '60s, for example, of trying to organize a peace movement at Teachers College. I especially remember when we had a vigil in front of Teachers College, a silent vigil for two hours. I remember what went into that for those of us who cared about it, even though nobody said, "Oh boy! You did this!" or nobody knew it was me and the four or five other people who did it. What is so interesting to me is this sign, this indication (today it's the marathon) of the need to commit ourselves to something, of the desire to really work at something. Do you realize what kinds of energy apparently that last six miles summon up? Imagine if that kind of interest and concern and self-testing were used in the creation of a better world?

I guess my future hopes include community created through the hard work of us all. I can see teachers and students beginning to create a space where meanings can emerge for diverse persons and where we all can choose to take the risks of questioning, of breaking through to another vision. And if we want to jog toward that future, that's fine; but let's create a direction and a project for that energy, and let's run together. (Miller, 1978)

REFERENCES

Miller, J. L. (1978, May). *An Interview with Maxine Greene.* Videotape. The Curriculum Collection, Museum of Education, University of South Carolina.

Greene, Maxine. (1995). *Releasing the imagination: Essays on education, the arts, and social change.* San Francisco: Jossey-Bass.

Shields, Carol. (1993). *The Stone diaries.* New York: Penguin Books.

10

On Doing
Something More

Deborah P. Britzman

Around 1965, the year of publication for Maxine Greene's *The Public School and the Private Vision: A Search for America in Education and Literature,* Bill T. Jones, an African American choreographer, dancer, and recent McCarthur Foundation recipient, was a student in elementary school. He would not begin dancing until college, but throughout elementary and secondary education, his interest was in theatre. He recalls directing a high school production of Arthur Miller's *The Crucible,* a text often censored in U.S. schools. And, he recalls a certain teacher:

> I was fortunate enough to have a very feisty teacher, Miss Mary Lee Shappee, a white woman, who was an "out" atheist. As an atheist, she considered herself slightly above everybody else in our small, bourgeois community, and she took a liking to me. She encouraged my scepticism and she emphasized, "There's something more than this." That was in the fourth grade. (Washington, 1994, p. 191)

Miss Mary Lee Shappee and Bill T. Jones may or may not have read Professor Maxine Greene's text. But what remains common after all these years is a collective insistence on imagining "something more" than staying put in the logic of official knowledge. All seem to share that contradictory sense of schooling as that great social accident *and* that haunted cultural sphere, where some are lucky enough to engage with

---

This essay originally appeared as "On Doing Something More": A Reconsideration of Maxine Greene, *The Public School and the Private Vision: A Search for America in Education and Literature,* in *Educational Studies* (1994, Winter), *25*(4), 273–282. An expanded version will appear in my book, *Lost Subjects, Contested Objects: Toward a Psychoanalytic Inquiry of Learning* (Albany: SUNY Press, in press).

"feisty teachers" while, more often than not, many others are left to fend off the temporality of the felt present—classroom time—that seems to move at a glacier rate. But in this space where disparate groups meet and collide, within the space in-between the teacher and the student, there must be moments when limits are exceeded, when an uncommon sociality can be invented in a common place.

Within Bill T. Jones's counter-memory of being affirmed through the cultivation of scepticism, within Miss Mary Lee Shappee's insistence on being known and on knowing others as an atheist during a time when daily Christian prayer was mandatorily broadcast in each public school classroom, and within Maxine Greene's restless search for the moments and movements between literature and the lived, one can still feel a sense of precarious danger and, perhaps, of transgressive pleasure. The danger has something to do with what Maxine Greene names early on in her text as the dream of public education and "the validity of the claim that a community of common men could be created in an open world and that it could survive" (1965, p. 4). It has, as well, something to do with the fact—and here is the space where danger and pleasure collide—that communities are something made and not magically received. And if in fact education could proceed without treating knowledge as category maintenance work, and attempt "an open world," its problems would not just be how education might recognize itself without its criteria of standardization, prediction, norms, and deviancies, but how communities become made from difference. And these problems, then as well as now, if I follow Maxine Greene's 1965 text, bothers the hell out of "the schoolmen," the engineers of that great confinement and romance known as schooling.

Maybe the heart of Professor Greene's text is the *Bildungsroman* of schools. But if it is a Bildungsroman, a building of selves and culture, a bringing up of education and life, it is not necessarily the heroic story of progress. In part, the stuff of this narrative is built from the dreary reports of "the schoolmen" and their collective efforts to keep the lid on the radical uncertainties of education and nation. There are uncanny and often cruel stories of identities being both made from and repressed within the knowledge and sociality known as schooling. But this Bildungsroman is also made from the anxious stuff of artists' visions, fantasies, and dreams. Theirs are also uncanny stories—of being lost and of losing things, of melancholy longings, and, perhaps, as Freud would say, of the work of mourning (A. Freud, 1969; S. Freud, 1915/1953). It is this part of Maxine Greene's text that troubles—then as now—even the best efforts of "the schoolmen."

As Professor Greene tells it, the stories of compulsory education are at once a problem of how culture works to differentiate and unify, of how subjection is lived under the banners of freedom, of individuality, and of opportunity, and even, of how "there was the 'single person' still to be accounted for."(S. Freud, 1915/1953, p. 45). But in writing within and against this incompleteness and in managing to be both suspicious of and hopeful for what education is and can become, Maxine Greene departs company from the majority of her contemporaries who, then as now, insist upon, for its metaphors of education, discourses of social science, psychometric measurement, and the military. In this text and, indeed, in all of her work, Maxine Greene casts her lot with those who refuse to close down their identifications in the name of social order, efficiency, mastery, and, yes, even community. This Bildungsroman of schooling, then, is also the dialogic of the discontent: the creative artists who offered, through their texts, the future stuff of curriculum—their anxious, celebratory, and transgressive dreams. What they offered, in their refusal to guarantee meaning, and what Maxine Greene engages, is the potential for literature to change how one sees the world and what one has yet to imagine.

A few years before the publication of Greene's text, James Baldwin addressed an audience of teachers. "A Talk to Teachers" began with the trauma of education:

> Let's begin by saying that we are living through a very dangerous time.
> . . . [Y]ou must understand that in the attempt to correct so many generations of bad faith and cruelty, when it is operating not only in the classroom but in society, you will meet the most fantastic, the most brutal, and the most determined resistance. There is no point in pretending that this won't happen. (1985, p. 325)

Within this room full of teachers, how many of them could notice that the very resistance to transforming education is an effect of educational design, not of education gone somehow wrong? And yet, within this vast educational design of what might now be called normalization, an artist addresses teachers.

It is this insistence on the arts as a method for thinking the unthought of education, of exploring what "the schoolmen" could not think precisely because of what they thought, that Greene develops in her 1965 text. And, read as a method rather than as content, that is, as a practice for doing something more, this text can be understood as in dialogue with present concerns. We might put it in dialogue with a question about reading raised recently by Shoshana Felman's 1993 text, *What Does a Woman Want?: Reading and Sexual Difference.* There, like Professor Greene, Professor Felman reads the stories of others to say something about her own. And the questions Felman asks about reading might as well apply to education:

If reading has historically been a tool of revolutions and of liberation, is it not . . . because, constitutively, reading is rather risky business whose outcome and full consequences can never be known in advance? Does not reading involve one risk that, precisely, cannot be resisted: that of finding in the text something one does not expect? (pp. 5–6)

How, then, does Professor Greene's method work? And, what is at stake in "the rather risky business" of reading the Bildungsroman of schooling through the discontented artists?

Maxine Greene narrates a noisy, overpopulated, and haunted history, one that privileges the hesitations, the uncertainties, the detours, and the grand and pitiful operatic gestures made from the dreams of public education. She narrates early stories of a nation built from the stuff of slavery, genocide of First Nation people, and global diaspora. These traumatic episodes schooling must bury and repress in order to preserve the brutality of its origins. This, after all, is the unconscious of education. But Greene, unsatisfied, yet still in dialogue with the official stories of the schoolmen, from Horace Mann to John Dewey, and with the popular news accounts of various moral panics between 1830 and 1914 that imagined the working class, the foreigners, and the rural populations as in need of containment, order, and Christian morality, places these official accounts in tension with fictional worlds of a burgeoning national literature. This other world imagines itself in all the wrong places, sometimes exploring the underside of the lived, sometimes exalting the promise of oneness, sometimes rendering impossible the contradictory humanist dream of transcendence and disinterestedness—of oceanic feelings and confession—and sometimes, insisting, in Greene's words, that "knowledge itself may be suspect" (1965, p. 65). The brutality of a nation's origins returns, like the repressed, in its literature.

There is, then, in all of this life, a fundamental contradiction that makes the project of education inconsolable. It has to do with the question raised earlier by Felman. What is actually occurring when education represses uncertainty and trauma if the very project of reading requires risking the self? How could teachers—of any era—teach its national literature if that literature itself broke apart the order, the punishments, the didacticism, the religiosity, the greed, the conformity, indeed, the very structure of disavowal? What would happen to this literature that admits—whether intentionally or not—its own traumas? How could the lid of education be held if the stuff inside was also taken as the stuff of revolt? Well, the reader might think, education has that peculiar talent for rendering as banal the uncertainties of the lived. We can all remember reading amazing texts in rather unamazing ways and perhaps even reading unamazing texts in amazement. Maxine Greene anticipates this tension when she observes repeatedly that the schoolmen must "necessarily lag behind the artists" (1965, p. 157). But this belatedness, or perhaps ignorance of the artists' concerns, still leaves its trace in schooling. The imaginative articulations of the artists, even if in fairly selective ways, stumble into the curriculum to become the stuff of canonicity, of the culture wars, and of discourses of multiculture. Education is always lived as an argument.

In casting the lot of the early history of compulsory education with that of the history of early U.S. literature, Greene offers her readers not a content (although the footnotes of educational history that Greene juxtaposes and critically comments upon are neither the story of romance nor progress) but rather a method of doing and reading the historicity of the present. It is a method that seems to take quite seriously Freud's concerns with civilization as the production of unhappiness and his decision to learn from and listen to discontents. It is a method that shapes the work of such educational theorists as Bill Pinar (1994), Janet Miller (1990), Jo Anne Pagano (1990), Madeleine Grumet (1989), Warren Crichlow and Cameron McCarthy (1995), Roger Simon (1992), Deanne Bogdan (1992), and Judith Robertson (1994), all of whom in very different ways open education with imaginative works. Imagination is, for Maxine Greene, a method, one that insists that neither the structure and dreams of schooling nor the desires of those who live there can be exhumed from its cultural matrix. In this method, history cannot be rendered as a discreet object, as that great differential alibi for the present. The method is structured by the refusal to detach herself with the congratulatory tone of how much better it is in her present, how different the present schoolmen are from those who first claimed that name, and how nice education has become. One finds, in this 1965 text, a responsibility, something more to do.

Writing within the great waves of civil rights in the United States, writing just eighteen years after the European genocides—the Shoah as Jewish historians now name it—writing within the great demands for relevancy in education that is the legacy of the student protest movement, writing within the U.S. war against Vietnam, and writing against, perhaps, the contemporary schoolmen of her times, those obsessed with new world orders and with what Maxine Greene calls, "the Hegelian need to resolve" (1965, p. 160), this text of Greene's is oddly a history of her present, perhaps a chronicle of her own library, perhaps her view from the window of her office at Teachers College, Columbia University, located "on the edge of the slums in the largest city of all" (p. 160).

And so we might find ourselves on the edges of Maxine Greene's own contemporary space. An example that stands out is when, in the midst of examining the racism of "the Schoolmen" and the National Education Association's refusals between 1870 and 1890 to challenge the structures of educational inequality between white and black children, Greene, in a chapter titled, "The Predicament of Freedom: The Negro, the Farmer, and Huck Finn," turns to Ralph Ellison's novel *The Invisible Man*: "You ache with the need to convince yourself that you do exist in the real world, that you're a part of all the sound and anguish." Then, Greene continues: "It was that way in the 1880's; it is that way now. And a variety of re-enactments are taking place, reminiscent of what was happening eighty years ago" (1965, p. 127). In the next sentence, Greene addresses her white readers, who are also living within the movements of civil rights, "to challenge their sense of themselves as persons as well as to their conception of democracy." This insistence, that history requires answerability, implication and not transcendence, is reminiscent of James Baldwin's "A Talk to Teachers." Greene asks educators to witness the self in relation to the other and hence grapple with who one is becoming when one subordinates another under the name of education. We are asked to imagine who we might become because there is so much to do.

This writing of history, then, is about the presence of a past as a return of the repressed, but without gathering the ground of repetition. It is *not* a story of certainty or conciliation. Nor is it the mere recovery of tiny social artifacts, occasionally dusted off for the museum of educational repression. Still, the social artifacts are there, described in uncanny ways, like the obscurantist McGuffey *Readers* that "built a hundred bridges between the Puritan past and the children of the unregenerate present, who were told they could only be American if they learned what was True" (Greene, 1965, p. 50). And such artifacts are not dusted off as examples of what can only be found in a distant and bad old past. Indeed, I could not help but think of those textual creatures in my own past—Dick and Jane, running in an ever orderly fashion into the whiteness of nuclear family value life—and then, the violence of their return in Toni Morrison's first novel (1970), *The Bluest Eye*. But in examining the footnotes and tiny social artifacts of educational thought, Maxine Greene's project is more akin to Michel de Certeau's (1988) examination of the function of history:

> [It] attests to an autonomy and a dependence whose proportions vary according to the social settings and political situations in which they are elaborated. In the form of a "labor" immanent to human development, [the documents and the writing of history] occupies the place of the myths by means of which a society has represented its ambiguous relations with its origins and, through a violent history of beginnings, its relations to itself. (p. 45)

As Maxine Greene notes in her conclusion, "This has been a book about illusions, about green lights and transcendent goals"(1965, p. 165). But the illusions she may be referring to are not merely the misconceptions or even the interminable betrayals of education. Rather, what is at work is something more central than attempting to survey a particular geography. At once, it has something to do with whether in fact education can be more than colonization, more than the impulse to set in proper place—through its technologies of correction—the needy student, the dangerous individual, the attention deficit, the ignorant parent, the docile body, the dysfunctional gender, and all the other tragic roles that spring forth from the moral panic that stages education. It also has to do with something quite intangible, something to be done. What seems to be at work in Greene's text, as I mentioned earlier, is a method for interpreting the unconscious of educational life, for puzzling over the dream of education, and for imagining education as something different then repression and normalization, something that is capable of surprising itself.

Toward the conclusion of this 1965 text, Greene discusses what might be now a mere footnote in "that slow moving river of educational theory" (p. 114): the self-taught sociologist, Lester Ward and his 1883 text, *Dynamic Sociology*. Ward was interested in the problem of freedom and believed education might be a site where its meanings could be humanly fashioned. Significantly, Ward was interested in engaging some of the problems the artists of his day confronted, and this, after all is the method offered by Maxine Greene. Continually, Greene returns to the preoccupations of artists in all of her writing and with what the arts might open in conversation. The sociologist Ward, according to Greene, worked with two problems—both of which are still a preoccupation, although in ways not imaginable, perhaps, to the Ward of 1883, or to the Maxine Greene of 1965. One had to do with the implications of science for people's visions of themselves. The other had to do with what had become of the hope of progress. Today these concerns collapse within the pandemic known as AIDS, within world-wide civil wars and global displacements and genocides of humans, and even within current debates about the human rights of those who happen to be disenfranchised by identity, by experience, by history. Here, I am thinking of collectivities—and they are not mutually exclusive—of children, women, gays and lesbians, First Nation people, people of color, refugees, and so on. And I'm thinking, how is it possible for education as a discourse and as a practice, as an institution and as an experience, to listen to its own exclusions, repressions, and silences?

Like Maxine Greene, we can decide to become addressed by the artists of our time—and in doing this, decide to make ourselves into new publics. The artists still worry about this thing called pedagogy, about what it means to teach and to learn, and about the detours known as history.

The protagonist Eve in *Eve's Tattoo* (Praeger, 1991) worries about how her New York contemporaries—the artists, the film makers, the advertisers, the rock singers, the people waiting, along with their pets, in a veterinarian office—will think about Nazism, the desire for fascism, and the Shoah. On her fortieth birthday, she has tattooed on the inside of her wrist a concentration camp number, first explaining it as a sort of MIA bracelet. Eve is missing in action, and she spends the rest of the novel in a failed pedagogy of educating others about what she herself cannot bear to know. Tony Kushner's (1992) two-part play, *Angels in America: A Gay Fantasia on National Themes* (*Part One: Millennium Proposals* and *Part Two: Perestroika*), offers a sort of queer diorama of imagined identity performances, all in incomplete acts of community. Characters from different histories confront one another in our time of the pandemic known as AIDS. They meditate in fits and starts about how to live and love within immense suffering and loss. The play collects an accidental sociality in its most vulnerable moments. And like the pandemic known as AIDS, the old boundaries of inside and outside no longer hold any sense. Gracefully and ungracefully the characters become caught in change and loss. And for Tony Kushner, the tension we are asked to bear concerns how it is possible to care for the self in a way that one cares, as well, for another.

In Toronto, where I now live, Canadian artist Bruce Eves investigates homosexual desire. He calls his exhibit, "Theoretical People," and, perhaps in spite or maybe because of this artist's edgy and transgressive attempts, he made me think about education, stalled in its own attempts to make certain the uncertainties of theory and practice. Elaine Shape's photo exhibit, also in Toronto, elicits a sort of fascination and repugnance toward the traditional roles of women in contemporary Western culture. I think, along with Shoshana Felman, of how these women suffer from too many stories, none of which can be their own. Then, there is Bianca Nyavingi Brynda's feature-length documentary that examines, under the title *Roots Daughters,* Rasta-women in social, political, and economic contexts as they fight for equality within Rasta culture and within larger worlds. I am reminded of Jyl Lynn Felman's haunting essay (1994) titled, "If Only I'd Been Born a Kosher Chicken," a sort of Kaddish for Jewish lesbians denied membership, forgotten in our own Jewish communities. Then there is the film *Go Fish,* also playing in Toronto. It magnifies some minuscule daily anxieties and pleasures of a small lesbian community in the process of making itself. There, I study this new generation, marvelling over the public accessibility of a film about lesbians doing nothing more than making an everyday, than figuring the problem of love.

The method here is free association, and, in this all too brief sampling, we have artists unafraid to imagine differences within, to address those who may or may not understand, to fashion communities yet to become, and to engage life at its most incomplete. Unlike educators, they seem to offer only the stuff for interpretation and then no guarantee. They are interested in the mistakes, the accidents, the detours, and the unintelligibilities of identities. Unlike educators, they gesture to their own constructedness and frailties, troubling the space between representation and the real. And in doing so, the responsibility for new meanings, for making new projects, lies elsewhere: in the doing of dialogue, in the interminable arguments over what can constitute and undo in the Bildungsroman of schooling, authenticity, appropriation, and the limits of culture. They explore, then, that twilight of experience where every reading of the body is a misreading, where every search for self leads to the other. They refuse the simple and moralistic romance that we in education call self esteem, role models and childhood innocence. They are not the invisible hand that centers the child. Theirs are decentered concerns with desire gone awry, with the clash between the desire to represent and the representation of desire, and with the offer of making difference and hence provoking new imagined communities from the limits of experience and history. And with these insistences, none of which offers any guarantees, perhaps education can begin.

It may be that the problem of bringing these new artists into schools and into schools of education requires a great deal from teachers and students. But this work of learning, as Maxine Greene's 1965 text reveals, has always been a problem in education. Learning and teaching requires something of us because, as Anna Freud reminds, education in its widest sense "comprises all types of interference with . . . development" (1969, p. 317). But maybe precisely because reading is risky business in that selves and cultures are interfered with, there can be made an interest in leaving the notion that knowledge is a settled and affirming space of answers. There can be provoked—and this, after all, is the problem of pedagogy—a decision to listen to stories of another in order to do more with the stories one already holds. And if this can be the start, maybe it will begin with an ethical concern for examining the structure of one's own worries, fears, and desires when one is surprised. Maybe then, education can engage in that difficult study of its own unconscious, with what it cannot bear to know with an interest in implicating itself in its own fragilities. At the very least, and this, without her ever saying it directly, is what I learned from Maxine Greene's text: one can respond to what the artists require of us within the arts, one can find something more to do. It may have something to do with understanding that imagination can exceed what an everyday tolerates as normal.

Still, to return for a moment to the Toronto art offerings one summer, crowded with all kinds of publics, one can notice something being made. Maybe each individual had a feisty fourth grade teacher that affirmed through the cultivation of scepticism, or maybe not and still figured a way to confront "something more." But what these artists ask those of us in education, and what Maxine Greene writes, is whether education can tolerate the arts even as the arts must necessarily exceed education.

REFERENCES

Baldwin, J. (1985). A talk to teachers. In *The price of the ticket: Collected nonfiction, 1948–1985*. New York: St. Martin's, pp. 325–332.

Bogdan, D. (1992). *Re-educating the imagination: Toward a poetics, politics, and pedagogy of literary engagement*. Portsmouth, NH: Heinemann.

Certeau, Michel de. (1988). *The writing of history* (T. Conley, Trans.). New York: Columbia University Press.

Crichlow, W., & McCarthy, C. (Eds.). (1995). Toni Morrison and the curriculum [special issue]. *Cultural Studies, 9*(2).

Felman, J. L. (1994, July/August). If only I'd been born a kosher chicken. *Tikkun: A Bimonthly Jewish Critique of Politics, Culture, and Society, 9*(4), 47–50 and 78–79.

Felman, S. (1993). *What does a woman want? reading and sexual difference*. Baltimore, MD: Johns Hopkins University Press.

Freud, A. (1973). About losing and being lost. In *The writings of Anna Freud: Indications for child analysis and other papers* (Vol. IV 1945–1956, pp. 302–316). New York: International Universities Press. (Original work published 1953).

Freud, S. (1953). Mourning and melancholia. In J. Strachey (Ed. and Trans.), *The standard edition of the complete psychological works of Sigmund Freud* (Vol. 14, pp. 239–258). London: Hogarth Press. (Original work published 1915)]

Greene, M. (1965). *The public school and the private vision: A search for America in education and literature*. New York: Random House.

Grumet, M. (1989). The beauty full curriculum. *Educational Theory, 39*, 225–230.

Kushner, T. (1992). *Angels in America: A gay fantasia on national themes (Part I: Millennium proposals and Part II: Perestroika)*. New York: Theatre Communications Group.

Miller, J. L. (1990). *Creating spaces and finding voices: Teachers collaborating for empowerment*. Albany, NY: SUNY Press.

Pagano, J. (1990). *Exiles and communities: Teaching in the patriarchal wilderness*. Albany, NY: SUNY Press.

Pinar, W. (1994). *Autobiography, politics, and sexuality: Essays in curriculum theory.* New York: Peter Lang.

Praeger, E. (1991). *Eve's tattoo.* New York: Vintage Press.

Simon, R. (1992). *Teaching against the grain.* Hadley: Bergin & Garvey Press.

Robertson, J. (1994). *Cinema and the politics of desire in teacher education.* Unpublished doctoral dissertation, Ontario Institute for the Study of Education, University of Toronto.

Washington, E. K. (1994). Sculpture in flight: A conversation with Bill T. Jones. *Transition, 62,* 188–202.

11

Notes on the Intellectual: In Praise of Maxine Greene

William F. Pinar

Like many of you, I have studied the work of Maxine Greene since graduate school (which for me began in June 1969). Her "Curriculum and Consciousness," published in the famous 1971 issue of *Teachers College Record,* was stunning; I reprinted it in the 1975 *Curriculum Theorizing* collection. After graduation, I had the chance to invite her to my campus, and in 1973 I did. Even today I can remember being seated next to her on the podium; she was, clearly, a most remarkable person. I thought then and I think now that Maxine Greene is the preeminent philosopher of education of her generation, one of the most important figures of any generation to have written and taught and lectured in our field.

Here, I want to examine the character of our work as teachers, as scholars, in a word, as intellectuals. To focus upon the intellectual, I will use Edward Said's (1996) *Representations of the Intellectual* as my sourcebook. The essays in this collection were originally given as the 1993 Reith Lectures, for which there is no equivalent in the United States. Several Americans, among them J. Robert Oppenheimer, John Kenneth Galbraith, and John Searle, have given them since Bertrand Russell started the series in 1948. Broadcast over the BBC, these lectures have been heard by millions. Summarizing Said's lectures provides an occasion to honor Maxine Greene by focusing our attention on what it might mean, as the century closes, to be an intellectual in the field of education.

Of course, to be an intellectual is a good thing, possibly, depending upon the extent of the accomplishment, a great thing. But intellectuals were and are not universally appreciated. Indeed, "until the middle twentieth century unfavorable uses of *intellectuals, intellectualism* and *intelligentsia* were dominant in English." "And," Raymond Williams (1976/1985) adds, "it is clear that such uses persist" (p. 170). One might ask, why would that be? To ask this question presupposes ignorance of what an intellectual is. As Said (1996) explains, "intellectuals are precisely those figures whose public performances can neither be predicted nor compelled into some slogan, orthodox party line, or fixed dogma" (p. xii). Expressing skepticism, even criticism, of the status quo does not win membership in local country clubs, even the university kind.

But the problem intellectuals in our time face is not so much an uncomprehending, unappreciative, sometimes hostile public. Rather, as John Carey (1993) discusses, the problem the intellectuals face have now to do with their own kind, the "insiders" and experts, those professionals who mold or would mold opinion. Intellectuals have a problem when they want to *become* insiders, and this is a problem precisely because intellectuals are obligated to be those who question insiders' privilege, especially when they are based, as they so often are, on class, race, or gender (Said, 1996). The cult of the expert is classed, racialized, and gendered. In education it is to be middle (aspiring to the upper-middle) class, white, often male, certainly heterosexual (or passing as such).

James Baldwin and Malcolm X suggest to Said the order of work the intellectual performs. "The challenge of intellectual life," Said (1996) says succinctly, "is to be found in dissent against the status quo" (p. xvii). Dissent is not a knee-jerk reaction to whatever is, however, but rather an informed, considered analysis. Indeed, being an intellectual requires "a relentless erudition" (Foucault, quoted in Said, 1996, p. xviii). Further, the intellectual's work, in Said's words, "will neither make them friends in high places nor win them official honors. It is a lonely condition, yes, but it is always a better one than a gregarious tolerance for the way things are" (p. xviii).

DEFINITIONS

Said (1996) reviews the two basic concepts of the modern intellectual. One is associated with Antonio Gramsci (a name familiar to students of curriculum), one with Julien Benda. In Gramsci's analysis of the intellectual there are two kinds of specialists who perform the intellectual functions in society. First, there are those traditional intellectuals such as teachers, priests, and administrators. These tend to perform similar work from generation to generation. Second, there are organic intellectuals, whom Gramsci saw as directly linked to those classes or enterprises that employ intellectuals to represent their interests in order to gain more power.

Regarding the organic intellectual, Gramsci wrote: "The capitalist entrepreneur creates alongside himself the industrial technician, the specialist in political economy, the organizers of a new culture, of a new

legal system, etc." (quoted in Said, 1996, p. 4). The advertising or public relations specialist, for instance, would count as an organic intellectual, using Gramsci's definition. Such a person works to gain the consent of potential customers, wins their approval, marshals consumer or
voter opinion. Unlike teachers and priests, to Gramsci's mind, organic
intellectuals are always on the move, in a sense always on the make (Said,
1996). Philip Wexler once asserted, in my Baton Rouge living room in
fact, to a small group of astonished graduate students, that those in the
advertising industry *are* the revolutionary class in America, exactly because
they are actively engaged in the transformation of existing society.

At the opposite end of this definitional spectrum is Julien Benda's
characterization of intellectuals as a small group of extraordinarily gifted
and morally endowed philosopher-kings who personify the conscience
of humankind. Benda's religious term for intellectuals—clerics—denotes
a status and performance that distinguishes the intellectual from the laity,
those ordinary citizens who spend their lives busily pursuing material
advantage, status advancement, and, sometimes, close relationships
with those in power. Authentic intellectuals, Benda reminds, are not in
pursuit of practical aims. Authentic intellectuals seek pleasure in their
art or science without regard to material advantage, and by doing so
they communicate: "My kingdom is not of this world" (Benda, 1928/1969,
p. 43). Said's (1996) concept of the intellectual seems to be a mix of Benda's
and Gramsci's. He is interested in the moral high-ground of Benda's
idea, without its elitist connotations or its gender-blindness. (Benda never
mentions women or non-Europeans, except Jesus.) Said is drawn to teaching but in an "organic" way that links intellectuals to the wider world,
that is, to history and politics.

Intellectuals, it is clear, have to be thoroughgoing individualists with
strong personalities, able to follow their individuated paths, sometimes
amidst skepticism if not outright opposition. Indeed, by vocation, intellectuals tend to be in a state of almost constant opposition to the status
quo: political, cultural, and—this especially pertinent to academicians—
to the status quo within their own specialized fields. The image of morally
positioned, socially estranged intellectual remains a compelling one. When
we think of "intellectual" we tend to think of someone set apart, a person able to speak the truth to both secular and ecclesiastical powers.
This person is often eloquent, always unintimidated, and sometimes angry.
No site of power, including the individual's own field, can be exempt
from critical analysis (Said, 1996). There is, additionally, the expecta-
tion that the intellectual will say something "new." As Richard Rorty
(1991) puts the matter: "[O]ne should see the intellectual *qua* intellectual as having a special, idiosyncratic need—a need for the ineffable,

the sublime, a need to go beyond the limits, a need to use words which are not part of anybody's language-game, any social institution" (p. 176).

Despite the appeal of the image of the cleric, Gramsci's idea of the intellectual as someone who fulfills a specific set of functions in the society is more typical today. Especially now, near the end of the twentieth century, many professions—Said (1996) lists broadcasters, academic professionals, computer analysts, sports and media lawyers, management consultants, policy experts, government advisers, authors of specialized market reports, and journalists—seem to illustrate Gramsci's model. Anyone who works in a specialized field involved either in the production or distribution of knowledge is an intellectual in Gramsci's sense, and in this "information age," in our "semiotic society," that covers a wide range of activity indeed.

The era of what Foucault called the "universal intellectual" (nearly everyone including Said thinks of Jean-Paul Sartre) is gone. Now is the time of the "specific" intellectual, someone who works inside a discipline and makes use of his or her expertise in carefully circumscribed ways. Intellectuals today are almost never individuals of independent means who address a wide lay public. Almost invariably, intellectuals are now members of what Alvin Gouldner (1979) has called a culture of critical discourse.

Despite this variegated image of the "organic" intellectual today, Said (1996) insists that the intellectual must be someone whose role in society cannot be reduced to that of a faceless professional, merely a competent member of a class going about his or her business. True, the central fact is that the intellectual is a person endowed with a gift for representing, embodying, articulating a message, a view, an attitude, philosophy, or opinion to, as well as for, a public. But, as Said (1996) says,

> this role has an edge to it, and cannot be played without a sense of being someone whose place it is publicly to raise embarrassing questions, to confront orthodoxy and dogma (rather than to produce them), to be someone who cannot easily be co-opted by governments or corporations, and whose *raise d'etre* is to represent all those people and issues that are routinely forgotten or swept under the rug. The intellectual does so on the basis of universal principles. (p. 11)

And when the intellectual raises these questions, obstacles blocking movement toward a more just order are exposed. Bernard Yack (1986) cites this as characteristic of the intellectual's task:

> One of the most characteristic activities of the intellectual . . . is the definition of obstacles to our satisfaction. Intellectuals search out the con-

nections between seemingly unrelated phenomena and thus provide us
with deeper explanations of our dissatisfaction with the world. In this
way the concepts which they develop redefine objects of desire and
longing. (p. 6)

Because we deal with obstacles in the world, there are, strictly speaking, no private intellectuals. Nor are there only public intellectuals,
those who exist exclusively as figureheads or spokespersons for or symbols of causes, movements, or moral and intellectual positions. In the
intellectual's self-representation there is always what Said (1996) describes
as "the personal inflection and the private sensibility, and those give meaning to what is being said or written" (p. 12). Least of all, Said continues,
should the intellectual perceive his or her job to be only to please the
audiences. "The whole point," Said reminds us, "is to be embarrassing,
contrary, even unpleasant" (p. 12).

   Intellectuals are individuals, then, whose vocation is the art of representing knowledge, whether through the medium of talking, writing,
teaching, appearing on television, and so on. And in this representation
there is some critique of the status quo, a critique individually signed.
Note that the emphasis in this definition is equally upon vocation, representation, and individual. "[W]hen I read Jean-Paul Sartre or Bertrand
Russell," Said (1996) explains, "it is their specific, individual voice and
presence that makes an impression on me over and above their arguments
because they are speaking out for their beliefs. They cannot be mistaken
for an anonymous functionary or careful bureaucrat" (p. 13).

   While the expertise and the representation of that expertise is of
course crucial, expertise itself is insufficient to qualify as "intellectual
work." It is the individualistic and critical character of that representation that signals to us that an intellectual is at work, not merely an expert
or competent professional. Again, Said (1996) thinks of Jean-Paul Sartre:

> In the outpouring of studies about intellectuals there has been far too
> much defining of the intellectual, and not enough stock taken of the
> image, the signature, the actual intervention and performance, all of
> which taken together constitute the very lifeblood of every real intel-
> lectual....When we remember an intellectual like Sartre, we recall the
> personal mannerisms, the sense of an important personal stake, the sheer
> effort, risk, will to say things about colonialism, or about commitment,
> or about social conflict that infuriated his opponents and galvanized his
> friends and perhaps even embarrassed him retrospectively. (p. 13)

The purpose of the intellectual's individual, often irreverent activity is
to advance the intertwining causes of human freedom and knowledge.

The purpose is *not* to advance careers, strengthen egos, or celebrate status. The intellectual's representations are not intended exclusively for service within those bureaucracies in which the intellectual works. Nor are they designed only to please employers. "Intellectual representations," Said (1996) indicates, "are the activity itself, dependent on a kind of consciousness that is skeptical, engaged, unremittingly devoted to rational investigation and moral judgment; and this puts the individual on record and on the line" (p. 20).

Being an intellectual does not mean that one is *always* a critic of government policy, of course. Occasionally governments and mainstream institutions do things right. The intellectual's vocation requires a state of alertness, "wide-awakeness" Maxine Greene might say, a perpetual determination not to allow half-truths, however fashionable, or popular ideas, however self-serving, to seduce one. The vocation of the intellectual requires a never-ending vigilance, a seemingly inexhaustible rational engagement, a strong sense of self in-the-world "not yet." This last requirement Said (1996) usefully describes as "a complicated struggle to balance the problems of one's own selfhood against the demands of publishing and speaking out in the public sphere [and this] is what makes it an everlasting effort, constitutively unfinished and necessarily imperfect" (p. 23).

In 1927, "intellectuals" meant, at least for Benda, Europeans. The cultural center of gravity has shifted since then. Europe and the West are no longer the unchallenged intellectual center of the world. The astonishing acceleration both of travel and global communication has supported a somewhat greater awareness of what now gets called "difference" and "otherness." To speak of intellectuals as the century comes to a close requires speaking of national, religious, and even regional versions of the intellectual, each dimension worthy of separate consideration, yet functioning together nonsynchronously (McCarthy, 1993). To some extent this localization of the generic concept of intellectuals is due as well to the proliferation of specialized studies (Said, 1996), of which our own field is, of course, but one example.

SIGNATURES AND STRANGERS

Each of us is born into a language. Generally one spends the rest of one's life in that language, which is the principal medium of one's intellectual activity. Certainly an important aspect of the intellectual's signature is his or her use of language. But there is another element of one's linguistic medium: its association with national identification. One creates "others" through a series of discursive moves, moves which also structure oneself: "To tell, for example, that the Russians are coming, or that the Japanese economic invasion is upon us, or that militant Islam is on the march, is not only to experience collective alarm, but also to consolidate 'our' identity as beleaguered and at risk" (Said, 1996, p. 32).

Nationalism, patriotism, and other forms of group identification function to divide peoples across a series of discursive divides: race, gender, ethnicity among the most prominent. The intellectual, Said tells us, has a specific responsibility toward these phenomena:

> With regard to the consensus on group or national identity it is the intellectual's task to show how the group is not a natural or god-given entity but is a constructed, manufactured, even in some cases invented object, with a history of struggle and conquest behind it. . . . In the United States Noam Chomsky and Gore Vidal have performed this task with unstinting effort. (p. 33)

In the field of education, Maxine Greene has performed this work, questioning, not only specific national issues such as America 2000, but school reform generally, including the military/industrial-based embrace of mathematics and science as the curricular center, and a corresponding devaluation of the arts and humanities. Indeed, probably no one person has served the educational cause of the arts more than Maxine Greene.

Of course, not only national identities are socially constructed, intellectuals' responses to them are as well. Said regards a certain self-reflexive grasp of one's views as qualifying for the status of intellectual. That autobiographical consciousness is well developed in our field. Said remembers Virginia Woolf's essay *A Room of One's Own* as reminding us that:

> one can only show how one came to hold whatever opinion one does hold. . . . One can only give one's audience the chance of drawing their own conclusions as they observe the limitations, the prejudices, the idiosyncrasies of the speaker. (Woolf, quoted in Said, 1996, p. 34)

As Frantz Fanon (1952/1967a, 1964/1967b, 1961/1968) argued for the native intellectual, we might recall for those of us in the metropole: We cannot simply become replacements for hegemonic policemen. We must strive pedagogically for what Fanon called the invention of new souls. I would add the new soul we must seek is our own, a soul to then be witnessed to our students. In fin-de-siècle America, to seek our souls situates us, to use Oscar Wilde's description of himself, in a contrapuntal symbolic relationship with this soulless time (Said, 1996).

Exile can be a sad fate, as Said himself knows. But it is not only a literal, geographic experience. Exile is also a metaphorical condition, one with pedagogical potential. Said speaks of famous exiles such as Jonathan Swift and, in our time, Theodor Adorno. Adorno in particular reminds us that the intellectual's consciousness must not rest easily or for long in any one spot, that it must be on guard against the comforts of success, the temptations to play that tune one time more: "It is part of morality not to be at home in one's home" (Adorno, quoted in Said, 1996, p. 57).

The intellectual in exile, the teacher as stranger (Greene, 1973): We journey through ideas via reading, writing, and teaching. S/he does not reside in a specific country, or in any one practice: "For a man [sic] who no longer has a homeland, writing becomes a place to live." Especially when there is success, there must be no flight to the role ("the great man"), no retreat from self-analysis. Adorno writes that: "The demand that one harden oneself against self-pity implies the technical necessity to counter any slackening of the intellectual tension with the utmost alertness. . . . In the end, the writer is not allowed to live in his writing" (quoted passages in Said, 1996, p. 58).

Being an exile is not all heroics, of course. There can be pleasure in being a stranger, "those different arrangements of living and eccentric angles of vision that it can sometimes afford" (Said, 1996, p. 59). Not being submerged in experience, as Maxine Greene (1995) observes, allows one to live more fully, more consciously, more aware of contingency, choice, and the "otherwiseness" of daily life. Said (1996) notes: "An intellectual is like a shipwrecked person who learns how to live in a certain sense *with* the land, not *on* it" (p. 59).

Being an outsider permits one to act the beginner in one's circumstances, and this "innocence" allows an unconventional style of life, if one wishes, a different, possibly eccentric career. Said (1996) explains:

> For the intellectual an exilic displacement means being liberated from the usual career, in which "doing well" and following in time-honored footsteps are the main milestones. . . . If you can experience that fate not as a deprivation and as something to be bewailed, but as a sort of freedom, a process of discovery in which you do things according to your own pattern, as various interests seize your attention, and as the particular goal you set yourself dictates: that is a unique pleasure. (p. 62)

As I mentioned in another text, living on the margins may be dangerous, but at last you can breath there (Pinar, in press).

But how marginalized can the university intellectual be? Are we not always implicated by the institutions we serve? Even those of us who do not run after fame, government contracts, who do not belong to the country club networks, does not the question remain: Can there be anything like an independent, autonomously functioning intellectual, "one who is not beholden to, and therefore constrained by, his or her affiliations with universities that pay salaries, political parties that demand loyalty to a party line, think tanks?" (Said, 1996, p. 67). Vincent Leitch (1992) sees us all implicated in "regimes of reason," which code our work:

> In my understanding, intellectuals are situated amid determining historical, social, and political matrices that proffer vocational patterns sanctioned by society. Within regimes of reason, conformity and resistance are alike coded. . . . Being subject to "reason" does not involve thorough-going subjection. . . . The complicated bottom line is that academic intellectuals are intricately and inescapably implicated in regimes of unreason, that they can more or less unwittingly serve the established order both by attempting to avoid and to criticize it, and that they can, nevertheless, transform it. (p. 168)

Nineteenth-century and early twentieth-century representations of the intellectual, as we have seen, tended to stress individuality. The intellectual was represented as a solitary, somewhat aloof figure, one who refused to conform, who sometimes chooses the role of rebel, living and thinking outside mainstream opinion. However, to accuse intellectuals of being sellouts because they earn their living working in universities or for newspapers is, as Said (1996) says, a meaningless, self-serving charge. Maxine Greene is an example of an intellectual whose employment by a university in no discernible way undermined the independent, often against-the-grain direction of her intellectual career.

PRESSURES

To be an intellectual is to be continually subjected to pressures of many kinds. What are a few of these pressures today? Specialization is one. In the postwar period, expertise and the cult of the expert function as specific pressures upon the vocation of the intellectual. Expertise has little to do, necessarily, with knowledge, but rather with self-positioning, claims to remuneration, and authority. Perhaps such tendencies are ever present among the intelligentsia, but in the postwar period they have seemed especially powerful. Said (1996) illustrates the point by reference to the staggering extent to which the agenda of the U.S. national security efforts during the "cold war" determined priorities and the mentality of academic research. A similar situation, he notes, occurred in the Soviet Union, but in the West no one had any illusions about free inquiry there. It is the undermining of free inquiry here that is disheartening.

In our field of education, there is the unquestioned assumption that grants legitimize research, and that the closer the grant is to Washington, or to other sites of authority and power, where policy is formulated, the more significant the research. The image of professor as corporate executive, always more evident in business schools than in education departments, has been alluring for some, especially for those in the fancy private schools where institutional pressure for "external" funding is sometimes relentless. Even in the prestigious public universities, there is a tendency for administrative staff—especially but not only at the dean's level—to equate externally funded research with important inquiry. If the work is important, it will be funded. Said (1996) is speaking about research influenced by cold-war militarism, but what he writes applies to the situation in the various subfields of education:

> [T]he space for individual and subjective intellectual representation, for asking questions and challenging the wisdom of a war or an immense social program that awards contracts and endows prizes, has shrunk dramatically from what it was a hundred years ago when Stephen Dedalus could say that as an intellectual his duty was not to serve any power or authority at all. (p. 82)

The complicity of intellectuals within education schools and departments with administrative expectations for policy-oriented or parent-discipline research undermines the autonomy of our discipline and restricts the intellectual gains we can make. This is not to say we should abandon the university, even with its sometimes shameless badgering of education schools, its contradictory demands ("serve the schools" and "act like business professors" and "act like arts and sciences scholars"). The university, Said (1996) is right to say, remains a relatively free place in which to follow one's intellectual passion: "To my mind the Western university, certainly in America, still can offer the intellectual a quasi-utopian space in which reflection and research can go on, albeit under new constraints and pressures" (p. 82).

Is there a model of the intellectual we might remember as we try to find our way at the end of millennium? Said (1996) offers us one, one from which we in education might shy away, given our persisting anxieties over the quasi-autonomy of our discipline, the integrity of our efforts, the disregard in which we are held by colleagues across the university, by politicians, and by not a few members of the public. He suggests the idea of "amateurism," by which he means: "an activity that is fueled by care and affection rather than by profit and selfish narrow specialization" (p. 82). He goes on to say:

> The intellectual today ought to be an amateur, someone who considers that to be a thinking and concerned member of a society one is entitled to raise moral issue at the heart of even the most technical and professionalized activity as it involves one's country, its power, its mode of interacting with its citizens as well as with other societies. In addition, the intellectual's spirit as an amateur can enter and transform the merely professional routine most of us go through into something much more lively and radical; instead of doing what one is supposed to do one can ask why one does it, who benefits from it, how can it reconnect with a personal project and original thoughts. (pp. 82–83)

The intellectual as amateur might restore a certain innocence and integrity to the intellectual project.

Certainly the idea allows Said to ask the basic questions the intellectual must ask regarding his or her activity: "How does one speak the truth? What truth? For whom and where?" (p. 88). In answering these questions one keeps in mind, as does Said, that "one of the main intellectual activities of our century has been the questioning, not to say undermining, of authority" (p. 91). And to pursue this activity, to question the taken-for-granted, one must sometimes question the accepted practices of one's field:

> Nothing in my view is more reprehensible than those habits of mind in the intellectual that induce avoidance, that characteristic turning away from a difficult and principled position which you know to be the right one, but which you decide not to take. You do not want to appear too political; you are afraid of seeming controversial. . . . For an intellectual these habits of mind are corrupting *par excellence.* (pp. 100–101)

Finally, Said observes that it is one's own taken-for-granted ideas and practices that function to undermine intellectual work. One's very successes, one's most admired contributions, one's identity as a scholar and teacher: All that comprises one's accomplishment can turn on one, eating away at one's freedom, one's relentless drive to know more, to understand more:

> It is difficult to face that threat on one's own, and even more difficult to find a way to be consistent with your own beliefs and at the same time remain freed enough to grow, change your mind, discover new things, or rediscover what you had once put aside. The hardest aspect of being an intellectual is to represent what you profess through your work and interventions, without hardening into an institution or a kind of automaton acting at the behest of a system or method. Anyone who has felt the exhilaration of being successful at that *and* also successful at keeping alert and solid will appreciate how rare the convergence is. But the only way of ever achieving it is to keep reminding yourself

> that as an intellectual you are the one who can choose between actively
> representing the truth to the best of your ability and passively allow-
> ing a patron or an authority to direct you. For the secular intellectual,
> *those* gods always fail. (p. 121)

Said's standards for the title of intellectual are high. They lead to me think,
appreciatively, of Maxine Greene.

JUNE 27, 1996

While Maxine Greene has achieved iconic status for many of us, while
we know her to be one of the most important scholars and intellectuals
in the field today, she has not succumbed to our veneration of her. Her
vitality, her wide-awakeness, her erudition were all evident, once again,
on Thursday, June 27, 1996, when she spoke (not for the first time) at LSU,
to an overflow crowd packed into the old Hill Memorial Library. She
had been invited to speak about her "present passions." And what were
they, as she faces her eightieth year?

Maxine Greene began by acknowledging that, as an existentialist, she
prefers to look to the future, to cultivate hope for a better time, to find
ways to the next situation, that which is not yet. As an aging person,
she said, smiling at us, the trouble is that the future shrinks, at least that
portion of it she will know. And so, she admitted, she finds herself looking at the past. When she does, she is troubled.

"I ask myself," she confided publicly, "what is the meaning of what
I have done?" When she surveys the current scene, when she sees the
continued prominence of, for instance, those who proclaim "family values" while making life even more difficult for teenaged mothers, the prominence of those who assert the right to life of fetuses while parenting
abusively in the name of the Father, when she watches efforts at educational reforms not a one of which points to that which she knows to be
central to the educational project—imagination—she is somber. In this
era marked by the continued deterioration of many of the nation's schools,
the degradation of the public sphere generally, a deepening disillusion-
ment regarding the progressive project itself, "what," she asked herself,
looking at us, "has my work meant?" There was no hint, either in tone
or content, of self-pity: only the feeling-filled, engaged voice of a serious
intellectual, committed to her cause, the cause of education.

The future awaits her, still. She is rewriting, she tells us, her first
book, *The Public School and the Private Vision*. That profound division
during the nineteenth century between an uncritical endorsement of

American culture personified in Horace Mann and the sober, skeptical study of a culture haunted by what it could not face, epitomized in the work of Nathaniel Hawthorne, remains vivid for her today. As right as she is about that question—the cultural divide between the boosters and artists/intellectuals—Maxine Greene does not stay there long. She confesses to us her embeddedness in the canon, in being a Barnard graduate before the cultural revolution and the civil rights movement of the 1960s. That's another reason for rewriting the book. Her authorities in *The Public School and the Private Vision,* first time round, reflected that canon; they were Europeans or European-Americans, save Ralph Ellison. Now she sees a much more multicultural canon; still her educated vision does not obliterate those great writers who first meant liberation to her as a young woman, the great names of European and European-American philosophy and literature.

It is late morning now, and she has been speaking for an hour. I am watching her finger shake slightly as she makes a final point through her nearly eighty years, and I know, at that moment, I am in the presence of education personified, imagination exemplified, an intellectual *engagé.* No doubt she knows we venerate her; she must see it in our faces. Isn't she tempted to rest in that gaze, I wonder, returning it, saying, yes I know I am your great one? No, that would be like being Sartre's waiter in the café. No, like Adorno, like Said, like Woolf, Maxine Greene remains the stranger, the one in exile, thinking of what might be next, not playing to our gaze, not collapsing, as a more ordinary mortal might, into our admiration for her. How *does* she think of herself? She asked that question that morning, toward the end of the speech. "Who am I?" she posed, half to us, half to herself, then paused before the answer: "I am who I am not yet." *Not yet* . . . the phrase hung in the air. Maxine Greene is, not yet. She may be not yet, but for me, for us, she is now, she is courage, strength, stamina; she is a continual questioning not only of the world but of her world. These are, unmistakably, signs of an intellectual.

REFERENCES

Benda, J. (1969). *The treason of the intellectuals* (R. Abington, Trans.). New York: Norton. (Original work published 1928)

Carey, J. (1993). *The intellectuals and the masses: Pride and prejudice among the literary intelligentsia, 1880–1939.* New York: St. Martin's Press.

Fanon, F. (1967a). *Black skin, white masks* (C. L. Markmann, Trans.). New York: Grove Press. (Original work published 1952)

Fanon, F. (1967b). *Toward the African revolution* (H. Chevalier, Trans.). New York: Grove Press. (Original work published 1964)

Fanon, F. (1968). *The wretched of the earth* (Preface by Jean-Paul Sartre. C. Farrington, Trans.). New York: Grove Press. (Original work published 1961)

Gouldner, A. W. (1979). *The future of intellectuals and the rise of the new class.* New York: Seabury Press.

Greene, M. (1965). *The public school and the private vision: A search for America in education and literature.* New York: Random House.

Greene, M. (1973). *Teacher as stranger.* Belmont, CA: Wadsworth.

Greene, M. (1975). Curriculum and consciousness. In W. Pinar (Ed.), *Curriculum theorizing: The reconceptualists* (299–317). Berkeley, CA: McCutchan. (Reprinted from *Teachers College Record, 73*(2), 253–269, 1971)

Greene, M. (1995). *Releasing the imagination: Essays on education, the arts, and social change.* San Francisco: Jossey-Bass.

Leitch, V. B. (1992). *Cultural criticism, literary theory, poststructuralism.* New York: Columbia University Press.

McCarthy, C. (1993). Multicultural approaches to racial inequality in the United States. In L. Castenell & W. F. Pinar (Eds.), *Understanding curriculum as racial text: Representations of identity and difference in education* (pp. 225–246). Albany: State University of New York Press.

Pinar, W. F. (1975). *Curriculum theorizing: The reconceptualists.* Berkeley, CA: McCutchan.

Pinar, W. F. (in press). Regimes of reason and male narrative voice. In W. Tierney & Y. Lincoln (Eds.), *Voice and educational research.* Albany: State University of New York Press.

Rorty, R. (1991). *Essays on Heidegger and others:Vol. 2. Philosophical papers.* Cambridge & New York: Cambridge University Press.

Said, E. W. (1996). *Representations of the intellectual: The 1993 Reith lectures.* New York: Vintage.

Williams, R. (1985). *Keywords: A vocabulary of culture and society.* New York: Oxford University Press. (Original work published 1976)

Yack, B. (1986). *The longing for total revolution: Philosophic sources of social discontent from Rousseau to Marx and Nietzsche.* Princeton, NJ: Princeton University Press.

12

Landscapes, Biography, and the Preservation of the Present

Craig Kridel

I grew up in a family that discouraged intellectual adventure and risk. To me, the opera and the Sunday concerts in the Brooklyn Museum Sculpture Court and the outdoor concerts in the summer were rebellions, breakthroughs, secret gardens.

Maxine Greene
"Curriculum and Consciousness"

I have long been struck by these opening lines of Maxine Greene's (1975) autobiographical statement, preceding her chapter, "Curriculum and Consciousness," in *Curriculum Theorizing*. Perhaps it is her recognition of the wonderment of knowledge and learning. Perhaps it is the public disclosure—the making known of a private fact—that I find so powerful. Her statement offers a rare glimpse at an educator's life and an invitation to the specialness of Maxine's writings. Wide-awakeness, transcendence, and landscapes—such are her invitations for creating possibilities and "releasing the imagination." Yet, when her work is coupled with such autobiographical facts, another "secret garden" forms between reader and writer. Increasingly, I am struck by the power of autobiography and biography—the construction of landscapes and the act of making history become personal. As Maxine underscores the importance of "being grounded in one's personal history and lived lives," autobiographical and biographical writing serve as a critical way not only to become grounded but, also, to preserve, maintain, and understand our contemporary heritage.

I will not discuss the work of Maxine Greene but, rather, reflect on the significance of certain aspects of her writing and how this relates to my professional life. Her impact on me is quite dramatic. Maxine's work in foundations of education and aesthetic education have had profound influence. However, I wish here to explore her implicit call to the auto-biographical voice which, when preserved in an archival setting, becomes the crucial material—artifacts and documents—for the biographer. Moreover, I call for the recognition and development of biographical work as a way of attending to certain issues and problems of postmodern educational research. Ultimately, this call addresses basic concerns about the preservation of the present.

QUALITATIVE RESEARCH AND BIOGRAPHY

Ours is a postmodern age where educators clearly recognize the importance of personal narrative, the power of stories, and the general recognition of not only perspective but also whose voice is being expressed and whose is being heard. Authoritative knowledge becomes an antiquated conception as an emergence of multifaceted research methodologies, embodying interpretive, naturalistic inquiry, now takes center stage. As the field of education explores further various forms of qualitative research—ethnographies, case studies, life histories, interpretive practice, participative inquiry, narratives and "narrative reasoning," and teachers' stories—the possible contributions of biographical research have yet to fully manifest themselves in this examination. This is not to say that biographical research does not exist in the field of education but only to suggest that a prominent biographical perspective is not as clearly visible as other forms—namely, autobiographic, narrative, and ethnographic. One should not be surprised since biography has always been viewed with some degree of suspicion among the academic disciplines—too fictional to be viewed as history and too historical to be viewed as literature—not quite a social science and not quite part of the humanities. Cursed and blessed, biography was "a disease of English literature" to George Eliot while being "the most delicate and humane of the branches of the art of writing" to Lytton Strachey.

Yet, public interest is beginning to grow as an increasing number of academic fields direct their attention to biographical inquiry. "Good biographies deal with the ways people faced living—tell how they met problems, how they coped with big and little crises, how they loved, competed, did the things we all do daily—and hence these studies touch familiar chords in readers" (Oates, 1986, p. 61). One needs little convincing of such "touched chords" as one observes teachers and researchers discussing case studies—all biographical in nature—and other teacher narratives. Moreover, biographical writings often permit readers to explore the imaginative while learning of the intimate, as "the biographer, once content with the public events in a life, wrestles now with its private meanings" (Pachter, 1981, p. 14). Such is biography's power that captures our imagination.

Writing about another's life holds many difficulties and problems. Too often, our thoughts of biographies turn to "great-man history" or hagiographies of past eras where a "detached" biographer prepares a work seemingly supported by various facts and a variety of commonly accepted descriptions. The absurdity of such work, conducted in years past as well, alas, as recently, is now quite clear. "Its narrative is built through rising action, recounting the subject's accomplishments and accolades, to a comfortable denouement that parallels the physical winding down of old age. . . . Complex issues that might interfere with the readers' response to the intended effect of the narrative . . . [are] softened or . . . entirely omitted" (Wagner-Martin, 1994, pp. 5–6). However, biography at its best still can hold the reader spellbound within the power of its voice—of its narrative, prose, and style.

> Because it must make the people of history live again, pure biography must be more than the compilation of research notes—more than the presentation of what one has gleaned from letters, interviews, journals, diaries, reminiscences, and other contemporary accounts. The prose of the biographer must radiate a sense of intimacy and familiarity, quite as though the author . . . has lived the life and walked the ground. (Oates, 1986, p. 129)

Research problems arise, of course, from such statements; yet, as the biographer seeks to construct this "intimacy and familiarity," the recognition and acceptance of interpretation—and dramatically different interpretations of biographers—has been generally assumed for some time. Among contemporary biographers, the determination of truth, as well as the existence of facts, has always been questioned; such differences of interpretations are continually viewed as part of the biographical process and suggest that a definitive biography is merely an allusion.

As interest in biographical research grows in our education community, research methodology—viewed by some as having moved from postmodernism into "post-postmodernism"—becomes increasingly complex. Denzin and Lincoln mention the "means for interpretive, ethnographic practices is still not clear, but it is certain that things will never be the same. We are in a new age where messy, uncertain, multi-voiced texts, cultural criticism, and new experimental works will become more common, as will more reflexive forms of fieldwork, analysis, and intertextual representation" (1994, p. 15). The possibilities for biography emerge as one struggles with such problems and issues; answers—as with facts—are illusive. Yet, it is this messy, experimental work that suggests such promise:

> As postmodern ethnography increasingly defamiliarizes the genre of life-writing into a voracious apparatus of textualized selfhood, . . . the primary function of biography is to disseminate a plethora of *selves* who might instantiate this integrity of selfhood as achieved against a more or less recessive social background. (Wilson, 1991, p. 167)

Perhaps biography—never fully accepted in the humanities or the social sciences—now has a chance to develop more fully in this period when old division lines are disintegrating and "new constellations" are emerging (Bernstein, 1992). Perhaps now, in an ever emerging postmodern period, biography can explore some of the many newly developing research directions that must be examined to provide a broader context for interpretation and critical analysis. In effect, biography offers a perspective that differs from other research paradigms—a fresh sense of tradition and structure, tempered with the complexity brought about by postmodern thought, yet reconciled, as Wagner-Martin asserts, "in this age of fluid moral positioning, when a subject can be praised by one group of readers and reviled by another, it is finally the biographer's conviction that directs the narrative" (1994, p. 10).

While issues of representation and interpretation have been a constant source of concern for the educational researcher, throughout these struggles a sense of purpose continues to appear to the biographer—to share in the examination of a life—with all of its commonalties, idiosyncrasies, and interpretations. While much narrative and autobiography in education seeks to tell a story—described by the author and deconstructed by the reader—the constructed meaning of the reader may be far from the intent of the author. At times it seems as if there may be little relationship or even little effort to share in a reciprocal gesture of meaning between author and reader. Biography, however, continues to aim at making history become *personal*—of telling the story of another person's life for a purpose—one that may change as the research process unfolds or as information and interpretations become apparent—but one with a purpose—a point—to offer the possibility of establishing shared meaning with the reader. The biographer becomes a mediator by presenting the lived experiences of the biographical subject to others. Shared meaning becomes terribly problematic; however, such is the quest and elusiveness of attempting to engage in biographical research. Such is the effort, perhaps ill-fated in this postmodern age, to attempt to bridge communities and to address a commonality, a heritage of values, that per-

mit others to come together, to engage in the "impassioned and significant dialogue" about which Maxine Greene speaks (1988, p. 4). Such
efforts of biography, more difficult today than ever before, may belie a
commonality. Yet this is the call put by John Dewey to our contemporary generation:

> We who now live are parts of a humanity that extends into the remote
> past. . . . The things in civilization we most prize are not of ourselves.
> They exist by grace of the doings and sufferings of the continuous
> human community in which we are a link. Ours is the responsibility
> of conserving, transmitting, rectifying, and expanding the heritage of
> values we have received that those who come after us may receive it
> more solid and secure, more widely accessible and more generously
> shared than we have received it. (1934, p. 87)]

As naive as it may be to seek to establish a common faith and a sense of
shared meaning, biographers continue to frequent archives and vaults full
of "facts"—the ill-begotten anachronism of our technological and postmodern society. In what might be construed as an ironic twist of methodological fate, biographers continue to place emphasis on issues of fact—
gaining access, determining copyright, filling gaps, developing an ethics
of documentation, and maintaining a sense (perhaps better viewed as a
"notion") of accuracy. Such attention to facts, or perhaps more accurately stated the "selection of facts," with a constant vigilance of interpretive perspective, is crucial during this age "where messy, uncertain,
multi-voiced texts, cultural criticism, and new experimental works will
become more common" as Lincoln and Denzin describe. However, the
role of archives as a repository of lived lives, of landscapes, and of professional portfolios for educators—such a role remains crucial.

ARCHIVAL REPOSITORIES AND THE
PRESERVATION OF THE PRESENT

While many forms of research rely predominately upon that material gathered by the investigator, the biographer relies in part on those documents
that have been preserved. Diaries are the blessing; however, assorted
local newspapers, institutional descriptions, church and civic records, and
various ephemera are all gladly examined once their existence is known.
Such archival repositories may take any form—attics, garages, libraries,
and museums—where large amounts of "stuff" are kept—stuff that permits the biographer to create and re-create a lived life. Perhaps the most
delightful attitude toward archival repositories is stated by Leon Edel:

> I do not disparage archives. I simply groan when I see one. Those great cluttered masses of papers . . . Who is to say what should be kept and what shouldn't? I remember finding a fur neckpiece in a box that contained letters of Henry James in the Library of Congress. . . . It told me merely that the lady who had received the letters got her archives mixed with her wardrobe. Yet perhaps that mangy little fur had its place. . . . No, we must allow papers to accumulate in a laissez-faire spirit. . . . Our concern is how to deal with this clutter. (1981, p. 24)

And while a few collections of individuals, typically political or literary figures, reach substantial proportions, such clutter of bureaucracies, of state and national government, is overwhelming. Our federal government generates in a four month period records equal in size to those of the first 124 years of our government—from the Washington to Wilson presidencies. Yet the accumulations of the lives of anyone other than acknowledged political and literary figures—of known national educators or of unknown local teachers, for example—is rapidly dwindling if extant at all. The existence of archival materials (and of archival repositories) are fundamental since all biographers realize that such paper trails provide more material from which to fill the gaps.

> That paper trail, extending from the birth certificate to the death certificate, is never continuous or complete. . . . One of the great triumphs of Boswell is the consummate biographical tact with which he resolved gaps. He spent less than a year—scattered over several years—in Johnson's company, . . . Yet he succeeds in giving the reader a sense of Johnson's life unfolding, a sense of that life being lived, from the beginning to the end. . . . The right way to fill gaps is unknown; the wrong ways are legion. (Kendal, 1986, pp. 41–42)

Such talk of tangible documents becomes somewhat of an anomaly in most educational research circles where perhaps the few artifacts of current educators and schools are the accumulation of audio and video tapes. Yet, preservation of such artifacts becomes crucial, even during our postmodern age where "facts" may not be all they are believed to be. Ironically, it is the "present" and the immediate past that are being lost; documents are being lost in a technological age where a false sense of assurance is suggested with each technological advancement. In fact, technology has complicated the storing, arranging, and retrieving of information. While paper lasts for decades (if not centuries) and vertical files may be "accessed" by anyone, new forms of technological storage create complications while often having a short life. CD-ROM storage has a life of just twenty years; audio/video tape are most likely nonfunctional from as little as ten years.

And as computer technology advances, the dangers of storing data in irretrievable, "antiquated" forms will increase.

Transferring electronic information from one medium to another has even been termed "technology refreshing." Yet to the researcher, "refreshing" involves not just ensuring the retrieval of documents but also, according to the Research Libraries Group's Task Force on Archiving of Digital Information, the retrieval of untampered documents: "Another concern we have is assuring an authenticated version of it [information]. If you don't preserve data in a certain fashion it's possible that it could be edited or altered perhaps without anyone realizing it" (Rogers, 1995, p. 35).

With the increasing glories of technology, new concerns have been expressed most notably about e-mail and its effect upon personal correspondence and future biographical research. And the loss of first drafts (and accompanying marginalia)—the adrenaline rush for any biographer— is acknowledged as an elusive set of materials rarely to be obtained during our computer age. "Few creators of documents consciously keep a copy of every version of every change. With the use of paper, retention of older drafts required only procrastination and a minimum of forethought. With electronic format, the author must consciously make a new file for every new version" (Sweetland, 1992, p. 800).

In the field of education—institutions, organizations, and individuals—such contemporary materials are often misplaced or not accessible—somehow they just seem to disappear. For those many settings at the school and classroom level where we, as researchers, see the genuine dimensions of school life and the individual lives of teachers, not enough is preserved—perhaps not due to bureaucratic inefficiency or administrative ineptness but, instead, to the pretentiousness of living in a technological age where we assume copies abound and will always be preserved. This has become quite apparent in my work on school studies of the late Progressive Era (Eight Year Study, Southern Study, Secondary School Study). I have accumulated an extensive collection of primary documents, oral histories, and narrative accounts from individuals—teachers and students—of the various participating schools. In addition, I am in contact with those extant schools as I seek materials to document the continuation of their life after this 1930s project. For some of the schools, such materials cannot be located from the early 1980s. Other than a few brochures or yearbooks, little exists. Institutions with a distinguished and distinctive past—yet the recent is lost.

Unlike Leon Edel, educators need not elicit groans upon seeing archives; however, carte blanche privileges should not be given to anyone to go out and start "collecting." To restate the primordial caveat of archivists: "There is little virtue in mere acquisition if it is divorced from intelligent purpose." Yet, in this complex, often messy, era of post-modernism, the plight and fate of future biographers must not be determined by our faith, and perhaps arrogance, in contemporary preservation. Equally important, documents and artifacts must abound, for as biographers attempt to transmit any sense of shared meaning and lived lives, the perceived meanings of diaries and memory (via oral history) must be supplemented—triangulated, if you will—with assorted clutter and ephemera. This clutter must be substantial and must be assorted. Too many examples of distorted perspectives (if not outright incorrect facts), questionable motives, and idiosyncratic views have been heard from the past as well as from the present. Ellsworth Collings's noted report of the "project method" (what served as an early twentieth-century dissertation and influential publication, *An Experiment With a Project Curriculum,* 1925) proves to have been "fiction" (Knoll, 1996). William H. Kilpatrick's diaries and scrapbooks serve as a not-too-camouflaged effort to enhance his role in the history of American education.

Diaries and memories serve as an initial archival venue from which a biographer steps—walking through the clutter of artifacts and the messiness of assorted interpretations—to seek to present the experiences of others. And it is this theme that takes us back to Maxine Greene as she calls for new perspectives—"perspectives on the past, on cumulative meanings, on future possibilities" (1978, p. 165). The call for persons to awake to their freedom is often a private act, yet such acts—gestures, perceptions, beliefs—take their form in tangible means, in documents, in diaries, and in narrative statements that portray the private and public voice of our contemporary age. While the difficult qualitative research issues continue to complicate our contemporary age, we must seek to preserve, in all different manners and means, the artifacts of our age—the tangible acts of individuals seeking their wide-awakeness, their landscapes, their freedom.

HISTORICAL PERSPECTIVE AND THE HERITAGE OF VALUES

Research issues of fact, truth, and interpretation; methodological problems of biography; technological concerns of archives; moral problems of transmitting a heritage of values—such are a few of the many issues and tensions of our postmodern age. As Maxine calls for public dialogue, such discussions seem to take place without a shared knowledge of pasts. Yet, I wish not to belabor why an historical perspective is not part of the educational dialogue. Instead, I continue to wonder if today's educational leaders will be remembered forty years from now. I am not hopeful as I find individuals from the immediate past—Lawrence Cremin, Lou LaBrant, Joseph Schwab, and Hilda Taba, for example—already unknown by doctoral students, recent graduates, and select faculty from their respective institutions. What this suggests for education and for the nature of the educational professoriate—serving as an education professor and maintaining any sense of tradition and meaning—cannot be good.

> The disintegration of a sense of historical community is amazing. It is not just that key dates are missing, hooks upon which prior generations have hung a panoramic and coherent view of time and existence, however skewed or biased. Missing is any sense that anything is missing. (Wilshire, 1990, p. 12)

This is when a return to Maxine Greene's call for wide-awakeness becomes crucial and Martha Nussbaum's call for poetic justice becomes essential (Nussbaum, 1995). It is during this "moral collapse of the university" as Wilshire (1990) has underscored, that the construction of landscapes—the private visions and public spaces—become so important. And such perspectives may manifest themselves in autobiographies and diaries, in personal narratives and ethnographies, from students' writings and projects, in school and institutional documents, newsletters, annuals, yearbooks, audio and video documentaries, in the professional portfolios of educators that emerge from our offices as a result of neglecting to prune our filing cabinets—it is these materials, from vast unbridled accumulations, that must be preserved.

As we live our lives and seek, in this complex age of reconciliations/ruptures, to come to grips with shared meaning for ourselves and of others, it is our contemporary age that must not be lost. Those special, autobiographical gestures—the "secret garden" between writer and reader, among individual, biographer, and reader—become so important. Such material—the personal as well as public—must be preserved for "the making and remaking of a public space, a space of dialogue and possibility" (Greene, 1988, p. xi). Such efforts are not merely to preserve information—to collect facts that have little purpose. The researching of life-histories, the writing of personal narratives, and the preserving of materials (and other documents) in archival settings permit biography to take on its power, in the words of Phyllis Rose, "to inspire comparison. Have I lived that way? Do I want to live that way? Could I make myself live that way if I wanted to" (1984, p. 5). This is when the power of biography leaves the realm of history and qualitative research—where the sweeping gestures of the biographer, the power of the narrative, no longer seeks to merely preserve or interpret. And this is when the complexities and convictions of biography attend to Maxine's central questions: "How can we reconcile the multiple realities of human lives with shared commitment to communities infused once again with principles? How can we do it without regressing, without mythicizing?" (1995, p. 197) We are left with her and Dewey's call to accept "the responsibility of conserving, transmitting, rectifying, and expanding the heritage of values we have received that those who come after us may receive it more solid and secure, more widely accessible and more generously shared than we have received it."

REFERENCES

Bernstein, R. (1992). *The new constellation.* Cambridge, MA: MIT Press.

Collings, E. (1925). *An experiment with a project curriculum.* New York: Macmillan.

Denzin, N., & Lincoln, Y. (1994). *Handbook of qualitative research.* Thousand Oaks, CA: Sage Publications.

Dewey, J. (1934). *A common faith.* New Haven, CT: Yale University Press.

Edel, L. (1981). The figure under the carpet. In M. Pachter (Ed.), *Telling lives* (pp. 16–34). Philadelphia: University of Pennsylvania Press.

Greene, M. (1975). Curriculum and consciousness. In W. Pinar (Ed.), *Curriculum theorizing* (pp. 295–317). Berkeley, CA: McCutchan.

Greene, M. (1978). *Landscapes of learning.* New York: Teachers College Press.

Greene, M. (1988). *Dialectic of freedom.* New York: Teachers College Press.

Greene, M. (1995). *Releasing the imagination.* San Francisco: Jossey-Bass.

Kendal, P. (1986). Walking the boundaries. In S. Oates (Ed.), *Biography as high adventure* (pp. 32–49). Amherst: University of Massachusetts Press.

Knoll, M. (1996). Faking a dissertation: Ellsworth Collings, William H. Kilpatrick, and the "project" curriculum. *Journal of Curriculum Studies, 28*(2), 193–222.

Nussbaum, M. (1995). *Poetic justice.* Boston: Beacon Press.

Oates, S. (1986). *Biography as high adventure.* Amherst: University of Massachusetts Press.

Pachter, M. (1981). *Telling lives.* Philadelphia: University of Pennsylvania Press.

Rogers, M. (1995, April 1). RLG task force will study the preservation of digital info. *Library Journal,* p. 35.

Rose, P. (1984). *Parallel lives.* New York: Knopf.

Sweetland, J. (1992). Humanists, libraries, electronic publishing and the future. *Library Trends, 40*(4), 781–803.

Wagner-Martin, L. (1994). *Telling women's lives.* New Brunswick, NJ: Rutgers University Press.

Wilshire, B. (1990). *The moral collapse of the university.* Albany, NY: SUNY Press.

Wilson, R. (1991). Producing American selves. In W. H. Epstein (Ed.), *Contesting the subject* (pp. 167–192). West Lafayette, IN: Purdue University Press.

13

Restaging the Civil Ceremonies of Schooling

Madeleine R. Grumet

The ringing of the bells, the politics at the faculty meeting, the mise en scène of the standardized test, open your booklets, NOW, all constitute the sequences and segments that order school time, space, and the human interactions that occur within their scaffolding. What has disappeared is the deliberate, aesthetically conceived and produced ceremony.

If we take an anthropological view of ritual, we may assume that school communities get the rituals they deserve. From this view, it follows that if schools have become still and sterile places, with drama and feeling erupting only in their boundary precincts, as violence erupts in the cafeteria or on the streets nearby, well, this emotional geography maps our culture's construction of its meritocracy and economy, class and race relations, and moral codes will have to change before we find another theater of schooling.

If we take an aesthetic view of ritual, we may assume that schools are liminal places, not isolated from the social systems of which they are a part, but set aside to comment on that system even as they participate in it. Here the art of ritual points to freedom rather than to the repetitions and traditions that we identify with its forms.

What follows is a meditation on the school play. I mine my memories of it, seeking the sensuality, the embeddedness, the performance, and the expressivity that could educate children to speak for freedom. The work of Maxine Greene has decried the silence of our public places. In *The Dialectic of Freedom,* she notes the absence of the "articulate public" that Dewey envisioned: "Messages and announcements fill the air; but there is, because of the withdrawal, a widespread speechlessness, a silence where there might be—where there ought to be—an impassioned and significant dialogue" (1988, p. 3).

In Greene's work the arts are calls to social criticism, invitations to explore identity, to challenge perception. They are always unavoidably social and they point to freedom, the direction that animates this excerpt from a lecture that Maxine Greene delivered to the Lincoln Center Institute:

> We want to enable the young to see and to hear more reflectively, more intelligently, more critically. We want to help them come awake to deception, to mystification, to distortion. We want them to overcome passivity as well as mere conventionality. We want them to take their own initiatives as they come together in dialogue about what they see and what they hear and what they feel. We want them to care, to wonder, to become. (1992, p. 2)

This standard guides this memoir of my second-grade class play about George Washington, produced in 1947, in P.S. 93, in Brooklyn, New York—and the sense I will make of it.

Any time I hear a few bars of the Polonaise in G, the play comes back to me. My mother wrote it, and she worked with some of the other mothers to make the costumes at card tables set up in the living room of our apartment on Ocean Avenue. I remember the wonder of seeing these mysterious people, other people's mothers, all crowded into that small room. But most of all I remember the minuet, and our stiff and endlessly rehearsed attempts to move to its courtly phrases in our long skirts. The boys wore high socks, their pants tied up around their knees to resemble colonial knickers. And I remember our Betsy Ross hats, circles of soft white cloth, gathered with elastic, the ruffles falling around our brows.

Ruffles were a major costume element in those days. They were featured in the Mexican dress my mother sewed for me when I participated in a summer pageant in Prospect Park run by the Parks Department. This time the ruffles were gathered along the neckline of the off-the-shoulder peasant blouse sewn for the occasion. The fabric was heavy, and I can still feel the rough press of the material gathered around my shoulders as I twirled around on the grass (we danced on the grass!), my right arm linked with the left arm of the eight-year-old girl who was my partner, one hand on my hip and the other held high in the air.

Each of these memories, the softness or roughness of the cloth, the stately music, is saturated with a sense of dearness, of moments so highly saturated with sensation, that they have spilled over into lingering memory. They involve the thrill and anxiety of performance, of display, equalled in intensity only by sense memories of books I read around this time. There was one about the daughter of a Canadian Royal Mounty stationed in the Northwest Territories or maybe it was the Yukon (or maybe I am confusing the book with the radio program, *Sergeant King of the Yukon*), where their time was spent planning a trip to attend a jubilee in honor or Queen Victoria and Prince Albert. This little girl's red tunics and riding boots filled my world with color, the scent of oiled leather, the sting of snow on chapped cheeks, the aroma of hot chocolate. My body memories of her experience, performative and fictive, are, strangely enough, more vivid than the memories of my own daily life. I cannot tell you what I wore each day to school, nor what we ate for dinner. I could not tell you what I used to have for lunch, day after day, in the steamy basement cafeteria, or in the kitchen on the days when I walked home, although I do remember sometimes listening to episodes of *Helen Trent* or *Our Gal Sunday* on the radio.

There is one more memory I must mention because it is not associated with the role of performance, but that of audience. Later, in another school, maybe it is the sixth grade, I have a dear memory of a white blouse that I would wear on assembly days. I think we all had to wear white blouses with green ties. (I also remember frantic searches for the repeatedly misplaced green tie, and the last minute fabrication of outrageous substitutes.) This blouse was nylon I think, or some kind of synthetic stuff that had just become available, not gauzy, but slippery and a little shiny. It had puffed sleeves and pearly buttons. (I may be making up the buttons.) But I remember the sense of the special day, marked by this costume and by the assembly itself, the gathering of all of us by class in the wooden chairs, teachers at the end of the aisles, for plays, musical recitals, and on bad days for documentary films on the pasteurization of milk or first aid demonstrations from the fire department.

I am a little embarrassed by the prominence of clothing in all these memories, fictive and actual. Was I, at the age of eight or nine, fixated on presentation, on style? Am I now? I would rather think it is about texture, about feeling a new skin. I think the gathered cap, the Mexican costume, and the blouse are tactile memories of moments when music, event, and ensemble performance extended the boundaries of my daily world, and I moved to the melodies of the minuet, the Mexican hat dance, and the national anthem. Maxine Greene's sense of freedom is anchored in such specificities:

> Stunned by hollow formulas, media fabricated sentiments, and cost-benefit terminologies, young and old alike find it hard to shape authentic expressions of hopes and ideals. Lacking embeddedness in memories and histories they have made their own people feel as if they are rootless subjectivities—dandelion pods tossed by the wind. What does it mean to be a citizen of the free world? What does it mean to think forward into a future? To dream? To reach beyond? (1988, p. 3)

My own children's schooling was, it seemed to me, sadly lacking in the ceremony and theater that filled my own public school days. Although as I utter this nostalgic critique, I am suspicious of it. We tend to be very selective about what we remember about the good old days. We tend to forget the bad old days, and we tend to employ today's loneliness, confusion, and bleakness as our routes to the past, looking for compensation and comfort, as we once ran home to Mom, instead of standing here, now, where the trouble is and meeting it head on.

Nevertheless, there is some architectural evidence to suggest that the contrast is not the product of nostalgia. The schools of the seventies were often built without the grand and ornate theaters that had been the center of the Brooklyn schools that I had attended in the forties. In the new schools there were smaller performance spaces, or none, and the gymnasium or cafeteria became the locus of collective ceremonies.

Perhaps, the suburban school district, intent on achievement and scores, was hesitant to surrender the precious hours of dittoes and drill to rehearsals. Perhaps the union contracts precluded the extra hours that teachers would donate to these enterprises. Perhaps the patience and attention of children habituated to television, to entertainment situated in the private domain of family, could no longer be adapted to the requirement of stillness that the assembly sessions required of their young audiences. (Even then we had row monitors commissioned to write down the names of anyone who talked, chewed gum, or passed notes.)

Perhaps the religiously oriented Christmas and Easter plays, the historically outrageous and distorted depictions of Columbus, Thanksgiving, and Presidents Lincoln and Washington could no longer be celebrated by educators and communities alert to bias and stereotyping.

In the absence of these ceremonies and displays, performance became the prerogative of athletes and troublemakers, the common citizen of the school cast as occasional spectator. In the curricular and semiotic life of the school, letters and numbers and codes reign supreme, displacing the gestural fluency and protean possibilities contained in more ludic forms: The word ate the body.

This emphasis on the specular and on the representation of thought disassociated from body, from identity, from event and context has always been essential to what makes the public school public. Michael Warner has argued that it was the development of print that made a public possible, for with the advent of print and text it became possible to be present to others without being identified as a body:

> The bourgeois public sphere claimed to have no relation to the body image at all. Public issues were depersonalized so that, in theory, any person would have the ability to offer an opinion about them and submit that opinion to the impersonal test of public debate without per-

sonal hazard. Yet the bourgeois public sphere continued to rely on features of certain bodies. Access to the public came in the whiteness and maleness that were then denied as forms of positivity, since the white male qua public person was only abstract rather than white and male. (1993, pp. 382–383)

The illusion that literacy is disembodied, and, as a result, accessible to all, has been used to rationalize our growing reliance on codes for communication and instruction that repudiate particularity and designate our bodies as excess, as well as to obscure the differential access to these codes available to citizens in relation to their race, class, and gender.

THE DEFIANCE OF GESTURE

In schools, the domination of language, and now of codes, creates a kind of gestural aphasia, for there are possibilities that dwell in gestures that words can never say. Our mimetic genius qualified us for human company long before we funded our smiles with humor or our cries with hope. Children playing grown up display an embodied grasp of adult relations years before they will choose to seduce or nurture someone else. Our bodies always anticipate what we only later come to know. Words and language scurry to catch up, providing rationales, justifications, assertions for what has already declared itself in our stomachs, the warm flush that creeps up our neck and around our earlobes, the tear, the itch, the shiver.

The mute body holds a silence that only death can impose, for no matter how circumspect we wish to be about what we think and feel about what is going on around us, our bodies give us away—in the tapping of a little finger, in the stretching of a tight muscle, in the wince and flicker of the eyes. And it is a gesture, caught in just a glance, that confirms our identities. I'd know that walk anywhere. Always pointing to someplace, someone, or something in the world, it literally, or gesturally, gives us away. And so it is particularly poignant when we coax our gesturing, declarative bodies, costumed and painted, on to the stage, pretending to be someone else.

The speaking of another's words is easy compared to the task of exchanging her walk for mine, discovering what her tongue does when she isn't talking, and what her toes do when she isn't walking. What mercy we extend to each other when we witness these attempts at transformation, and what pleasure there is when mimesis of another succeeds. It is the moment when we affirm our desire to make ourselves, to make more of ourselves, as Sartre would say, than what has been made of us. And the audience who witnesses this reach beyond the limit of one's own history and habit finds hope for its own possibilities in such a performance.

These moments of transcendence require presence. Wondrously fluid and protean are film images sliding in and out of each other, sliding from one space and time to another, but it is action that takes place in shared space and time that, I maintain, challenges its audiences to imagine the possibilities enacted before it, for itself.

There are always risks in these moments, as we edge out beyond what is familiar and common among us, to what Richard Schechner calls "dark play" (1993, p. 36). The suspension of cautions, the inversion of hierarchies and roles, is thrilling as they bring elements that our identities deny within our reach. But dark play is, at the same time, threatening, for we have not only walked out beyond ourselves, we have been witnessed as other, and we may be marooned in the performance. It must be horrifying to be frozen in persona, to lose one's passport back to Norma Jean. But if one successfully makes the passage between person and persona and back again, then one's humanity has been fully witnessed, as actual and possible identities mingle in social space. These are the moments of vulnerability and ecstasy that bond the members of a troupe or company, that link the members of a chorus together in a sound that none could make alone. Then we are not alone on the stage but share that moment of transcendence with others.

Hear this account of communion from Gitta Sereny, who recalls Hitler's arrival in Vienna in 1938:

> What I remember most clearly—to my horror—is how excited I felt myself as, part of this seemingly emotional crowd, I had listened to that man four years earlier, Nuremberg. I had sat high up in the stands and found myself shouting with joy. Small as I was, I was aware that my pleasure derived not from any person or words but from the theatrical spectacle. But now? I had heard the Austrian Chancellor Kurt von Schuschnigg announcing the plebiscite of 13 March, his voice breaking at the end: "Austrians, the time for decision has come . . . I had heard those raucous voices, *Deutschland erwache, Juda verrecke.* And here I was, standing before this man whose orders had sent troops into Austria and who had followed those troops so as to seal the deed with his presence. What was it that made me join the mindless chorus around me, welcoming this almost motionless figure to our Vienna? What was it in him that drew us? What was it in us—in me too, that day—that allowed ourselves to be drawn? (1995, p. 55)

Sereny would spend the rest of her life trying to answer the questions that she poses in this memoir. Her question, her image of being drawn, raises the spectre of fascist theater. How can we bring back a sense of community, of communion? How can we bring back the magic of the body, the richness of gesture and music to the community of our schools without reinstating the fascist drama?

It is clear to us that time and history cannot exempt us. Once, again, it appears, we are ripe for fascism. Maybe we are always ripe for fascism. David Harvey has argued that the inevitable reaction to the fragmentation, the loss of sense of place and identity associated with postmodern economy and aesthetics, is the longing for "secure moorings in a shifting world":

> Place-identity, in this collage of superimposed spatial images that implode in upon us, becomes an important issue, because everyone occupies a space of individuation (a body, a room, a home, a shaping community, a nation), and how we individuate ourselves shapes identity. Furthermore, if no one 'knows their place' in this shifting collage world, then how can a secure social order be fashioned or sustained? (1990, p. 303)

In recent years, in the United States of America, the strength of the militias, the separatism of fundamentalist schools, the burning of black churches, the repudiation of immigrants and their children remind us that the desperate assertion of identity associated with place, with body, with gesture is always at the service of fascism. The desire for connection, for affiliation, for rootedness is the stuff from which subordination, fear of ambiguity and difference and exclusion are fashioned. And even when there has been a negotiated peace, when an abstraction like Yugoslavia seems to prevail for decades, ancient memories of insult to body, to spirit, to hearth and home simmer and reappear to assert the identifications that have grown greedy root systems under the surface of their suppression.

We have not developed a democratic polity by turning from presence to print. Bodies do not go away, nor will our passions and yearnings to be part of something we share with other people dissolve because we are spending hours in isolated cubicles seated in front of our computer screens.

How can we educate bodies as well as minds so that emotion and feeling can be understood and so that choice and action can be informed by passion without being ruled by it? How can we use the theater of schooling to provide opportunities for the experience of communion that establishes connections between people without obliterating our specificity and respect for our diversity?

As we all well know, the theater of schooling has been deployed to induce compliance. Foucault has helped us to understand the ways our institutions and their cultures induce us, body and soul, to relinquish impulse and to surrender spontaneity. The white blouse and the minuet are not my only memories of schooling. There is standing in line on freezing winter mornings, silently, of course silently, until at the sound of the whistle we could walk, silently, into the building and up the stairs to our classroom. Silently. And long legs, hitting the underside of desk. And nausea in the steamy cafeteria, grey formica, grey trays, grey apples.

And my children's schools were not much better. The single floor sprawling design of the local elementary school admitted children without the long wait on lines; there was more sunlight, better ventilation in the cafeteria. But there were no doors on the stalls in the boys' bathrooms. And when I complained, the principal, surprised, claiming that no parent had ever mentioned it before, confided that even his private bathroom stall had no door. I should not have been surprised six or seven years later when, during the national hysteria about drugs in the adolescent peer culture, the high school provided a box where students could anonymously leave notes identifying their classmates whom they suspected of drug use so that the school could intervene and help these students to get the help they so badly needed.

In *Hopes for Great Happenings,* Albert Hunt poignantly portrays the naive, unreflective theatricality of our schools:

> The sense of other people, with mysterious knowledge, controlling your life is what our education system is structured to communicate. The form of that communication is *theatrical,* ritualistic. The lining up in the playground when somebody blows a whistle; the morning assembly, where power is displayed, . . . the rituals of moving from room to room when the bell rings; all these are theatrical in their effect. That is to say they work in the way the theatre works, making the abstract concrete, demonstrating in physical terms where the power lies. Even a lesson is theatrical, with the teacher playing a role in public. Until we begin to understand that the education system itself works in terms of theatre to communicate a particular experience of society, we won't get very far in saying what the role of theatre, *our* theatre, not the education system's—can be in contributing to the true aim of education, that of giving pupils understanding, control, and the power to make decisions about changing their environment. (1976, p. 121)

For our purposes, I would like to consider Stanton Garner's phenomenological grasp of theater, for he finds this heightened awareness of partial truth of any objectification at the very heart of any performance:

> Hamlet holds Yorick's skull, though individual Hamlets will hold it in a potentially infinite number of ways. In this sense the dramatic text

effects a version of the *epoche* or 'reduction,' whereby phenomenology suspends awareness of the object's actual existence in one place and
one time in order to disclose this actuality in its own parameters and
tolerances, its dialectic of the variable and the invariable. Drama, in
short, presents "the thing itself" as a bounded (or floating) facticity,
available to a variety of specific actualizations. (1994, p. 6)

"'The thing itself' as a bounded (or floating) facticity, available to a variety of specific actualizations." This is an important phrase, for it holds
the distinction between a democratic theater and a fascist ritual. It names
the fullness of the presence of the body at the very same time as it invites
the variation of meaning and interpretation that is inevitably part of every
theatrical event.

Drama invites the whole person into its spotlight. There is no leaving bodies behind, and no matter how costumed or made up, the bodies
are always there, feeling the ruffles against the skin, looking for the
green tie. This degree of presence, dancing to the music, squinting under
the lights, or feeling the dread of time and mortality in the weight of
Yorick's skull, invites the education of emotion as well as cognition.
Nevertheless it not only brings bodies on stage, it also brings these bodies, our bodies, into play.

Let us think, for a moment, of what might be possible if this sense
of theater were alive and well in schools. The *Oxford English Dictionary*
indicates that one early sense of the word "performance" was to carry
something through to full realization. The embodiedness of theater
demands this fullness. It draws the public and the private into an enacted
moment as word and action issue from particular persons situated in time
and space. Theater is so full that the only aspect that distinguishes the
theatrical moment from every day life is the frame that names it observ-
able and gathers an audience to witness. But as soon as that frame is
constructed around our everyday world, our taken-for-granted comings
and goings are set off for our attention, comment, and interpretations.

To the degree that school is set off from the office, the field, the
kitchen, it is a place in our society where a moment can be taken to
watch ourselves learning. An instant frame materializes as soon as one
class becomes the audience for another. How might students reflect on
their own attention, or lack of it, their discourse with each other and
with their professor if they regularly visited another class and returned
to speak about what they had seen. And if the visits were exchanged
you would have an instant seminar ready to address the theater of higher
education. Greene has called for this mindfulness when she says that "it
is because of the apparent normality, the givenness of young people's
everyday lives, that intentional actions ought to be undertaken to bring

things within the scope of students' attention, to make situations more palpable and visible. Only when they are visible and 'at hand' are they likely to cry out for interpretation" (1988, pp. 121–122).

This example of the class visits has a feature that is missing in the fascist spectacle, and that is the presence of the audience. There must always be an audience that is not involved in the performance. The presence of the audience is what discriminates theater from ritual, for while rituals have the virtue of involving everyone and filling in the criteria of *full participation,* that fullness precludes the antic observation of the onlooker who says, this is all very interesting, but is it necessary to do things this way?

Fascist spectacle never invited such debriefings. Bertolt Brecht yearned to disturb the trance of ritual, or of what we have called integrationist propaganda. He identified dramatic theater with the theater of indoctrination, and the dialectical theater, he called epic theater:

> The dramatic theatre's spectator says: Yes, I have felt like that too— Just like me—It's only natural—It'll never change—The sufferings of this man appall me, because they are inescapable—That's great art; it all seems the most obvious thing in the world—I weep when they weep, I laugh when they laugh.
>
> The epic theatre's spectator says: I'd never have thought it—That's not the way—That's extraordinary, hardly believable—It's got to stop— The sufferings of this man appall me, because they are unnecessary— That's great art; nothing obvious in it—I laugh when they weep, I weep then they laugh. (1964, p. 71)

Another feature of this theater must be its multiplicity. It was Victor Turner (1967) who insisted that we see the repetitions of rituals as dynamic rather than static events. The very repetitions of a set of actions make any changes, and change is inevitable, visible. In his studies, he offered readings of those changes, although it was clear that one would have to be present at many rituals over time to discern them. This kind of variation was visible even in the elementary school of my memories. One could tell when the teacher responsible for the assemblies changed, and it was instructive to us kids in the long rows to see how the world changed when different personalities were installed as its director. Remember, we were the audience and we watched.

Bruce Wilshire reports a theatrical event, Robert Whitman's *Light Touch,* where the audience is seated in a warehouse and looks through a loading door, framed with curtains out to the street:

> Cars appeared occasionally, framed by the door, as they passed on the street directly outside. Appeared, but appeared transfigured, as if a spell

had been cast over them. Details of their shape and movement, ordinarily not noticed, leapt out, as if from a numinous aura. It was as if cars were being seen for the first time. (quoted in Carlson, 1990, p. 83)

I am looking for ways that we can bring the curtains that framed the loading door to the door of the classroom, and to the door of the boardroom. We will never strip schools of their theatrical and ritual character. We would not want to, for with these orderings of time and space and movement, we have the opportunity to communicate a sense of order, a sense of place and of community. But we also have the opportunity to remember that schools are liminal places. You know that the limen is the top beam of a doorway, a passage that designates movement between one space and another. So the limen, or liminal, experience is experience in the middle, experience that is situated somewhere special, where it can be felt and thought about and played with. When schools forget they are liminal spaces, they forget that schools are places for inquiry, not indoctrination. Toward the end of *The Dialectic of Freedom,* Maxine Greene reminds us that the arts of education must point to freedom:

> Teachers, like their students, have to learn to love the questions, as they come to realize that there can be no final agreements or answers, no final commensurability. And we have been talking about stories that open perspectives on communication grounded in trust, flowering by means of dialogue, kept alive in open spaces where freedom can find a place. (1988, p. 134)

REFERENCES

Brecht, B. (1964). *Brecht on theatre* (J. Willet, Ed. and Trans.). New York: Hill and Wang.

Carlson, M. (1990). *Theatre semiotics.* Bloomington: Indiana University Press.

Garner, S. B., Jr. (1994). *Bodied spaces.* Ithaca, NY: Cornell University Press.

Greene, M. (1988). *The dialectic of freedom.* New York: Teachers College Press.

Greene, M. (1992). *Lincoln Center Institute report,* p. 2.

Harvey, D. (1990). *The condition of postmodernity.* Cambridge, MA: Blackwell.

Hunt, A. (1976). *Hopes for great happenings.* London: Eyre Methuen.

Schechner, R. (1993). *The future of ritual,* New York: Routledge.

Sereny, G. (1995, Autumn). My journey to Speer. *Granta,* (51).

Turner, V. (1967). *A forest of symbols.* Ithaca, NY: Cornell University Press.

Warner, M. (1993). The mass public and the mass subject. In Craig Calhoun (Ed.), *Habermas and the public sphere* (pp. 377–401). Boston: MIT Press.

14

Autobiography and the Necessary Incompleteness of Teachers' Stories

Janet L. Miller

No one of us can see the whole or sing the whole. Since I was a little child, I have known that all perspectives are contingent, that no one's picture is complete.

Maxine Greene
"The Shapes of Childhood Recalled"

I first read some of Maxine Greene's writing when I was studying for my master's degree at the University of Rochester, 1973–1974. Newly divorced, living alone in a strange, cold city, substituting instead of teaching English full-time to high school juniors and seniors as I had during the seven previous years, I clung to the familiar processes of being a student. Unclear about where or how I would live, I knew only that I could read and study.

But, even as I derived some comfort in knowing how to be a student, nothing I was studying was familiar to me. I initially read Maxine's work within the contexts of what William Pinar, my academic advisor at Rochester, was characterizing as the just emerging "reconceptualization" of the curriculum field. That reconceptualization shifted the emphasis on linear and technologized versions of curriculum as "content" to an understanding of curriculum as also encompassing personal and political dimensions of educational experience (Pinar, 1975).

I first met Maxine and heard her present academic papers at curriculum theory conferences identified with the reconceptualization. Dressed in her New York black, leaning into the rhythm of her words, periodically gazing toward the ceiling as she spoke, Maxine articulated personal as well as political imperatives in conceptualizing curriculum as means by which to take "a stranger's vantage point on everyday reality" and to look "inquiringly and wonderingly on the world in which one lives" (Greene, 1973, p. 267).

Such perspectives had in no way informed my undergraduate teacher preparation or my high school teaching experiences. There, I was pressured to present predetermined, sequential, skills-oriented, and measurable versions of "English" to my students—hardly ways to encourage looking "inquiringly and wonderingly on the world."

I immediately was drawn to Maxine Greene's compelling philosophical and political analyses of education, and to her uses of literature as one means of engaging in such analyses. When I taught high school English for those seven years, I had only a few colleagues who would discuss with me why and how to side-step pressures to teach mechanics of grammar and even literature in detached, scripted, and officious ways. In Maxine's writing, I at last found theoretical, philosophical, and political imperatives for what had been considered among some of my colleagues as "subversive" attitudes and perspectives about teaching. Reading and hearing Maxine, I no longer felt apprehensive or even guilty about knowing that "all perspectives are contingent, that no one's picture is complete."

Simultaneously, I found joy, familiarity, and challenge in the countless literary examples that illuminated Maxine's work. Literature provided one means by which I could look "with a stranger's vantage point on everyday reality" at both my life and those influences of political, social, and cultural contexts in which I lived and taught. I had studied Camus's *The Plague* with my high school seniors—ah, I could make immediate associations with Maxine's insistence on "wide-awakeness" as a form of moral vigilance and action against the plagues of habit, passiveness, indifference, and alienation. I also had taught Ibsen's *A Doll's House,* and was reading Kate Chopin's *The Awakening* in one of my graduate classes— surely I could continue to consider what, in the 1970s, these literary representations of women's lives had to do with my own.

My most immediate readings of Maxine Greene's work, then, were responses to passions for and about imaginative literature and teaching and their capacities to move individuals to see and to act against habit and indifference. Thus inspired to pursue my own academic passions, I wrote a dissertation at The Ohio State University on the relation of Maxine's work to the fields of curriculum theory and English education. Maxine distanced herself from any one categorization of her intentions and perspectives, and so I attempted to read and to situate her work contingently, and as exceeding the confines of the label, "reconceptualist."

During the late 1970s, I also began working in and with autobiography because it was one mode of inquiry that initially characterized "the reconceptualization" of the curriculum field. I focused my autobiographical research on issues of being and becoming a woman who teaches, issues that Maxine earlier had begun to address from her stance as an existential and phenomenological educational philosopher. Maxine's use of historical analysis and imaginative literature to conceptualize "predicaments" as well as "the work" of women (1978, 1988) provided impetus and challenge to me as I explored critical possibilities of feminist autobiographical inquiry.

SHAPINGS OF SELVES

A recent essay, in which Maxine Greene (1995) recovers literary experiences that have been significant at various times in her life, exemplifies disruptions of fixed identities, and the resulting political agency that can emerge through such disruptions. Further, in detailing her various responses to imaginative literature, Maxine also challenges normative categories on which versions of autobiography that supposedly tell "the one true story" rest. Maxine's work thus continues to inform my explorations of both tensions and potentials in the uses of autobiography as a form of feminist educational inquiry.

In evoking "the shapes of childhood recalled," Maxine explores the resonance of various images from particular works of literature and what these images and stories "had to do with the patterns I was constructing as a child, the horizons toward which I was extending my hands" (p. 80).

Through her recollected responses to imaginative literature, Maxine also explores aspects of her "life story" as a woman and an academic by refusing any one definitive construction of that story. Maxine has not "spiderlike, . . . somehow spun a web solely from the stuff" of her own being, nor does she "claim to be free from the shaping influences of contexts" (p. 74). Rather, Maxine acknowledges the *impossibility* of constructing her life story outside "a whole variety of ideologies and discursive practices," including those related to gender, sibling and maternal relationships, political and professional phenomena (p. 74). In so doing, she provides provocative challenges to any simplistic version of autobiography as a "memory game" (p. 77), or as a merely self-indulgent endeavor, or as a reinforcer of already known and determined constructions of "selves." And, as always in her work, there are political imperatives attached to her unique enactment of autobiography:

> If I can make present the shapes and structures of a perceived world, even though they have been layered over with many rational meanings over time, I believe my own past will appear in altered ways and that

my presently lived life—and, I would like to say, teaching—will become
more grounded, more pungent, and less susceptible to logical rational-
ization, not to speak of rational instrumentality. (1995, pp. 77–78)

Further, Maxine contends that "the narratives we shape out of the materials of our lived lives must somehow take account of our original landscapes" where there is "a sense of consciousness being opened to the common" and where we might "recognize each other" (p. 75) in order to "take
the kind of initiatives that relate perspectives into a more or less coherent, even if unfinished whole." For, it is "incompleteness . . . that summons us to the tasks of knowledge and action, . . . putting an explanation into words, fighting a plague, seeking homes for the homeless,
restructuring inhumane schools" (p. 74).

Maxine, in imposing her own order on the shapes of childhood
recalled, also provides glimpses of contradictions, disjunctures, and ambiva-
lences—the "incompleteness" that she experiences within and toward her
"self" as a woman who desires both to "merge and to be outside" (p. 84),
as an academic who dares to do educational philosophy in unconventional
ways, and as a scholar who reads imaginative literature as one way of
disrupting and questioning any one final version of her self or the world.

At the same time, Maxine gestures toward possibilities of taking action
against unjust and inhumane conditions even as individuals face the "incompleteness" and "unfinished whole" of their actions, their knowledge, their
"selves," and their lives. I take this to mean that, in recognizing that I
have a responsibility to act in and against an unjust world, and in accepting the possibility that I might "recognize" another with whom to take such
actions, I am not paralyzed by the limits or "incompleteness" of my "selves,"
or my commitments, or my inability to "see the whole or sing the whole"
(1995, p. 82).

I particularly am drawn to Maxine's essay on "the shapes of childhood recalled," then, because it so evokes possibilities as well as tensions
in the doing of educational autobiography that resists closure or paralysis around issues of identity and agency. And, as always, I am drawn to
Maxine's encounters with imaginative literature as means by which to
break with the taken-for-grantedness of one's "self" or of one's world.

AUTOBIOGRAPHY AND THE INCOMPLETE SELF

My reading of Maxine's "shapes of childhood recalled" obviously reflects
my interest in current issues in autobiography as both genre and method.
These issues focus on postmodern challenges to the unity and coherence of an intact and fully conscious "self" and to the limits of its rep-

resentation. As Shoshana Felman (1993) notes,"We can neither simply 'write' our stories nor decide to write 'new' stories, . . . because the decision to 'rewrite' them is not simply external to the language that unwittingly writes us" (pp. 156–157).

At the same time, concerned with questions of action and agency, many feminist theorists of autobiography are grappling with how to conceptualize "self" and "woman," not as permanently essentialized or naturalized through language and culture, but rather as sites for cultural critique and social change.

In constructing a feminist theory of women's self-representation, Leigh Gilmore (1994), for example, frames the "I" as situated simultaneously in multiple identity constructions and argues that autobiography can demonstrate "how gender identities are specified in cultural identities, how racial identities are sexualized, how ethnic identities are gendered, and how sexual identities are inflected by class, . . . how the 'I' shifts within those places and how power is distributed" (p. 184).

Many feminist theorists find Judith Butler's (1992) discussion of the possibilities for working the very notion of identity categories to be helpful here:

> Identity categories are never merely descriptive, but always normative, and as such, exclusionary. This is not to say that the term "women" ought not to be used, or that we ought to announce the death of the category. On the contrary, if feminism presupposes that "women" designates an undesignatable field of differences, one that cannot be totalized or summarized by a descriptive identity category, then the very term becomes a site of permanent openness and resignifiability. (p. 16)

But where is the "permanent openness and resignifiability" in many versions of "teachers' stories," which now represent one of the most visible uses of autobiography in education? Both William Pinar and Madeleine Grumet, in their groundbreaking work in autobiography as a form of curriculum theorizing (1976), have drawn attention to the necessity of rendering multiple accounts of selves and experiences in education in order to "cultivate our capacity to see through the outer forms, the habitual explanation of things" (Pinar, 1988, p. 149). Those multiple accounts "splinter the dogmatism of a single tale" (Grumet, 1991, p. 72). Thus, one singular version of "self" or story will not do, as Maxine Greene so eloquently has demonstrated through her "shapes of childhood recalled."

But in recent years, some troubling "teachers' stories" have appeared in educational literature. The form they take often assumes one singular version of self and story. Nevertheless, they often are accompanied by claims about transformative possibilities of the reflective, the autobiographical, and the narrative (terms often mistakenly used synonymously in educational research) as forms of educational inquiry. In the graduate program in which I teach, as in many education programs, teachers are encouraged to "tell their stories" of their teacher-researcher investigations into issues and problems in their classrooms. And they also are expected to write autobiographical tracings and reflections on sources of, changes in, and questions about their assumptions, expectations, and enactments of themselves as teachers. And many instructors try to encourage such work by saying to teachers, "just tell your story."

But obviously I think something is missing in the invitation to teachers to "just tell your story." One difficulty arises when autobiographies, or narratives, or stories in and about education are told or written as unitary and transparent, "so that the fabric of the narrative appears seamless, spun of whole cloth. The effect is magical—the self appears organic, the present the sum total of the past, the past appears as an accurate predictor of the future" (Benstock, 1991, p. 10).

Such "teachers' stories" often offer unproblematized recountings of what is taken to be the transparent and linear "reality" of their experiences from identities that are perceived as unitary, fully conscious, and non-contradictory. Of course, these are modernist notions that most of us in the United States have grown up with, where the dominant narrative includes belief in linear and sequential progress as well as "personal" development. That is, many of us grew up with Western cultural norms that reinforced notions that "I" was an always "accessible self," one completely open to observation, rational analysis, and even "correction" by myself and others. It is not surprising, then, that many educators approach the uses of autobiography with an assumption that there is a simple one-to-one correspondence between a "self" and "rememberings" and the encoding of these in writing. And it is not surprising that such forms of autobiography proliferate in the field of education, where strong emphasis is placed on the present as sum total of the past and on the past as predictor of the future in terms of student achievement and teacher effectiveness.

One difficulty that I see with such "stories," then, is that many do not explore and theorize social, historical, or cultural contexts and influences, including language and discourse, on constructions of the "selves" who have those "experiences." Such autobiographical work does not incorporate situated analyses of specific contexts that influence the constructions and representations of selves and others. Nor do such "seamless narratives" analyze the work "that language does to limit, shape, and make possible one world or another" (Davies, 1993, p. xviii). As a result, unified and essentialized versions of "self, experience, and other" continue to be produced in the field of education.

Therefore, I no longer think it's possible to "do" autobiography without asking some questions about the ways in which its uses as a "factual" recording of memories—or as a means by which to find, celebrate, or interrogate a complete and whole "self"—are problematic. One goal of autobiography, as conceptualized by Felman (1993) for example, is to create, use, and explore readings and writings of autobiography that recognize their own social construction and cultural conditioning, and that simultaneously call attention to interpretations as always incomplete, always caught up in repression, always interminable.

If we as educators were to recognize constructions of our "selves" as mediated by social and cultural forces and contexts, as well as by the unconscious, then the uses of autobiography in and as one form of educational research necessarily could move beyond just the "telling of teachers' stories" as an end unto itself.

Nor should autobiography be used only in the service of simply adding "teachers' stories" into already established educational research and literature. Autobiography, whether in the form of "teachers' stories" or researchers' examinations of the filters through which we perceive our work, must move through and beyond traditional framings of educational situations and issues in order to "take us somewhere we couldn't otherwise get to" (Behar, 1996, p. 14).

Such traditional framings usually have encouraged teachers to resolve discrepancies between theory and practice, between competing versions of our teaching and "personal" selves, or between school-reform goals and objectives and teachers' enactments of them. Rather than encountering "contradictions, gaps, views from the margin, views from the center, . . . a field of multiplicities" (Greene, 1997, p. 391) that require rearrangements and reconsiderations of "the self" and of cultural and social normalizations of that self, many uses of autobiography in education encourage the creation and sharing of "teachers' stories" that simply reinforce static, predetermined, and resolved versions of our selves and work. Unlike imaginative literature or other art forms in which, as Maxine Greene reminds us, there are "no clear-cut either/ors, . . . neither truth nor resolution, . . . no firm conclusion" (p. 391), such autobiographical renderings close down rather than open possibilities.

Now, I am not arguing that autobiography as one form of educational inquiry be regarded as literature, per se. However, I do want to consider what might happen to the forms and purposes of autobiography in education if they assumed the potentials of imaginative literature to disrupt rather than reinforce static versions of our "selves" and our work as educators. In fact, this may be the only reason to use autobiography as a form of educational inquiry. Just as informed encounters with literature can lead to what Maxine calls "a startling defamiliarization of the ordinary" (1995, p. 4), so too can autobiography call into question both the notion of one "true," stable, and coherent self and the cultural scripts for that self. Such challenges to the normative, the ordinary, the taken-for-granted can lead to "reconceiving," "revisualizing," and "revising the terms" of one's life (p. 5). Maxine shows how such "defamiliariza-tion" and "revising" can enlarge our capacities "to invent visions of what should be and what might be in our deficient society, on the streets where we live, in our schools" (p. 5).

Autobiography in education could become one means by which to "get us to someplace we otherwise couldn't get to" by providing both form and context for examining the surprises, juxtapositions, contradictions, and incomplete stories of our "selves" and our work.

For this is one of the challenges, I believe, in working with and in auto-biographical research in education contexts. To "tell your or my story" as singular, unified, chronological, and coherent, is to maintain the status quo, to reinscribe already known situations and identities as fixed, immutable, locked into normalized conceptions of what and who are possible.

Instead, addressing "self" as a "site of permanent openness and resig-nifiability" opens up possibilities for speaking and writing into exis-tence ways of being that are obscured or simply unthinkable when one centered, self-knowing story is substituted for another. Changing what it means "to be" or "to become" a teacher, or a student, or a researcher cannot happen by "telling my or your story," if that story simply repeats or reinscribes the already normalized and descriptive identity categories of "woman," "man," "student," "researcher," or "teacher."

Reconstituting the world in significant and needed ways requires us "as" educational researchers to presuppose that such categories as teacher, researcher, and student can point to "undesignatable fields of dif-ferences." And further, that teacher, researcher, and student cannot and should not be "totalized or summarized" by unproblematized exhorta-tions to "tell our stories."

AUTOBIOGRAPHY AS ACTION

Thus, I want to consider uses of autobiography in educational inquiry in ways that allow the identity categories of researcher, teacher, student, woman, man, and so on as permanently open and undesignatable fields of differ-ences—fields that can be read from the cross-cultural perspective of their dif-ferences and the interactions between different languages and cultures (Felman, 1993)—so that these become available as sites that can be resignified in the name of and for the sake of specific social and political projects.

These are the tensions with which I currently am working in my own attempts to "do" autobiography as a form of educational inquiry. And, as always, Maxine's scholarship provokes me to ask my own questions and to pursue these tensions. Not that I could ever arrive at any final and complete resolution of method or identity. Rather, pursuing tensions generated by "the irreducibly complex and paradoxical status of identity in feminist politics and autobiographical writing" (Martin, 1988, p. 103), I am grappling with ways of constructing and using autobiography as a form of educational inquiry that does not reinforce what seem to be collective desires "to know, define, and sum up" (Benstock, 1991, p. 5) the practices of both education and autobiography.

At the same time, I still wish to "take initiatives" by recognizing that it is "incompleteness that summons us to the tasks of knowledge and action." What political projects can I, can teachers, make from uses of autobiography that refuse closure and that posit the constructing and reconstructing of experience and identities as interpretive? That is, subject to the interpretive conventions available to us and to the meanings and identities imposed on us by on-going uses in culture and language.

Such conceptions of autobiography point to the "telling of stories" and to the constructions of "selves" in those stories as never-ending, complex, culturally and linguistically conditioned processes. It is to such complexities as well as to possibilities for agency even in the face of "incompleteness" that Maxine's (1995) uses of autobiography in "The Shapes of Childhood Recalled" point.

For it is, as Maxine Greene always reminds me, our "incompleteness—the open question, perhaps—that summons us to the tasks of knowledge and action" (1995, p. 74). Maxine's vision of the possibilities to be found in "incompleteness" certainly points to forms of autobiographical inquiry that challenge any fixed or predetermined notions of who one "is" or "could be." But more than that, Maxine's commitments to constantly "becoming," her grace amidst the unknowability of "self" and life, her desires to be connected to people who make "fighting a plague, seeking homes for the homeless, restructuring inhumane schools" their life-projects—all of these aspects of her "incompleteness" at the same time have constructed a life that has made a difference.

REFERENCES

Behar, R. (1996). *The vulnerable observer: Anthropology that breaks your heart.* Boston: Beacon Press.

Benstock, S. (1991). The female self engendered: Autobiographical writing and theories of selfhood. *Women's Studies, 20,* 5–14.

Butler, J. (1992). Contingent foundations: Feminism and the question of "post-modernism." In J. Butler & J. W. Scott (Eds.), *Feminists theorize the political* (pp. 3–21). New York: Routledge.

Davies, B. (1993). *Shards of glass: Children reading and writing beyond gendered identities.* Cresskill, NJ: Hampton Press.

Felman, S. (1993). *What does a woman want? Reading and sexual difference.* Baltimore, MD: Johns Hopkins University Press.

Gilmore, L. (1994). *Autobiographics: A feminist theory of women's self-representation.* Ithaca, NY: Cornell University Press.

Greene, M. (1973). *Teacher as stranger: Educational philosophy for the modern age.* Belmont, CA: Wadsworth.

Greene, M. (1978). *Landscapes of learning.* New York: Teachers College Press.

Greene, M. (1988). *The dialectic of freedom.* New York: Teachers College Press.

Greene, M. (1995). *Releasing the imagination: Essays on education, the arts, and social change.* San Francisco: Jossey-Bass.

Greene, M. (1997). Metaphors and multiples: Representation, the arts, and history. *Phi Delta Kappan, 78*(5), 387–394.

Grumet, M. R. (1991). The politics of personal knowledge. In C. Witherell & N. Noddings (Eds.), *Stories lives tell: Narrative and dialogue in education* (pp. 67–77). New York: Teachers College Press.

Martin, B. (1988). Lesbian identity and autobiographical difference. In B. Brokzki & C. Schenck (Eds.), *Life/lines: Theorizing women's autobiography* (pp. 77–103). Ithaca, NY: Cornell University Press.

Pinar, W. F. (Ed.). (1975). *Curriculum theorizing: The reconceptualists.* Berkeley, CA: McCutchan.

Pinar, W. F. (1988). "Whole, bright, deep with understanding": Issues in qualitative research and autobiographical method. In W. F. Pinar (Ed.), *Contemporary curriculum discourses* (pp. 134–153). Scottsdale, AZ: Gorsuch Scarisbrick.

Pinar, W. F., & Grumet, M. R. (1976). *Toward a poor curriculum.* Dubuque, IA: Kendall/Hunt.

IV

WHEN FREEDOM IS THE QUESTION

And when freedom is the question, it is always time to begin.

Maxine Greene
The Dialectic of Freedom

In a society that claims a large and entirely settled notion of freedom as birthright, it is ironic to find so much human suffering and everyday misery at its heart. But this is precisely the American predicament: Massive, gaudy displays of our commodified freedom—the blaring brass bands, the smothering folds of flags waving lazily above us, the bombs bursting in air, thrilling, terrifying, suffocating—the insistent claims of a kind of fixed freedom that is simply there—become themselves obstacles to the accomplishment of actual freedom. Certain that we *are* free, people become paralyzed in the search for freedom

When freedom is posited as pageant, when our sense of it follows a script already written, we find ourselves reduced, unnerved, befuddled. The trappings of freedom, oddly, entangle us; they are themselves walls that must be breached in our search for freedom as an achievement of consciousness and action, freedom as a collective accomplishment to overcome what stands in the way of our humanity.

Maxine Greene reminds us again and again that freedom is linked to the capacity to imagine a better world, linked as well to a coming together of many people to identify deficiencies and obstacles and the unendurable. Freedom, then, requires consciousness and collectivity and action.

In a recent conversation she said:

155

If you release more and more voices, if you hear more and more stories, you cannot but touch upon histories of resistance. There is the need to pay heed to what is being said, what is trying to break out of the silences, where the critique is—and the pain. What is there that people find they hold in common? What social visions do they share? Do they rise out of what they want for their children, for their parents, for their neighborhoods? Or are they visions of domination, of seizing power? And then there is the demand to talk about feasible action, what can be done to heal, to equalize, to repair. I am over-reaching, perhaps, trying to integrate a notion of social action with responses to the arts and the humanities in a dialogical space—where the contradictions are allowed to find expression, even as people strive towards some kind of unity.

The focal idea, still, is to introduce the idea of imagination as thinking about what ought to be. It is to create the possibility of social vision at a moment when people seem to have given up when it comes to conceptions of utopia, of heavenly cities, all those images that informed what we still call the "American Dream." Facing what we are facing in our state and federal governments, we have to work locally, pondering decent and humane ways of coming together, opening a public sphere where multiple perspectives play a part and multiple voices open the way to the "articulate public" Dewey used to describe. We have to sow seeds of outrage, I think, wherever we are: outrage at death penalties; outrage at the existence of boat people (allowed for, I keep thinking, by a holocaust mentality that screens out the human face). This has to be a part of what we try to make. There have to be confrontations, refusals, even as there have to be moments of commitment and hope against hope. . . .

Imagination . . . needs to be ascribed a new centrality in this time of cynicism and hopelessness. Imagination seeks meaning and widening perception; but it also gives rise to glimpses of possibility, to what is not yet, to what ought to be. It is beyond prediction. Imagination opens windows in the actual, releases people from the coercion so characteristic of this media-dominated time. Saying that, however, I think we have always to remember that imagination does not only open to visions of the beneficent and the decent. It can lead to terrible things—Auschwitz buildings, "contracts with America," devices that humiliate and exclude. Associated with the nurture of imagination, therefore, must be a critical self-reflectiveness, a demand that people ponder what they imagine, that they articulate the principles that govern the choices they make as they live. What, after all, is the relation between imagination and the moral life? . . . I try to connect it, for example, to a kind of face-to-face morality—the morality that finds expression in coming towards another person, looking her or him in the eyes, gazing, not simply glancing. It finds expression in one person communicating to another that she/he does not need to know that other's credentials or the particulars of the other's identity. It is a matter of affirming that one person is *there* for the other, looking her/him in the face, answering the situation's demand. It may be empathy that makes such an encounter conceivable, the ability to cross a distance and be *with* another person, to imagine, as Cynthia Ozick has written, "the familiar heart of the stranger." It is important that she stressed imagination, the capacity to move beyond the confinement even of privacy, to reach beyond the wall. . . .

Social imagination involves looking at the world as if it could be otherwise; but we are fully aware that we must always confront the question of whether "otherwise" is always better. (We need only recall what free market means in parts of Russia, what the future signifies for Newt Gingrich.) Still, I am obsessive about social imagination as a way of thrusting towards a better, fairer social order by means of language, imagery, and action. Like Jean-Paul Sartre, I believe that it is only when you have a vision of a better social order that you find an existing set of deficiencies "unendurable." Finding them "unendurable," you then may act to heal, to repair. It is a matter of recognizing the space between what is and what could be; and it is in that space that I choose to work.

We are sadly aware of the feeling in our schools and outside them that nothing can really change, that the most we can hope for is to consume a little more. On all sides people are feeling they require things, but they do not want to become mere things. There is a dearth of the kind of concern that will move persons towards their own humanization, towards a refusal of objectness. . . . Social imagination . . . involves far more than "caring," far more than compassion. It can be active and communal and directional, stemming from but going beyond the poetic imagination. We think constantly, for example, of what it signifies to be in a world becoming increasingly diverse and multiplex, rich with contending values and competing ways of life. It takes an enormous act of imagination to attend to the lived reality of so many different persons without subsuming them in groups and categories. It takes an enormous act of imagination to grasp a world that is pluralist, relativist, perspectival and, at once, yearning towards community. There is no chart for this. We are living through new beginnings; we require imagination to light "the slow fuse of possibility." (Greene, quoted in Ayers, 1995, pp. 320–322)

Freedom is an enduring theme of Maxine Greene's life and work. Never entirely settled, it is always an ideal, a hope, and a practical challenge to take up.

REFERENCE

Ayers, W. (1995). Interview with Maxine Greene. *Qualitative Studies in Education,* *8*(4), 319–328.

15

Ethics and the Imagination

Nel Noddings

Philosophers and educators have different interests in moral theory and the discussion of moral life. Educators, it seems to me, have the more compelling concern; for them, it matters what their readers and students *do* with the discussion, what it means for the kind of lives they will lead. In contrast, for at least the past two centuries, philosophers have concentrated primarily on problems of justification and clarification. In this century, they have been greatly influenced by Wittgenstein's notion that "philosophy leaves everything as it is." When the philosopher and educator exist in the same body, the educator ought—for moral reasons—to prevail, and this is a message made manifest in the ways Maxine Greene has courageously and regularly crossed disciplinary boundaries to contribute to her own growth and that of her students and readers.

Following Maxine, I want to explore the role of the arts, especially literature, in the teaching of ethics and, more generally, in the effort to develop ethical imagination and motivation in students. This chapter, then, is at least in part a plea for an approach to the teaching of philosophy (and other subjects) that will invite and inspire students to engage in a quest for moral excellence while maintaining a deep respect for others whose similar quests may lead in different directions.

VALUING A MORAL LIFE

Aristotle argued long ago that the only students who could profit from his teaching of moral reasoning and theory were those who already had sound characters and an appreciation for moral life. For him, philosophical instruction required a starting point in real-life appreciation that certain ways of behaving are virtuous and others not. An understanding *that* must precede study of the *because* (Burnyeat, 1980). How to achieve this starting point for philosophical study was a matter of great interest among the Greeks. Aristotle, Plato, and Socrates seemed to agree that children need fine models of moral behavior and that they should be instructed to behave virtuously. Aristotle put the greater emphasis on learning to be virtuous by behaving virtuously. Plato was so deeply concerned about providing good examples that he advised censorship of those poetical and dramatic works that might have an adverse effect on the young. Thus in classical Greek thought, we find two ideas that we will pursue further here: first, that effective philosophical study requires a starting point and, second, that the arts can be a powerful influence on moral development.

More recently, Simone Weil also sought a way of bringing students to a heightened moral sensibility. Her idea was that school studies should teach children how to attend. A heightened capacity for attention could then be turned to God in prayer, and communion with God should produce moral concern for one's fellow human beings. Her reasoning is not confirmed by empirical evidence, and I think she was plainly wrong in making a fast connection between intellectual and moral attention, but listen to what she says:

> The love of our neighbor in all its fullness simply means being able to say to him: "What are you going through?" It is a recognition that the sufferer exists, not only as a unit in a collection, or a specimen from the social category labeled "unfortunate," but as a man, exactly like us. . . .
>
> This way of looking is first of all attentive. The soul empties itself of all its own contents in order to receive the being it is looking at, just as he is, in all his truth.
>
> Only he who is capable of attention can do this (Weil, 1977, p. 51).

What seems clearly right in this is Weil's emphasis on attention and her identification of the question, "What are you going through?" as a central question of moral life. Asking such a question fastens our attention on the living other and not on a set of principles or our own righteousness. However, the question still remains how to develop the capacity for such attention.

In essay after essay, Maxine Greene has suggested the judicious use of literature to awaken imagination in both students and their teachers and also "to arouse them to some degree of committed rationality" (1978, p. 22). Not only does literature provide a possible starting point for critical thinking, it also gives a place to passion and to passionate commitment. Through it, students may come to question the "givenness" of their own lives—"to take an initiative, to refuse stasis and the flatness of ordinary life" (Greene, 1988, p. 123). With Walker Percy's narrator, they may move from being "sunk in everydayness" to a willingness "to learn again to see the world" (Greene, 1988, p. 123).

In our search for a starting point that will both enrich the philosophical discussion of moral education and further a commitment to develop moral behavior, we might agree that some consideration should be given to the development of virtues. In many places, I have recommended, for example, that adults should show children how to care, engage regularly in dialogue with them about care, and provide many opportunities for them to practice care. In these recommendations, the care perspective resembles character education. But forms of character education that put great emphasis on the norms of the community or personal virtue or both run the risk of producing people whose self-righteousness draws strong lines between themselves and "others" whose values and ways of life may be judged inferior. Overly vigorous obedience to authority and hypocrisy may also result. Now, of course, I am not claiming that deplorable traits and behaviors are a necessary, or even frequent, result of character education. But it would be dangerous to suppose that instruction in the virtues would by itself provide a starting point for careful reasoning about moral matters.

To develop the form of attention described by Weil and Greene, we may have to cultivate the moral sentiments as David Hume advised. We have to *feel* something that prompts us to ask, "What are you going through?" and we have to feel something again when we hear the answer, if we are to respond appropriately. Hume suggested that stories and the arts help in cultivating the moral sentiments. They tend to humanize us and make us more agreeable.

But, clearly, there is no guarantee that love of the arts will produce morally sensitive people. People evil to the point of depravity have enjoyed the music of Beethoven and Wagner. Hume was careful to include virtues such as temperance and decency in his discussion, and in both Greene's work and this present discussion, the recommendation is not merely for literature and art appreciation, but for the use of literature to deepen self-understanding. As we attempt to cultivate moral sensitivity through the arts, we have to acknowledge that other sentiments can also be aroused.

It is not surprising that educators have so often tried to avoid arousing emotions. Many have become afraid even to discuss values, and those who do engage in such discussion try hard to avoid indoctrination. There are good reasons why educators have turned to the so-called cognitive approaches to moral education, and today there is increasing emphasis on critical thinking. But my thesis here is that critical thinking needs a starting point in both character and feeling, and most episodes of critical thinking should be liberally sprinkled with turning points—points at which the thinker reaches toward the living other with feeling that responds to the other's condition.

And, when reasonable people differ, when there really is an *issue,* I believe that we have a pedagogical obligation to balance the accounts. Instead of shunning emotion, we have to tell stirring stories on both sides. This provides a situational starting point for critical thought.

I want to say more about starting points in just a bit, because I've used the expression in at least two ways. But, before doing that, I must address a worrisome problem. In suggesting that teachers have an obligation to present all sides speaking on an issue, am I suggesting (with that unfortunate candidate for congressional historian) that the Nazi side of the Holocaust be somehow represented in the history we teach our children? The idea is so appalling that, once again, we are tempted to flee from all emotion-laden discussion. But as the hairs on the back of our necks slowly settle, we should explore carefully what might be meant by including the Nazi side.

If, by such a suggestion, we mean that perpetrators and opponents of the Holocaust should be treated as two groups of reasonable people with differing views, then I think the suggestion is truly appalling. But notice that it is moral sensibility that is aroused here. We feel so strongly on the matter that we do not want even to engage in debate with those who might try to justify the Nazi position.

However, I believe there is a way in which the Nazi experience should be included in studies of the Holocaust. Students should be helped to understand how martial music, heroic stories of sacrifice for the state (or cause), fiery speeches, propaganda posters, and the like can be used to induce fierce commitment to causes that turn out to be evil. As a psychological study, that experience could play a vital role in promoting moral understanding and growth, and I'll return to an extended example in the last part of this paper.

Let's turn back now to my use of "starting points." In one sense, I'm using the expression in an Aristotelian way. With Aristotle, I believe that the rudiments of moral character provide a foundation for moral reasoning. But I would add to this a well-developed capacity for moral sensibility, the capacity for attention and fellow-feeling described by Hume, Weil, and Greene. Some, I realize, would include this capacity in their description of character, but I think it goes beyond character into personality and is perhaps even better described as a "way of being in the world." Although I cannot develop the idea here, such development requires that we turn from ethics of virtue to relational ethics— Martin Buber's (1958, 1965, 1966) ethic of response, the ethic of care that several of us are trying to develop (Gilligan, 1982; Noddings, 1984, 1992), and perhaps elements of Emmanuel Levinas's (1989) face-to-face ethic.

The second way of using "starting points" is more immediate. I believe that, if we are concerned with moral outcomes, most episodes of critical thinking must start with the arousal of feeling. We must care about the people, causes, and problems to whom and to which we will apply our thinking skills. The second sense is clearly pedagogical, and the first has a significant pedagogical aspect in its policy implications. We must ask how to establish the capacity referred to in the first sense, and we must press questions about the legitimate use of the arts in inducing the feelings that furnish starting points in the second sense.

THE POWER OF STORIES

Here I want to argue, first, for the use of stories in developing the capacity that might safely establish a starting point for critical thinking and the philosophical study of morality and ethics. Second, I'll argue for their episodic use—the use of particular stories to encourage self-examination and reflection on a specific social or ethical issue.

Several literature-based programs of moral education are in current use, and interest in them is growing. The basic idea is to choose literature of high quality that illustrates the virtues we want children to develop. In the best of these programs, a teacher reads to children (or the children may participate in reading aloud), a virtue is identified, and open discussion follows. In one lovely program, the Heartwood Curriculum, stories from all over the world are included, and children are asked to place colored pins representing a particular virtue on a world map in the area described in the story. At the end of a year's reading, children should see the world covered in the core virtues.

At this stage—elementary school—educators wisely leave aside the fact that the world is also covered in evil (although that point will inevitably come through to some degree), that the virtues are manifested in different ways, that not every possible virtue is discussed, and that some virtues may be emphasized more than others. The idea is not to argue, refine, or justify but to give children the thought-feeling that there is good in people everywhere and that people in every walk of life can exercise that goodness.

This approach—the use of stories—to moral education has a long and mixed history. Almost every form of religious education uses it, and parents choose it almost instinctively. The history is "mixed" because many advocates do not emphasize goodness everywhere but, instead, concentrate on the superiority of their own group and its values. It is mixed also because early exposure to stories of great emotional power has not often been followed up either by stories from the other side or by critical discussion. Indoctrination has been routine.

Even today thoughtful developers of such curricula are under great pressure to anchor their teaching in authority—in the word of God, or in the American way—and opposition to their "rudderless" way of teaching virtues is growing (Bates, 1995). Opponents do not want their children to exercise moral imagination; they want moral conformity and obedience. What we see here—in both advocates of literature-based programs and their opponents—is general recognition that stories have enormous power.

Both sides also want to accomplish something beyond the starting point I've so far emphasized. The developers of the Heartwood Curriculum, for example, really do want children to appreciate and exercise the virtues exemplified in their literature. Critics on the Christian right also want this, but they want something more—that their children should believe that the virtues can only be genuinely understood and exercised in a framework of Christian belief. Their message, quite literally, is "teach it our way or don't teach it at all" (see Bates, 1995). This attack will have to be courageously resisted. It will not do to give up the story phase and try to maintain the critical thinking phase, because the latter is, as C. S. Lewis (1955) claimed, empty without the former.

Consider, for example, the power of *Uncle Tom's Cabin*. At the time Stowe wrote her novel (1852), debate (reasoned dialogue?) raged over the rightness or wrongness of slavery. A conversation between two of Stowe's characters illustrates the difference between a rational-feeling approach and a rational approach that has escaped the domain of feeling entirely. Mrs. Shelby reacts with horror to her husband's decision to sell Uncle Tom and little Harry. Her husband argues financial necessity. When that is brushed aside, he accuses his wife of talking like an abolitionist and reminds her that "pious men" have argued for the justice of slavery. Mrs. Shelby refuses the invitation to argue abstractly. Rather, she points out that there are loving families involved here—human beings she herself has come to love—who care deeply for one another. Isn't this enough to forbid selling them? Doesn't moral sensibility give the answer directly?

The novel is its own best example. Stowe actually presented a brief argument against slavery, and the argument appears as an addendum, a last chapter, to the novel. But scarcely anyone remembers the argument. What moved a nation was the story. Think, too, of the political storm set loose by the novels of Charles Dickens.

When we advocate enhancing this imagination suggested by Stowe, Dickens, Lewis, and Greene, we can expect to encounter resistance. Further, we have to acknowledge that we could be wrong. In any given case, we might be on the side that will be judged ultimately wrong. However, despite our fallibility, we have to embrace a way of being in the world that, as Joseph Schumpeter said, we will "stand for unflinchingly" (Berlin, 1969, p. 172). I may, for example, in caring deeply, advocate nonviolence when a fight would better preserve those for whom I care; I might advocate action prematurely; or in reaching out to care for someone, I might inadvertently hurt several others. Because I could be wrong in a given case, I must, without ceasing to care, listen to others and exercise the best of critical thinking. But, at bottom, I cannot be wrong in choosing a way of life characterized by care, and it is that sensibility that we must be courageous enough to develop in the young.

AN EXTENDED EXAMPLE

So far I have argued that moral development depends as much on moral sensibility as on reasoning and that, further, sensibility together with the rudiments of moral character provide a starting point for critical thinking and the philosophical study of morality. I have argued also that the arts—especially literature—can be used to encourage moral sensibility. Now I want to argue for the episodic use of stories and to offer an example of the kind of story and discussion I have in mind.

The following story is told by Simon Wiesenthal. We may assume from what follows the story that the young Jew, Simon, in the story might have been Wiesenthal himself:

> A young Jew is taken from a death camp to a makeshift army hospital. He is led to the bedside of a Nazi soldier whose head is completely swathed in bandages. The dying Nazi blindly extends his hand toward the Jew, and in a cracked whisper begins to speak. The Jew listens silently while the Nazi confesses to having participated in the burning alive of an entire village of Jews. The soldier, terrified of dying with this burden of guilt, begs absolution from the Jew. Having listened to the Nazi's story for several hours—torn between horror and compassion for the dying man—the Jew finally walks out of the room without speaking (1976, cover).

After the war, Simon—who had not expected to survive—goes to visit the dead soldier's mother and, without telling her of his encounter with her son or the confession he had heard, listens as the mother talks about Karl, "a dear good boy." She describes Karl's religious upbringing and how she and her husband lost him to the Hitler Youth. Out of compassion, Simon remains silent about Karl's confession. Years later, Simon—still agonizing over whether he did right or wrong in leaving the Nazi soldier's bedside without speaking—gathers together a symposium of distinguished thinkers and asks them: Did I do right or wrong?

The question itself is typical of the traditional approach to ethics. Either answer—"right" or "wrong"—demands justification and, although it is useful to engage in debate as part of moral education, such debate by itself fails to get at the deepest existential questions: Why do we harm others? Why do we fail to meet the living other with Weil's deeply moral question? Can we imagine ourselves as Simon? as Karl?

Most of the respondents were able to identify sufficiently with Simon so that they could express sympathy and understanding for his predicament. Recognizing the extremity of Simon's condition and the horrors he experienced, no one on the panel was willing to judge him. Thus there was, at least initially, evidence that the panelists were sensitive to what the young Jew had gone through. But this approach was quickly put aside by most of the respondents as they turned to their own traditions, symbols, and moral codes to answer the question: right or wrong?

One set of responses focused on the religious requirement to forgive the truly penitent. Most respondents believed that Karl, dying in physical and psychic agony, was genuinely penitent; his remorse was not questioned. Therefore, although these speakers could understand why Simon was unable to do so, their considered judgment was that, if he had not been in such peril and misery himself, he would have and should have granted forgiveness.

Another approach centered on symbols. The two actual men meeting in a face-to-face encounter were forgotten. Simon became a symbol of "all Jewry" and Karl a symbol of Naziism. On this level, forgiveness was seen as impossible.

The last respondent, Friedrich Torberg, assured Simon that his failure to forgive was not a sign of moral failure:

> If today, after all your experiences you are still worried by the question whether you should have forgiven a Nazi murderer, that very fact is far more valid evidence of an intact morality than if you had actually forgiven him. It is in this intact morality . . . that we are superior to the others, to the murderers and to those who held their peace about the murders when they were committed and are still holding their peace today. (Wiesenthal, 1976, p. 208)

Here we can begin to encourage the exercise of care and ethical imagination. What is this "intact morality" of which Torberg speaks and how do we maintain it? Surely, people like Wiesenthal, Elie Wiesel, and many others who survived the horrors of death camps are to be credited with moral heroism when they emerge still able to care deeply for others. From the care perspective, Simon demonstrated his intact morality more convincingly in his compassionate treatment of Karl's mother than in his persistent concern to answer the question whether he was right or wrong.

Can we imagine ourselves without an intact morality? On the other side, is anyone really in possession of such a thing? In honest moments of introspection, we can readily acknowledge that we all make moral mistakes. In the language of religion, we commit sins. We, none of us, really possess an intact morality if we look at our lives in a case-by-case examination. However, if we retain a way of being in the world that allows us to respond to the other, to ask, "What are you going through?" and to act compassionately on what we hear, perhaps we have come close.

Our imaginations are challenged with a series of questions. How can we maintain a moral way of being in the world? How do we live it? As we give up the debate on justification and seek self-understanding, what can we learn from *The Sunflower* story?

Probably most students, like the symposium participants, could imagine themselves in Simon's position. We can usually see ourselves as victims, especially if the victims are recognized as good and innocent. However, it is harder to imagine ourselves as perpetrators—to imagine the suffering one is about to inflict. It may have been because he knew that he had added to Karl's suffering by his silence that Wiesenthal agonized all those years. But Karl was not an innocent sufferer. Was his suffering deserved? Should we cut the chain of suffering when we can? Some of Wiesenthal's respondents feared that forgiveness would somehow have excused the whole Nazi regime, that it would have betrayed the dead Jews and those still suffering. But that fear takes imagination too far and in the wrong direction. Wiesenthal and Karl were alone. It was an encounter between two suffering young men barely out of boyhood. We need to think on this, to exercise our imagination on the possibilities. Can we live so that we help to cut the chains of suffering, enmity, and violence?

Now for the hardest challenge to imagination. Can we imagine ourselves as Karl? Most listeners and readers find this very difficult. Indeed when I pose this question to live audiences, many suppose that I am pleading for an understanding of Karl that will arouse our sympathy and perhaps excuse his monstrous acts. But, although a form of sympathy may indeed be aroused, that is not the point. The point is to explore how a "good boy" became a Nazi. The point is to understand ourselves better and, through that understanding, to provide a moral climate in which our children are unlikely to perform violent acts.

Could I have been like Karl? Most of us deny the possibility. But, for myself, I am not so sure. Having been a child myself in that era, I can imagine being dazzled by the snappy uniforms, colorful flags, martial music, precision marching, fiery speeches, and the call to honorable comradeship. I—a child who adored her teachers—would have been especially vulnerable. If *they* had said, "This is right," or even failed to say, "This is wrong" . . . If I had been a boy . . .

What we see when we exercise the moral imagination is that good fortune plays a part in what Torberg called an "intact morality." It was my moral luck to be born an American girl and too young to be involved in armed service. But beyond luck, there is responsibility—Karl's, Simon's, and mine; perhaps above all, the responsibility of parents and teachers is to provide the healthiest possible moral climate for the young. In large part, we establish and maintain the circumstances in which it is possible for our children to be good.

We have now come back to our starting point. It is useful and interesting to study *The Sunflower* story critically—to argue the merits of forgiving or not forgiving, to endorse or reject the level of abstraction that turned Karl into "a specimen from the collection" of Nazis and Simon into a specimen of Jew, to argue for or against meeting Karl as a sufferer rather than a criminal enemy. All of this is instructive. But, at bottom, the story calls for an exercise of ethical imagination that forces us to consider the conditions under which we might lose our very way of being in the world.

When we imagine ourselves as victims, emotion is aroused, and that emotion may increase our compassion for other victims, or it may create hatred for oppressors, or both. Sometimes, in our horror of victimhood, we are comforted by the fact that *we* are not the actual victims; the actual victims are not as smart, not as innocent, not as blessed as we are. And when we look at the perpetrator, we are again comforted because we are not, could not be, that monster. But when we look at a scene of suffering and see *both* possibilities for *ourselves,* then a new horror is aroused, and that horror provides a starting point for real moral growth.

In Maxine Greene's discussion of literature and emancipation, she notes that the really fearsome figures in Flaubert's *A Sentimental Education* "are not the drifters and the dabblers . . . [but] those who have made themselves into one-dimensional creatures with fixed ideas" (1978, p. 34). In Flaubert's story, we follow the deterioration of several characters into moral deadness, stupidity, and cruelty. By concentrating on the more factual content of the story and its writer's technical strategies, teachers might well contribute to the moral and intellectual "slumber of vulgarity" that Lewis so feared (Lewis, 1955, p. 24). Greene wants the opposite:

> I am asking that attention be paid to a literature that seems . . . irrelevant to teacher education, a literature whose critical elements have been effectively absorbed. The reason, again, is that literature may have an emancipatory function for people whose selves have become attenuated, who have forgotten the function of the "I." I do not see how individuals who know nothing about "the powers of darkness," who account for themselves by talking about "chance, circumstances, and the times," can awaken the young to question and to learn. (1978, p. 39)

I would just add, in closing, that of course "chance, circumstances, and the times" do affect us deeply and indelibly. But we must remember, when we teach, that we are for our students a significant part of their "chance, circumstances, and time." Greene reminds us dramatically of our responsibility.

REFERENCES

Bates, S. (1995, January 8). A textbook of virtues. *New York Times,* Education Life, Section 4, p. 16.

Berlin, I. (1969). *Four essays on liberty.* Oxford, England: Oxford University Press.

Buber, M. (1958). *I and thou* (R. G. Smith, Trans.). New York: Scribner's.

Buber, M. (1965). *Between man and man.* New York: Macmillan.

Buber, M. (1966). *The way of response* (N. Blatzer, Ed.). New York: Schocken Books.

Burnyeat, M. F. (1980). Aristotle on learning to be good. In A. O. Rorty (Ed.), *Essays on Aristotle's ethics* (pp. 69–92). Berkeley: University of California Press.

Gilligan, C. (1982). *In a different voice.* Cambridge, MA: Harvard University Press.

Greene, M. (1978). *Landscapes of learning.* New York: Teachers College Press.

Greene, M. (1988). *The dialectic of freedom.* New York: Teachers College Press.

Levinas, E. (1989). *The Levinas reader* (S. Hand, Ed.). Oxford, England: Blackwell.

Lewis, C. S. (1955). *The abolition of man: How education develops man's sense of morality.* New York: Collier Books.

Noddings, N. (1984). *Caring: A feminine approach to ethics and moral education.* Berkeley: University of California Press.

Noddings, N. (1992). *The challenge to care in schools.* New York: Teachers College Press.

Weil, S. (1977). *The Simone Weil reader* (G. A. Panichas, Ed.). Mt. Kisco, NY: Moyer Bell Limited.

Wiesenthal, S. (1976). *The sunflower.* New York: Schocken Books.

16

Meandering and Mattering: Moving Toward Horizonal Persons

Louise M. Berman

Several women were sitting at the table with Maxine Greene. One person asked her: What do you think accounts for your appeal to diverse groups of persons? Maxine replied, "I have seen the darkness." Perhaps so many people resonate with Maxine as a person, an educator, a philosopher, a writer, and a speaker because she helps us to understand the joys and sorrows, the pain and ambiguities of being human. She also provides a crossroads where the inner life of the poet and storyteller intersect with the marketplace of ideas integral to the creation and recreation of democracies.

I first came to know Maxine Greene at a retirement conference held for Alice Miel, a longtime professor at Teachers College and a believer that all persons possessed capacities for imaginative thought and ethical social action (Miel, 1961). As conferees participated in the celebration of the departure from academe of one committed to creativity and its meaning for teaching, some of us also realized that a relative newcomer to Teachers College possessed faith in the human spirit to create and imagine new ways of being in community. Drawing heavily upon Dewey and his work on democracy, as well as the scholars in the arts and humanities, Greene has been a persistent and consistent voice reminding educators of the indomitable qualities of the human spirit, of the necessity of creating communities where that spirit can flourish, and of the ability of persons to deal with pain and suffering—the black and bleak periods—integral to our sojourns on earth.

As one encounters Greene in a one-to-one setting, in a small group, or in a large assemblage she is a constant reminder of our common humanity and yet of our countless individual gifts.

Although she journeys with us through the darkness, she has the rare capacity to help us see the light. She has the brilliance of mind to *mean-*

der with us through fields of ideas, yet she has the moral sense to point the beacon toward what *matters.* In a sense, she is what Hinson calls a *horizonal person* (1995, pp. 22–29), a person understanding of the age in which she lives, but not completely shaped by it. Greene reminds us that as educators we need to respond to what calls us to search more deeply, and to create spaces where the young are invited to join us in our searches:

> To feel oneself en route, to feel oneself in a place where there are always possibilities of clearings, of new openings. This is what we must communicate to the young if we want to awaken them to their situations and enable them to make sense of and to name their worlds. (1995, pp. 149, 150)

MEANDERING

Recently I was in a group in which I had to find a metaphor that seemed comfortable in describing my life. I began exploring the idea of meandering.[1] Being a person who likes to travel the main highways if I am anxious to make time, I am also one who gets a good deal of energy from exploring a country lane, from following a path along a winding river, from encountering persons in a neighborhood cafe in a land different from my own, or from perusing a piece of unknown literature that might provide an insight invitational to extending my thinking and feeling. I like to know approximately where I am in relation to my starting point or the superhighway, but I also like to feel free to move off the highway, to encounter the unexpected or the unanticipated.

At times my meanderings take me into the larger world as I explore a new community, converse with an unfamiliar person, or trek along a new-found trail. At other times my meanderings take me inward as I discover crevices where the inner river is hidden but deep, or where a rock knocks out my best-laid plans, or where a stifled emotion spills over the banks. Even as paths and rivers may be circuitous, so my inner life may have serendipitous and unexpected turns. Persistent values, my professional identity, and significant relationships may endure even as well-known highways provide familiar landmarks on a trip. But the unanticipated turns of the unfamiliar road or the sudden rapids or changes in the river tides provide newness, inviting reflective thought and action. Meandering makes the familiar strange and the strange familiar. It allows me to see the old in new ways; it permits the stranger to become friend.

Meandering is not always pleasant. Sometimes I hit upon a place where I would rather not be. My sense of direction, which would take me back to the highway, falters. Illness may overcome me, and at times death snaps a cherished idea or loved one. Yet, such loss along the way may beget new freedom and a keen willingness to trust my own encounters with life and death.

The freedom to meander may call forth gentleness toward those encountered along the way—toward their strengths, weaknesses, and foibles. At the same time my meanderings may cause me to rise up when I see wicked situations, acts of injustice, or intolerable treatment of the environment or persons. Distraught by incessant calls to matters for which I have no inclination or interest, I frequently search for that which will support explorations of my own inner geography (Norris, 1993) and the common spaces in which I meander with others. Inwardness, outwardness; privacy, togetherness; inner harmony, shared community—all of these contribute to the clarity of inner visions and the communication of ideas for shared meanderings.

Meandering may involve moving toward specific goals, objects, or realities that can be directly seen or grasped. I can will to be an author. On the other hand, meandering may involve movement toward those mysteries that cannot be fully seen, heard, or grasped. I cannot always will that my writing be poetic or imaginative. Grasping may destroy the art of meandering and move me toward directly defined outcomes in which will rather than imagination plays a more predominant part.

Kurtz and Ketcham (1992, p. 125) say we can:

directly will	*but not will*
knowledge	wisdom
pleasure	happiness
congratulations	admiration
reading/listening	understanding
going to bed	sleeping
meekness	humility

Meandering is being willing. Taking action is contingent on the will. Meandering is embedded in a limited freedom where life is seen not so much as a "problem to be solved" but rather "a mystery to be lived" (Kurtz and Ketcham, 1992, p. 128).

Situations in life reveal that chance, choice, and control are all necessary to life and the good society. How persons drive, how food is packaged, how buildings are constructed, how health care is administered involve chance and choice as well as control. Meandering involves choice and chance but in many areas of life would not be possible if controls were not in place.

When it comes to ideas, meandering can take many circuitous routes. Meandering invites the mind to twist and to turn as it deals with the intersection of thoughts from varieties of schools of study, as the mind fixes on ideas that create yearnings for new personal directions, or as new ideas call forth a re-look at ways of being. The mind can turn concepts developed during times of meandering into proposals for commitment and action.

I have been fortunate in having among my friends, colleagues, and acquaintances, persons who not only can meander among ideas, but who also define and delineate issues needing particular attention. Such persons often serve as a beacon to others to move toward collaborative constructive action on matters calling for change or creation.

Maxine Greene invites persons to inner probing and outward action. She can deal with ideas from varieties of fields and within multiple perspectives. Whether talking with superintendents, principals, teachers, small or large groups, she taps persons at the inner core, provides contexts in which they are energized, invites them to meander in their own inner geographies, and calls them to join with her in dealing with critical topics and issues. Her generous spirit is contagious as she quickens people to engage in inner dialogue and community discussion about imagination, arts and the spirit, possibility, and freedom. The themes are universal. Her appeal is to the one among many and to the many ones.

Why does Greene's message have such unusual appeal? My hunch is that she frees people to meander, but she also calls them to create and to be in lively communities concerned about complex dilemmas; she calls persons into conversations about what matters.

MATTERING

Experiences of pain, nurture, and time can each be seen as instances of mattering.

Pain can be vocalized, named, endured, suffered, or ignored. Pain matters when I see the interrelationship between your pain and my suffering.

> In times of injustice, the "subject" of pain is not me, but you. Your pain makes my own more bitter and more generous. Your pain restores my pain to me. For my pain when it is too great, exceeds, escapes me, grows alien to me, I can undergo it only dully, far inside me, where I am a stranger within me. It is only in your pain that I can suffer and weep, I need you to suffer my suffering. (Cixous, 1993, p. 24)

The restoring of pain to me through the suffering of others enables the building of community based not so much on my own suffering or woundedness, but rather on the suffering of those whom I encounter. To be attuned to mattering is invitational to compassionate action. Rich writes about "naming and mourning damage, keeping pain vocal so it cannot become normalized and acceptable" (1993, p. 242).

In a series of conversations I (Berman) held with new urban teachers in an alternative certification program, a poignant theme was that of their own pain, suffering, and woundedness. Sometimes such pain came forth loud and clear, as when individuals talked about being angry, about having their energy drained, and about being burned out or frustrated. Other times, pain was discerned in their tones of voice, inflections, pauses, and silences (1993, p. 18).

In these conversations, teachers frequently talked about "patience," a word meaning enduring with fortitude, being victimized, and suffering. These qualities were sublimated, in many instances, as teachers sought to convey a bearing of being in control, of accepting, or of showing fortitude.

Personal pain and the pain of others were intertwined. One teacher commented that the children have not seen the "splendor of life. They are sort of locked in a cubicle of life. . . . I still feel that I can identify with them. . . . I guess I heard what it was like, but I didn't touch it, feel it, or smell it like I am now, and it is very severe" (Berman, 1993, p. 22).

I was challenged as I talked with teachers suffering both their own pain and that of students. How can teachers endure situations in which their reactions and actions desperately matter? How does one help neophytes see possibility and hope when situations are such that teachers' very beings are racked with pain?

I was also challenged by teachers' pain in other kinds of situations. Conversations with experienced teachers deemed "good" by their superiors brought forth the pain and fear of becoming burned out or stale. These teachers longed for freshness and newness in their lives without having to leave classrooms to assume administrative and supervisory positions. I heard them asking for more possibilities, more ways to view teaching and life in classrooms that would enhance their visions and those of the students whom they taught. They seemed fearful of losing the vitality of their early callings into teaching.

A second instance of mattering is what I would call professional *nurturing*. Mattering involves educators seeing themselves as professional nurturers responsible for forming linkages with families, social institutions, art centers, and others who have a stake in the growth and development of the young. Eleanor Holmes Norton (1995) posits that one of the dilemmas of the teaching profession is that schools and teachers try to take on single-handedly the nurturing of the young. Rather, Holmes stipulates, teachers should reach out to others in the community who are in any way responsible for children and youth and invite such persons into partnerships in rearing the young. Nurturing matters. The collaborative nurturing of the young is essential to kindling and igniting the spirit so that the innate birthright of each individual to explore, imagine, care, meander, and create is not quenched. Seeing the faces of those in the community who might provide needed energy in rearing the young can set in motion a nurturing process beneficial to all.

Teachers also serve as nurturers to each other when they see their peers in compassionate and caring ways. Intellectually, teachers nourish each other when they look at larger issues that go beyond their own specialties, thus integrating a wider vision with their own "practical and emotional attitude to life" (Midgley, 1989, p. 8).

Teachers nurture each other by inquiring together: Teaching is uncertain; knowledge is uncertain; life is uncertain. It matters desperately that teachers and students abdicate frames of mind that value control and certainty over ambiguity and uncertainty. If such were the case, teachers might collaborate in producing stories, narrating case studies (Ornstein, 1995, p. 125) that highlight the voices of teachers. (For discussions of teachers inquiring into their own experiences, see Clift, Houston, and Pugach, 1990; Goswami and Stillman, 1987; Schubert and Ayers, 1992; and Manen, 1991.) Teachers can nurture each other as together they search for feelings of efficacy and strength in an uncertain world.

Third, within educational settings, what matters is that *time is held as sacred.* During periods of individual meandering, of reflecting, and of exploring, teachers and students have the right to be in time in ways that will contribute to their own growth and well-being. During times of group involvement, teachers and students have the right to follow trains of thought, develop ideas, or move in new directions.

When time is considered sacred, it is seen as whole. When thought is frequently disrupted, either by what is taking place in the classroom or by bombardment of messages through loudspeakers, persons do not have the continuity of thinking that permits good ideas to emerge and be developed. Writers who must frequently answer the phone or scientists interrupted in their experiments may not experience wholeness of thought.

Time—it can be seen in small or large chunks. It can be experienced as waiting, as anticipating, as reflecting, as dwelling in the moment. It can be seen as a psychological space waiting to be filled or space full of too much. It can be seen as significant or unimportant. For the imaginative person though, time is sacred—precious, whole, and matters greatly.

TOWARD HORIZONAL PERSONS

Horizonal persons have not been completely shaped by the "mold of the age in which they live. They are transformed by a recycling of understanding." (Hinson, 1995, p. 27). Through meandering, imagining, and mattering, such persons may see beyond what is to what might be—to see possibilities, as Maxine Greene frequently says. Horizonal persons wonder, ponder, act, and reflect.

The actions of horizonal persons move us ahead—at times by being revolutionary. Rich (1993) writes about people's confrontations with their deepest longings. In writing about poetry, she says, "A revolutionary poem is written out by one's individual confrontation with his/her own longings . . . in the belief that its readers or hearers . . . deserve an art as complex, as open to contradictions as themselves" (p. 241).

Rich goes on to talk about work as "a human blessing" (p. 242). Thus, horizonal persons see and hear what is around, but they can also use their work, their abilities and imaginations to create something that takes us beyond the here and now and adds a twist that enables viewers to see life in a new way. The creations may be poems, songs, stories, paintings, social inventions, deeper views of selves, new visions of the environment, or new medical cures. In other words, horizonal persons are poets in a broad sense. They reveal the present and the immediate (Kronenberger, 1969, p. 330), but they also express what is more enduring. Horizonal persons go beyond personal thoughts, pains, and joys to that which has more universal meaning. Horizonal persons are sensitive to the common good and to their own inner spirit. Their continuous rethinking and re-creating of self nurtures community ventures.

Horizonal persons are continuously dealing with meanings of concepts like goodness and morality. Reflection on such ideas provides the impetus for seeing beyond, for imagining things as though they might take a different slant, for helping to determine what on the horizon is worth devoting time and effort. Horizonal persons do not define goodness and morality in terms of sets of rules or regulations but rather in terms of increasingly more satisfying moral principles.

Tuan (1989) describes the moral being as follows:

> A moral being . . . is a thinking and reflective individual, alive to the paradoxes and dilemmas of life, critical of the crude generality of behavioral codes; and hence someone who, while he or she recognizes the need to attend to the difficulties of each case, also wrestles with the formulation of superior moral principles which can cope with problems of equity and justice for society at large. A moral person . . . is someone irresistibly drawn by the good. (p. 3)

Tuan later indicates that the good must be left undefined if it is not to deteriorate into a set of moral codes:

> The good is ineffable. Its very lack of specifiable content imparts to it the authority of the impersonal and the objective. A vision of the ineffable good, though it does not help resolve ethical dilemmas and problems of the day, provides a safeguard against intolerance and moral stasis. What we need is a powerful lure which limits the indecisiveness of freedom and yet does not enslave or blind. (p. 180)

When we deal with the good, the moral, the beautiful, or the problematic, what is real becomes important. The starting point frequently is something facing us that needs change or transformation. Tripp (1993) talks about making something problematic, because when problematics are realized, one can set out to "expose, understand and acknowledge (or, if necessary, transform) them" (p. 14).

Horizonal persons are sensitive to structuring and restructuring. They know when old structures need to be broken through, and when something new needs to be created (Greene, 1988, p. 17). Part of the dilemma is that as wise as any one person may become, it takes a community of real, of authentic persons working together to create many of the systems that renew the common good, which re-create democracy.

A true democracy is real. It is authentic. It is not monolithic, nor even a "distinctive identity" (Booth, 1993, p. 89). Rather, the identity "is the one we find when we *celebrate* addition of self to self, in an act of self-fashioning that culminates not in an individual at all but in . . . a kind of *society,* a field of forces; a *colony;* a chorus of not necessarily harmonious voices; a manifold *project.*" (Booth, 1993, p. 89). In essence, according to Booth, we are a "philiated" self (p. 90). We are part and parcel of one another.

Thus, our task as horizonal persons is to find in solitude that nerve that exposes what we can do and be as an individual self, but in community and in communion with others. At times we may be called upon to invent something new; at other times we may re-perform something that has been created. The re-playing of a Mozart sonata is not necessarily apelike or worthless.

If such a stance toward our society were taken, then rugged individuals may give way to horizonal persons, who are capable not only of meandering but also of carrying out what matters—whether it be creating a new classroom arrangement or seeing afresh the face of the other and the summoning of that face to my response (Levinas, 1963, p. 353). In the tradition of Maxine Greene, that response is imaginative, ever inviting persons to renew their faith in compassion, justice, creative intelligence, and democracy.

NOTE

1. *Meandering* comes from a Greek word *melandres* (now the Buyuk *menderes*), a winding river coursing through Turkey to the Aegean Sea. A meandering body of water flows into a larger space.

REFERENCES

Berman, L. M. (1993). *Conversations with teachers in an alternative certification program*. Unpublished manuscript, University of Maryland, Baltimore County.

Booth, W. C. (1993). Individualism and the mystery of the social self. In B. Johnson (Ed.), *Freedom and interpretation* (pp. 69–102). The Oxford Amnesty Lectures, 1992. New York: Basic Books.

Cixous, H. (1993). We who are free, are we free? In B. Johnson (Ed.), *Freedom and interpretation* (pp. 17–44). The Oxford Amnesty Lectures, 1992. New York: Basic Books.

Clift, R. T., Houston, W. R., & Pugach, M. C. (Eds.). (1990). *Encouraging reflective practice in education*. New York: Teachers College Press.

Goswami, D., & Stillman, P. R. (Eds.). (1987). *Reclaiming the classroom: Teacher research as an agency for change*. Portsmouth, NH: Heinemann.

Greene, M. (1988). *The dialectic of freedom*. New York: Teachers College Press.

Greene, M. (1995). *Releasing the imagination: Essays on education, the arts, and social change*. San Francisco: Jossey-Bass.

Hinson, E. G. (1995). Horizonal persons. *Weavings, 10*(2), 22–29.

Kronenberger, L. (1969). *Quality: Its image in the arts*. New York: Atheneum.

Kurtz, E. & Ketcham, K. (1992). *The spirituality of imperfection: Storytelling and the journey to wholeness*. New York: Bantam Books.

Levinas, E. (1963). The trace of the other. In M. C. Taylor (Ed.), *Deconstruction in context* (pp. 345–359). Chicago, IL: University of Chicago Press.

Manen, M. van. (1991). *The tact of teaching*. Albany: State University of New York Press.

Midgley, M. (1989). *Wisdom, information, and wonder: What is knowledge for?* New York: Routledge.

Miel, A. (Ed.). (1961). *Creativity in teaching: Invitations and instances*. Belmont, CA: Wadsworth.

Norris, K. (1993). *Dakota: A spiritual geography*. New York: Ticknor and Fields.

Norton, E. H. (1995). Paper presented at the annual meeting of the American Association for Colleges of Teacher Education, Washington, DC.

Ornstein, A. C. (1995). The new paradigm in research on teaching. *The Educational Forum, 59*(2), 124–129.

Rich, A. (1993). *What's found there: Notebooks on poetry and politics*. New York: W. W. Norton.

Schubert, W. H., & Ayers, W. C. (Eds.). (1992). *Teacher lore: Learning from our own experience*. New York: Longman.

Tripp, D. (1993). *Critical incidents in teaching: Developing critical judgment.* London: Routledge.

Tuan, Yi-Fu. (1989). *Morality and imagination: Paradoxes of progress.* Madison: University of Wisconsin Press.

17

Living Dangerously: Toward a Poetics of Women's Lived Experience

Mary-Ellen Jacobs

PROLOGUE: THE PARADOX OF FEMINIST PHENOMENOLOGY

I have long been attracted to phenomenology's focus on the "lifeworld" and, initially, derived profound satisfaction from meticulously recovering lived experience as if it were a unified, eminently graspable entity. Reveling in the challenge of identifying the universal "essence" underlying lived experience, I failed, at first, to recognize how phenomenology makes women invisible. Habitually gender-blind in its pursuit of "human" science, phenomenological research posits masculine ways of knowing and being as the norm and overlooks the notion that "gender is basic in ways that we have yet to fully understand, that it functions as *a difference that makes a difference*" (DiStefano, 1990, p. 78). Thus, engaging in phenomenology from a feminist perspective requires a radical recuperation of lived experience as gendered experience in which "we avoid buying into the neuter, universal 'generic human' thesis that covers the West's racism and androcentrism" (Alcoff, 1989, p. 326).

This essay draws on the writings of Maxine Greene to suggest how women's lived experience might be reenvisioned as a "poetics" that resists masculinist universals and acknowledges the densely tangled skeins of women's day-to-day existence. Ultimately, the heart of my project as a feminist is to rescue women's experiential knowledge from the genderless and apparently apolitical terrain of masculine theorizing: "Designating experiences as the ground for social transformation is central to a feminist politics because it is here—in our experience, not some abstraction of it—that we find both our subordination as well as our strength" (Lewis, 1993, p. 5).

RECLAIMING LIVED EXPERIENCE

By rigorously decontextualizing experience through reductive techniques like "bracketing," traditional phenomenology obliterates complexity, masks difference, and denies ambiguity. What remains is an ontological land-scape, sunless and deceptively smooth, stretching indifferently toward an empty horizon. As a feminist committed to recovering—rather than attenuating—the richness of lived experience, how might I find my way?

The root meaning of "experience" suggests not inertia (either epis-temological or ontological) but rather an existence poised precariously on the edge. Derived from the Latin *periculum* meaning peril or risk, "expe-rience" implies a sense of living dangerously, reminiscent of a passage from Greene's *Existential Encounters for Teachers*: "We see ourselves as teachers goading [the student] on to *live dangerously* for his own sake, to combat inertia, to take the risks of growth" (1967, p. 160).

Yet—in a patriarchal culture where norms of male agency and female passivity are firmly entrenched (Lerner, 1986), "living dangerously" for *one's own sake* is viewed as an exclusively male prerogative. Women, instead, are rewarded for their docility and are tirelessly socialized to assume the role of the "good daughter" who eschews unnecessary risk, exists entirely for others, and eradicates unruly desires. The idealized image of the deferential good daughter so pervasive in Western culture is troubling because it seems to legitimate patriarchal power relations by equating "goodness" with how readily women adhere to their subor-dinate position.

Distinguishing traits of the good daughter are her submissiveness and docility. "Submission," rooted in the Latin *submittere,* means "to set under." In patriarchal culture, women are considered the inferiors of men and, hence, under their domination. "Docility" is derived from the Latin *docere,* "to teach." Teaching, though, seems associated with mold-ing rather than with prompting individuals to realize their own gifts. Consequently, good daughters are expected to be compliant rather than creative. For example, in an essay on the history of women's education, Greene points out that if women "were to be educated at all, the pur-pose was to educate them for dutiful and dependent lives—for subordi-nation and powerlessness" (1978, p. 227). Women, thus, have tradition-ally been taught to conform—without complaint—to the expectations of a patriarchal universe.

What, though, becomes of the daughter who resists patriarchy, who risks living dangerously by relishing "lived experience" as "female expe-rience"? Greene grapples with these ideas in "The Lived World" (1978), an essay in which she deliberately resituates herself as an "ambivalent daughter" daring to speak her life and her differences into being. Greene's text seems emblematic of DuPlessis's sentiments: "For when the phenomenological exploration of self-in-the-world turns up a world that devalues the female self, when the exploration moves along the tacit boundaries of a social status quo, she cannot just 'let it be,' but must transform values, rewrite culture, subvert structures" (1980, p. 151).

"The Lived World" makes questionable the "social status quo" by poignantly chronicling the lifeworld of women oppressed by patriarchy. Drawing on Merleau-Ponty's concept of embodied consciousness, in which perception necessarily undergirds cognition, Greene presents lived experience as the continual forming and re-forming "of a primordial landscape in which we are present to ourselves" (1978, p. 213). What, Greene wonders, are the contours of that landscape for women negotiating the dailiness of their lives? By raising this question, Greene deliberately resituates phenomenology on gendered terrain, a honeycomb of hills and valleys reflecting her own emerging understanding of herself as a philosopher marked by difference: "The inescapable fact that I was female, aware that ordinary appearances presented themselves to me differently than they did to males, very vaguely aware that there were indeed 'multiple realities'" (1983, p. 3).

Greene points us toward a feminist reclamation of lived experience when she boldly announces: "I want to discuss the lived worlds and perceptual realities of women because I am so sharply aware of the degree to which they are obscured by sex and gender roles. I am convinced that the imposition of these roles makes women falsify their sense of themselves" (1978, p. 213). Patriarchal culture—a culture that defines woman as Other—denies women their perceptions of the lived world and, instead, confines them within socially prescribed roles: daughter, wife, mother. Roles themselves are social constructs that compel us, regardless of gender, to adapt ourselves to the reality of others. In so doing, "we are likely to lose touch with our projects, to become *invisible*, . . . to think of ourselves as others define us, not as we create ourselves" (pp. 216–217).

To prevent invisibility, Greene urges women to become truly present to themselves by reconsidering their own lived experiences: "I am arguing for an intensified awareness of women's own realities, the shape of their own lived worlds" (p. 219). How, though, might women come to view the lived world as a source of affirmation rather than negation? Should women seek to replace the "good daughter" with her antithesis, the "bad daughter"? At first, such a substitution possesses an exhilarating appeal; yet, even the "bad daughter," like her endlessly self-effacing sister, represents a socially prescribed role. Inevitability, the predictability of *both* female "goodness" and "badness"—polar opposites on the narrowly defined spectrum of patriarchy—promotes cultural invisibility.

Greene herself repeatedly resists the seduction of binaries: "My sense of the oppressiveness of gender roles does not move me to think about recovering a 'natural,' spontaneous, untrammelled self uncorrupted by the world" (p. 216). Instead, Greene encourages women to live dangerously by envisioning reality as a multiplicity of possibilities rather than a single, immutable way of being. Remaking the constituted world in all its complexity requires women to dare to view life as it might be otherwise, to actively seek out multiple perspectives. Yet such active seeking is impossible for women trapped in "good daughter" or "bad daughter" roles; instead, such questing seems the province of the "ambivalent daughter" who remains perpetually attuned to the nuanced shadings of the lived world. By embracing multiplicity rather than aligning herself with a single perspective such as "goodness" or "badness," the ambivalent daughter is infinitely more subversive to the cultural status quo than her more predictable sisters.

Above all, Greene reminds us, lived experience necessitates that we move beyond corporeal perceptions to consider how the body is entangled in webs of social, cultural, and political significance. Women live dangerously when, as ambivalent daughters, they question the strictures of the conventional and recognize the multiple realities woven into the tapestry of everyday existence. From these continually shifting particularities, women learn to "transform values, rewrite culture, subvert structures" (DuPlessis, 1980, p. 151) and, most importantly, to reclaim lived experience as their own.

RE-ENCOUNTERING THE AMBIVALENT DAUGHTER

A decade before Greene wrote so eloquently about the complexities of women's lives in "The Lived World," she explored the lifeworld of the classroom from an existential perspective. In *Existential Encounters for Teachers* (1967), Greene dramatically charged teachers to exhort students to "live dangerously." Although it is tempting to trace Greene's gradual awakening to feminist issues as a trajectory arcing gracefully from *Existential Encounters* to her later work, such exquisite linearity smoothes over the contradictions, hesitations, and silences within her texts. The ambivalent daughter, I now realize, has always hovered at the margins of Greene's prose, and it is to her story that I now turn to begin conceptualizing a poetics of women's lived experience. I start, though, with my own story of ambivalence—for I, too, am a deeply ambivalent daughter—to discover how I might learn to reread women's words and lives.

Years ago, I framed my interpretation of *Existential Encounters* as a quest narrative (Jacobs, 1991) that serendipitously (or so I liked to think) foreshadowed Greene's turning from depersonalized academic prose to a discourse style that acknowledged her own subjectivity:

> In 1967, Greene published *Existential Encounters for Teachers,* a collection of philosophical and literary readings—all male-authored—interspersed with her own commentaries which suggested "*possibilities* for looking at certain educational issues from an existential vantage point" (1967, p. 6). Greene's prose, characterized by a careful adherence to the stylized objectivity of academic writing, shifts slightly but unmistakably in the final pages of the book and, thus, seems to signal her sudden discomfort with the genderless realm of scholarly discourse. No longer the deferential good daughter abiding by the conventions of distanced academic prose, Greene momentarily inserts a female subject— a brief but telling textual rupture which may be indicative of her own growing consciousness of herself as a woman writing within the confines of male discourse. Because it is in *Existential Encounters* that I first detect the ambivalent daughter who both resists and succumbs to patriarchy almost in the same breath, the book itself seems to convey Greene's own inner turmoil. Though her ambivalence might be entirely subconscious, its eruption is significant enough to be volcanic, significant enough, as Cixous reminds us, to provoke "an upheaval of the old property crust, carrier of masculine investments." (pp. 57–58)

I alternately admired and scorned the ambivalence I detected in Greene's text. When I viewed ambivalence as a breaking out, a movement toward something that resembled the confident self-actualization I associated with feminism, I applauded what I perceived as Greene's emerging self-acceptance: "In the closing pages, the good daughter, as if discovering her own voice—a surge of speech after long silence, abandons the neutral discourse of scholarship and first speaks as a woman by boldly inserting the female pronoun" (pp. 63–64).

I celebrated Greene's rebellion against the universal male signifier and lauded the act as a triumphant leap forward for feminism. Alternately, when Greene relapsed—ambivalently—into the conventions of academic discourse, I felt betrayed:

> Though Greene identifies herself as a teacher and begins her introduction by specifying that *Existential Encounters* was written primarily for "the individual teacher or teacher-to-be" (p. 3), her language seems alienating to all women who teach. Throughout the text, "the teacher" to whom she refers is always male. Because teaching is such a thoroughly feminized profession (Grumet, 1981), Greene's ubiquitous, and

clearly incongruous, male pronouns are particularly disturbing in passages such as:

> Doing, acting, choosing—these are the watchwords of existential
> thinking and existential education. The world remains open; the world
> remains strange; and history is possibility. The teacher, then, may con-
> ceive himself to be a metaphysician, an ironist, an artist; but, from the
> first and last, must conceive himself as a living man. (1967, p. 152)

> Did Greene, as a teacher, think of herself as a "living man"? Ever
> the dutiful daughter who erases gender so completely, Greene has, with
> a peculiar flourish, managed to erase herself as well. (pp. 60–61)

Uncomfortable with what I viewed as Greene's failure to break through
the barriers of patriarchal discourse, I concluded my commentary of
Existential Encounters ambivalently:

> Ostensibly, Greene is discussing the existential plight of the individual
> but, subconsciously, she might also be evoking some of the tensions in
> her own situation as a woman attempting to reveal herself as a gendered
> subject within a patriarchal society. Yet, almost from habit, Greene dimin-
> ishes the gravity of her message by continually inserting qualifiers so that
> the demure voice of the good daughter persists—soft as silk, not expect-
> ing her words to be taken seriously by very many of her readers. Not
> surprisingly, Greene's own ambivalence is a haunting reminder of the
> "divided consciousness" experienced by women in a patriarchal culture:
>
> > For women, then, existing in the dominant system of mean-
> > ings and values that structure culture and society may be a
> > painful, or amusing, double dance, clicking in, clicking out—the
> > divided consciousness. . . . The shifting focus, bringing the world
> > into different perspectives, is the ontological situation of women
> > because it is our social situation, our relationship to power, our
> > relationship to language. (DuPlessis, 1980, p. 149)
>
> (pp. 68–69)

Reviewing my interpretation of *Existential Encounters,* I realize my own
complicity in creating—or at least desiring to create—a heroic masculinist
narrative where Greene as teacher and writer courageously claims her
gendered identity and, in so doing, becomes an inspiration to all women
struggling to undo the strictures of patriarchy. I had euphorically envisioned a predictable linear progression with textual ambivalence as the
means to a predetermined—and ultimately victorious—finale. In retrospect, I recognize that I had not yet learned to live dangerously but had,
instead, succumbed to my own need to bring closure. What I had failed
to grasp was that ambivalence was actually "the end" rather than merely
"the means." What I had neglected to explore was the convoluted, endlessly shifting landscape of women's "divided consciousness."

POETICS AND WOMEN'S LIVED EXPERIENCE

"Ambivalence," being strong both ways, seems central to women's sense of "divided consciousness"—the relentless tension between self and other, male and female, appearance and reality. Women are simultaneously pulled in two opposing directions, a situation Greene repeatedly acknowledges in *Existential Encounters.* From its opening sentence, Greene's 1967 text dwells in tension: "To teach in the American school today is to undertake a profoundly human as well as a professional responsibility" (p. 3). Existentially, we are continually torn between relating to others as persons and regarding them merely as objects. This subject/object duality, which Greene introduces in the book's initial pages, mirrors the situation of women who seem perennially caught at the crossroads of their desire to please (woman as object) and their desire to reveal (woman as subject) (DuPlessis 1980, p. 140).

As sites of contradiction and divided consciousness, the crossroads themselves might be locations where women can learn to think differently about themselves: "When women become feminists the crucial thing that has occurred is not that they have learned any new facts about the world but that they come to view those facts from a different position, from their own position as subjects (Alcoff, 1989, p. 324). Women positioned at the crossroads confront their own subjectivity in relation to the larger landscape of patriarchy and, thus, experience an unsettling ambivalence that can either be ignored or spark a feminist consciousness. For, "although the oppression of women is universal, feminist consciousness is not" (Bartky, 1990, p.12). What seems essential for developing a feminist consciousness is women's awareness of the multiple contradictions coloring their everyday lives as well as the possibilities for transformation (Bartky, p. 14). A feminist consciousness is necessarily "divided": Women aware of their victimization by patriarchal culture recognize that they have endured injustices, "but at the same time feminist consciousness is a joyous consciousness of one's own power, of the possibility of unprecedented personal growth and the release of energy long suppressed. Thus, feminist consciousness is both consciousness of weakness and consciousness of strength" (Bartky, p. 16).

Ambivalence—a consciousness of *both* weakness and strength—becomes a way of repositioning ourselves and of imagining the world as it might be otherwise: "Coming to see things differently, we are able to make out possibilities for liberating collective action and for unprecedented personal growth, possibilities which a deceptive sexist social reality had heretofore concealed" (Bartky, p. 21). At the crossroads, the personal and the political necessarily intermingle. By claiming—rather than meekly relinquishing—our divided consciousness, we retain our integrity as women committed both to living the contradictions in our lives and transforming debilitating patriarchal practices.

Thus, by embodying the divided consciousness and perceptual shifts possible at the crossroads, the figure of ambivalent daughter becomes integral to my understanding of Greene's text in ways I had never anticipated. For example, I now read Greene's movement between masculine and feminine pronouns as way of asserting both female subjectivity and the contradictions embedded in female lived experience. Substituting "she" for "he" throughout *Existential Encounters*—a linguistic sleight-of-hand for which I had initially yearned—negates the complexities of the crossroads and simplistically valorizes female rather than male existence. Such an either/or mindset numbs us to the perplexities of women's lived experience. Similarly, Greene's textual strategies of deferral, at first so disconcerting to me, now suggest a deliberate disruption of academic discourse. Greene repeatedly decenters herself by using the passive voice, by making self-references that are always in the third person, and by hedging her statements with qualifiers. Her deliberate self-marginalization throughout *Existential Encounters* might be reinterpreted as the antithesis of the dogmatic certitude of most scholarly prose. Greene, instead, undermines the certainty of academic discourse by creating a prose style open to possibility.

Throughout *Existential Encounters,* Greene resists the lure of dichotomous thinking and chooses, instead, to struggle with contradictions. Rather than accepting either/or distinctions, often synonymous with masculinist perspectives of the lived world, Greene deliberately blurs boundaries: "There is a sense, then, in which both an *inner* and an *outer* vision is required. There is a sense in which the multiple facets of the educational process can be described from both perspectives and when one perspective is taken, the facets from the other need be neither eroded nor denied" (p. 156).

As the consummate ambivalent daughter, Greene claims a both/and vision "born of shifts, contraries, negations, contradictions . . . linked to personal vulnerability" (DuPlessis, 1980, p. 132). Such ambivalence is for DuPlessis the hallmark of a "female aesthetic." Yet, like Rita Felski, I am wary of positing a purely female aesthetic because "multiplicity, indeterminacy, or negativity are not in themselves specifically feminist, or indeed specifically anything" (1989, p. 7). Instead, Felski insists on textual interpretation situated in a particular social, historical, and political context. This is similar to Alcoff's "positionality," which is sensitive to the shifting contextualities of women's lives: "The concept of positionality includes two points: first . . . that the concept of woman is a relational term identifiable only within a (constantly moving) context," and "second, that the position that women find themselves in can be actively utilized (rather than transcended) as a location for the construction of meaning . . . rather than simply the place where meaning can be discovered (the meaning of femaleness)" (1989, p. 324).

For me, the word "poetics" brings together aesthetics and positionality. From the Latin *poesis,* "poetics" literally means to make or create. This resonates with Alcoff's notion of actively constructing, rather than accidentally stumbling on, meanings. Reading Greene's texts as a poetics of women's lived experience resituates my interpretations at the crossroads of language and experience and acknowledges the innumerable contradictions that are the warp and woof of women's daily lives. A poetics challenges us to interpret lived experience deeply so that we might realize the multiplicity of possible constructions and the inevitable partiality—and even impermanence—of our own visions. "Poetics," thus, suggests a phenomenological way of being in the world that resists the search for a singular "essence" and, instead, requires we live dangerously by risking ambiguity rather than embracing certainty.

Greene's own writings point toward such a poetics, a breaking away from taken-for-granted categories and essences so that individuals might begin "authenticating themselves as persons, with acting in such a way as to realize themselves" (1967, p. 6). In *Existential Encounters,* Greene repeatedly stresses the primacy of the person—the individual responsible for her own actions and for creating her own destiny—startling ideas for female teachers schooled to reproduce rather than resist patriarchal values. For women, Greene's existential message was revolutionary—a call to replace abstraction with specificity, habit with imagination, complacency with curiosity.

Such a poetics of women's lived experience positions us irrevocably at the crossroads where multiple competing vistas intersect along the horizon: "The transformation of day-to-day living into a series of invitations to struggle has the important consequence for the feminist that she finds herself, for a while at least, in an ethical and existential impasse. She no longer knows what sort of person she ought to be and, therefore, she does not know what she ought to do. One moral paradigm is called into question by the partial and laborious emergence of another" (Bartky, 1990, p. 20). What seems vital for Greene and for us as ambivalent daughters is the struggle itself, the business of living dangerously so that we welcome tensions and ambiguities as occasions to illuminate and politicize, rather than perfunctorily resolve, the problematics of women's day-to-day existence. By daring to live within the complexities of the moment, we assert the authority of our own experiences as visible—rather than invisible—threads in the tapestry of the lifeworld.

REFERENCES

Alcoff, L. (1989). Cultural feminism versus post-structuralism: The identity crisis in feminist theory. In M. Malson, J. F. O'Barr, S. Westphal-Wihl, & M. Wyer (Eds.), *Feminist theory in practice and process* (pp. 295–326). Chicago, IL: University of Chicago Press.

Bartky, S. L. (1990). *Femininity and domination: Studies in the phenomenology of oppression.* New York: Routledge.

Cixous, H. (1981). The laugh of the Medusa. In E. Marks & I. de Couviron (Eds.), *New French feminisms: An anthology* (pp. 245–264). New York: Schocken.

DiStefano, C. (1990). Dilemmas of difference: Feminism, modernity, and postmodernism. In L. Nicholson (Ed.), *Feminism/postmodernism* (pp. 63–82). New York: Routledge.

DuPlessis, R. B. (1980). For the Etruscans. In H. Eisenstein & A. Jardine (Eds.), *The future of difference* (pp. 128–156). Boston: G. K. Hall.

Felski, R. (1989). *Beyond feminist aesthetics: Feminist literature and social change.* Cambridge, MA: Harvard. University Press.

Greene, M. (Ed.). (1967). *Existential encounters for teachers.* New York: Random House.

Greene, M. (1978). *Landscapes of learning.* New York: Teachers College Press.

Greene, M. (1983). How I came to phenomenology. *Phenomenology+Pedagogy, 1,* 3.

Grumet, M. (1981). Pedagogy for patriarchy: The feminization of teaching. *Interchange, 12,* 165–184.

Jacobs, M. E. (1991). *Diary of an ambivalent daughter: A feminist re-visioning of Maxine Greene's discursive landscapes.* Unpublished doctoral dissertation. The University of Maryland at College Park.

Lerner, G. (1986). *The creation of patriarchy.* New York: Oxford University.

Lewis, M. G. (1993). *Without a word: Teaching beyond women's silences.* New York: Routledge.

18

Voicing From the Margins: The Politics and Passion of Pluralism in the Work of Maxine Greene

Peter McLaren and Carlos Alberto Torres

AN UNFINISHED DIALOGUE BETWEEN PETER MCLAREN AND CARLOS ALBERTO TORRES

PETER: I have for many years admired Maxine Greene's work, especially its subversive potential. Her intellectual career has been impressive, and her contribution to education nothing less than exemplary. Early in her career she leapt off the plateau of academic convention, and she has not looked back—except in occasional retrospective musing. She has shown modern schooling to be an impoverishing, constraining, and domesticating environment, but also a place where hope intersects with subjective probabilities to create an arena of critical possibilities. Carlos, how would you characterize the intellectual profile of Maxine Greene in the context of contemporary philosophical dilemmas and intellectual challenges?

CARLOS: I feel that we are beginning a dialogue today about one of the most intriguing intellectuals that I have ever met. Multifaceted, with an enigmatic aura, a tremendous sense of love, in possession of a poetic language, a formidable memory, a creative and feverish imagination and a command of the language I have rarely seen, Maxine Greene stands tall amongst towering intellectuals in the United States and elsewhere. She cannot be described without mentioning the institution in which she spent twenty-nine years of her life, Teachers College at Columbia University. Teachers College is filled with a tradition of social struggles, social activism, and people such as John

Dewey who pursued the goals of education as a possible utopia, as a possible dream, as Paulo Freire would like to argue.

Yet among educational dreamers, philosophers, and social activists, Maxine has played a major role since 1969, when she began to dream, teach, and write about education for social change. When she retired formally a few years ago—although she continues to teach and is a leading force in the workings of the Center for Social Imagination, the Arts, and Education—she was the proud holder of the William F. Russell Chair in Philosophy of Education. Her work has inspired a host of philosophers of education, researchers and practitioners, including many of us. Her voice has a distinctive quality, nationally and internationally, and therefore I am not surprised that we are engaged in dialoguing about her, in a book that seeks to analyze but also to celebrate, and hopefully to extend, her own work.

PETER: Before we attempt to accomplish this, how would you define her work today?

CARLOS: In preparation to our conversation, I went back to her written production, which I constantly peruse for my own work, and I am impressed by the cohesiveness of her opus. Maxine's worldview is a rare and unique blend of Marxism, Deweyism, and European Existentialism à la Merleau-Ponty combined with Jean-Paul Sartre and Simone de Beauvior. Despite her prominence in the intellectual kaleidoscope of progressive thinking in the United States, she has stubbornly refused to be essentialized, more so in terms of her contributions to feminist theory. Maxine does not consider that her feminism reflects, in any measure, an assessment of the *essence* of womanhood. In fact, her feminism is more existential than what we may be led to believe in her elegant critical writing.

Perusing through her work, and in conversations with her, I am convinced that she became a feminist not because of her theoretical preferences, which may be extraordinarily important in this context, but because of her practical experience. As a woman in academia, she has endured so much discrimination that to develop her work into feminist discourse was an existential choice, perhaps her only choice. Remember that she had to work almost eight years in the Department of English at Teachers College before she was accepted as a full member of the Department of Educational Foundations. And this discrimination was happening while she was the editor of *Teachers College Record*—unbelievable.

I cannot understand any critical existentialist perspective without a solid ethical and political grounding, particularly in the domains of education. This is so because the increasing efforts for educational reforms cannot be dissociated from social reforms, as Maxine has discussed in many different places. In one of her forewords, she displays with characteristic wit her ecumenical view of social reform. With the care of the invited guest in a book that is not her own, Maxine (1989) writes in her foreword to *The New Servants of Power* the following: "Consciousness signifies a reaching out beyond, a refusal of objectiveness, a realization as well as a refusal, a move to transcend" (p. x).

Experiencing a book for Maxine is to take the book as part of a movement to transcend the written message and to act, practically, upon the social construction of reality. Maxine, in her unique style, suggests that the only way to read a book about social struggles and educational reform is to link consciousness with praxis. That is the reason she writes a foreword that calls for the consciousness of a reader who is neither a passive object nor someone who will remain untouched by the words, feelings, data, or felicitous phrases in the book. But she continues, and I think her point displays the power of her vision:

To read these chapters may well be to experience one's consciousness stirring a resistance and critique. What one can hope for is the launching of a dialogue. Who is to know whether the educational solution is to be found in Mortimer Adler's *Paideia,* in John Dewey's work, Paulo Freire's, Antonio Gramsci's, John Goodlad's, Ernest Boyer's? Who can be sure whether current proposals for civic education suggest the imposition of an unwarranted consensus? Who knows whether any such consensus can be thought to preexist or to emerge from what Jürgen Habermas calls competent communication, or from the ongoing 'conversation' so many thinkers propose today in the place of objective truth? (p. x)

Maxine has not given us a list of "must read" authors—although all of those listed above would help to engage in a fascinating discussion on educational reform. She is only asking herself, in a loud voice and in front of a public that she is constructing despite that this is not *her* book, how we can continue the democratic conversation in education. She inquires as to how we can accept the inevitability of our limitations, the fact that knowledge is always provisory, and that research findings are filled with a deep sense of uncertainty. For Maxine, reality is a social construction but it is not the product of our own imagination, alone. There is the "density" of material and existential conditions that Maxine wants to capture in her writings on philosophy of education, aesthetics, and art. As an existentialist and radical democratic thinker she suggests that we keep the dialogue going, that is, that we keep the conversation going. To continue the democratic conversation is, perhaps, one of the most important results to which we can aspire in promoting education for social change. Dialogue, consensus, and negotiation are instruments of struggle, hence pedagogical and political tools in the context of broader strategies, not ends by themselves.

PETER: We need to keep the conversation going, certainly, but I think this as an end-in-itself sounds too much like Rorty's liberal, consensual agenda. Dialogue—yes—but as a necessary if insufficient aspect of democratic struggle. Perhaps we could turn our attention to some of Maxine's epistemological and existential concerns.

CARLOS: Clearly, Maxine does not believe there is an "objective truth" waiting in the interstices of reality to be discovered by the researchers. For Maxine, the fact that there is no "essence" that can be discovered, analyzed, measured, weighed, synthesized, and presented through several sets of languages, including mathematical paraphernalia, should not preclude us to continue in our quest for knowledge. What better reason do we need to continue the democratic conversation, to continue the dialogue about reality, a dialogue like the one that has inspired our conversation about Maxine's philosophy, and to continue this dialogue in critical ways?

Indeed, the best way to acknowledge a powerful thought is to critically appraise its logic, breadth and depth, and possible contributions to historical and contemporary debates beyond the fascination of à la mode explanations. Peter, in your work—primarily your many texts written after your arrival from Canada to the United States in 1985—you have criticized liberal pluralist and humanist perspectives linked to bourgeois Enlightenment. It is evident that Maxine's discussion of a philosophy of consciousness throughout her work is linked to a humanist perspective. Can you apply a critique of liberalism and humanism to Maxine's work?

PETER: I am not among those Marxist critics who tend to treat humanism simply as a disease of the bourgeoisie—criticisms that, in the main, are ill-founded. I treat humanism with a healthy suspicion, but I do not dismiss it as simply a swindle of fulfillment, a trick of the Enlightenment. Let me tell you what I respect about Maxine's widely disseminated work—work that certainly can be characterized as humanistic. What I greatly appreciate about Maxine's work is the nuanced manner in which she embraces epistemological heterogeneity; her approach is not the search for a problem-solving discipline that Thomas Samuel Kuhn would consider "normal" science. I admire the finesse of argumentation she brings to urgent ethical issues, the wide range of interpretive frameworks she draws upon, and the sensitive strategies she employs when examining the myriad dimensions of social life: brushing them against existing proprieties and conventions without succumbing to a wispy, ethical relativism. Like the work of feminist poststructuralists, Maxine's writings constitute a form of revision, an act of looking back, of seeing the world with new, critical eyes. Her work is an opus *détourné,* an opus off the beaten track, so to speak. Like Hannah Arendt, whom Maxine admires, she emphasizes the role of memory, the act of remembrance—and this, I think, is the Heideggerian hint in her work— and she acknowledges, if only implicitly at times, that there exists an unreasonable moment of emancipation in every act and the promise of a nonviolative relationship to the other. For Maxine, texts and the acts of reading them are events that are invariably gendered, racialized, and mediated through capitalist logics.

CARLOS: Your remarks, Peter, strike a cord. In her foreword to *A Place for Teacher Renewal* (1992a), Maxine reiterates her concerns with consciousness and highlights a political and epistemological perspective that, you and I would agree, is useful for the political struggles of today: "Pulsating beneath the accounts of programs . . . is a consciousness of what it signifies for living persons actually to create identities by means of their projects, in this case projects of teaching, and —in so doing—to invent our lives" (p. viii).

There you have it again, reinventing our lives is a natural way of seeing and doing things for Maxine. She is, however, inviting us to be part of a specific project of reinventing teacher education: "Bypassed as a person, someone with a sense of agency, such a teacher, is altogether likely to rely on the predefined, the discrete, the fixed. We realize how frequently teacher reform movements have ignored the teacher as questioner, as beginner, someone caught in wonderment and uncertainty, reaching beyond to choose and to know. . . . Teacher's renewal is equally, wonderfully incomplete; there is always, always more. Like feminist thinking too, it refuses systematization, monologism, insularity" (p. viii).

PETER: I agree. Claiming that, for the most part, educational research has enabled practitioners to move beyond old factory models and mechanist claims, Maxine commented recently on "the growing disenchantment with technicism and bland behaviorist assumptions" (1992b) and cites an increased concern with social and economic contexts that affect the particularities of school life, as well as important gains made in educational inquiry with respect to gender, class, and ethnic identity. The existing "restiveness" with regard to educational research, Maxine maintains, involves the "uselessness" of mainstream research in responding to social inequality and the ravages of capitalism. Maxine suggests—and I am inclined in the main to agree with her—that questions surrounding epistemology have largely disappeared. Basically, Maxine reasserts the questions that need to be raised once again: What constitutes knowledge? How is truth understood? What validates knowledge claims? How does understanding differ from knowledge? And so on. She wants to assess the fresh perspectives on the horizon of epistemology that have been uncoiled by postmodernism, poststructuralism, critical hermeneutics, feminism, multiculturalism, and literary criticism. In my opinion, this is where Maxine is at her best—mining the rich and variegated terrain of these fields for their challenge to foundational epistemological stances, revealing mainstream epistemologies to be cataphracted discourses, walking her readers through the pitfalls of Plato, the Cartesian flight into the purity of objectivity, challenging Kant's universal reason, the dialectical reasoning of Hegel, the dialectical materialism of Marx. From Kohlberg to Charles Taylor, to Rorty, to Habermas, and then back to Dewey—Greene is there as a consummate cartographer of systems of intelligibility, mapping out for educators the signposts of a changing epistemological universe. She is able to relate, for instance, issues in the philosophy of science to contemporary issues in educational research.

CARLOS: Are you claiming that Maxine's central strength is that of a synthesizer?

PETER: I have heard some of Maxine's critics dismiss her as a mere synthesizer of various vectors in contemporary philosophy and social criticism, but, no, that is not what I am saying at all. I hardly agree that her creation of such syntheses can be dismissed with the adjective "mere." What her critics often miss is the way she brings herself to her synthesizing practices in a way that highlights her own moral and gendered universe, her own exercise of historical agency. Her work, in my mind, exemplifies the agency she writes about so passionately and approvingly: the subject of existential phenomenology; a subject that is negotiated through forms of discursive reformulation and theoretical resignification. For Greene, this subject is decidedly feminist, decidedly left-liberal, too. She is very much a modernist in her stress on art and agency, collective memory, on action, on public commitment; in her emphasis on embodied subjectivity; in her multifarious ways of thematizing and symbolizing the world, of reenchanting the universe. She is fearful of the future yet fearless in facing it. I do, however, believe that Maxine tacitly endorses a form of political agency that I would describe as left-liberal, an agency born out of a commitment to the major tenets of liberal democracy: hybridity, difference, and diversity. The interweaving characteristics of her work—including her stance against commensurability, against premature narrative closure; her commitment to dialogue, to public spaces where freedom can thrive; her faith in faith; her commitment to a common space, to shared public places of mutuality and concern; her struggle to keep open conditions of possibility for political life, for caring, and for community; her regard for all sides of the question, for a critical open-mindedness, for theoretical exploration—all of these are commendable, and they speak to a many-sided educational project: political, philosophical, aesthetic, and cultural. Yet despite these admirable characteristics of her work, I feel that Maxine's political project suffers from what I shall call an over-saturation in and overestimation of the power of experience. In me summarizing a critique position, I am not attempting to deemphasize or denigrate the major importance of Maxine's work. In fact, I believe Maxine would be disappointed if I failed to engage her work honestly from my own positionality as a Marxist theorist.

I think the problem is that Maxine truly believes that if only individuals could cease from being alienated from their own landscapes, and if only they would try to be less unreflective, and if only they could be more capable of interpreting lived situations, democracy would then be workable. I am oversimplifying Maxine's work here, I agree, in order to highpoint a tendency in Maxine's work to restore a view of democracy that is, I believe, tacitly grounded in a liberal view of consensus. Recently Howard Gardner (1995) discussed creativity as a dynamic process that involves interaction among the individual, a domain or discipline of knowledge, and some sort of institutional field composed of a collection of individuals that makes judgments. Gardner asserted that creative people have some kind of pull toward novelty, and they often need cognitive and affective support from others; they are usually possessed with a probing, iconoclastic personality; they need to get reaction from the gatekeepers and judges of their disciplines or domains, and they need to push the boundaries of their domains, often creating new ones. Gardner did not discuss the relationship between creativity and social justice. Somehow creativity is kept as a discrete interactive process. There is an ideological presupposition about creativity here that appears in my mind to speak to the capitalist repression of class antagonisms. Creativity is a substance that can easily be absorbed by the political mediation of the bourgeoisie. It can be turned into some kind of patriotism, some kind of emblem or slogan for solidarity: *we shall all become creative!* I feel that Maxine sometimes shares this position in that her work reveals at times a repression of class antagonisms. Similarly, there is little discussion of creativity in relationship to working-class struggles in her work. Despite her references to work being done in feminist poststructuralism, I believe that the subject-as-origin still surfaces in her work. I believe that creativity needs to be revealed in terms of its own conditions of existence within the circuits and production of labor value.

In other words, for Maxine dissension, rupture, and disarticulation are important, but the procedural movement of capital guaranteed by the social division of labor suggests that its broadest constituent movements are always recuperated at a higher level. She writes: "Multiple interpretations constitute multiple realities; the 'common' itself becomes multiplex and endlessly challenging, as each person reaches out from his/her own ground toward what might be, should be, is not yet" (1988, p. 21). Interpretation is never wholly free since the truth of any text is related to the rhetorical power of the reader to make the text speak in her or his own voice or image. While all points of view may be, epistemologically speaking, equally real, equally contingent, critical theorists do not believe that all points of view are equally valid or legitimate since interpretations of society as a social text still have material effects whose assets and liabilities are distributed asymmetrically in the social field. Knowledge always works in somebody's interest for a particular "we"—something conceded in Maxine's work, I admit—yet at certain times in her work, Maxine lapses into an unreconstructed humanism, into an idealist faith in the social and political power of reason. I would like to see more emphasis in Maxine's work on the culture of the indigene as it has been constructed within the disabling narratives of the ethnographic imagination and underwritten by a liberal pluralism and created by research practices that over-determine the narratives of the indigene herself. How do our research practices override her resistance through the provision of counter-narratives that actually domesticate indigene's own voice?

CARLOS: Your point, Peter, is well-taken. However, I know you would agree with me—and this has little to do with the overall discussion about Maxine's work—that rather than domesticating narratives from researchers—which as you and I know very well exist in academic environments—the logic of domination, the narratives that domesticate human lives, and the overall process of oppression emerges in a number of symbolic and material terrains in society. The academy is just a minor player. In other words, I am reminded here of Karl Marx's (1867/1971) powerful message (despite his sexist language) that "In the social production of their life, men enter into definitive relations that are indispensable and independent of their will; relations of production that correspond to a definitive stage of development of their material forces. The sum total of these relations of production constitute the economic structure of society, the real foundation, on which rises a legal and political superstructure and to which correspond definite forms of social consciousness. The mode of production of material life conditions the social, political and intellectual life process in general. It is not the consciousness of men that determines their being, but, on the contrary, their being that determines their consciousness" (pp. 20–21).

You and I, Peter, have discussed this statement of Marx on many occasions. We agree that despite formulations of Marxists who have taken the dynamic, dialectical, and historically nuanced sense of Marx's formulation away and fossilized a sizable part of his analysis, the narratives of the indigene herself, of the popular sectors, of the middle classes, of the upper classes, are not freed from this "conditioning," nor can they be understood without considering these multiple symbolic and material determinations. While not considered in a totally reductive way, individual consciousness cannot be free from the overall set of contradictions set in motion by capitalism, patriarchy, slavery; that is to say historical and political processes that have altered the potential sense of agency in individuals. These are individuals who, consciously or unconsciously, are part of classes, and are gendered, raced, have assumed specific choices in their sexuality, profess specific religious creeds, beliefs, or understandings. All of this takes place in the context of definitive relations that are indispensable and independent of people's will.

PETER: Carlos, I would like to take advantage of your special vantage point as a scholar trained and working in different intellectual traditions than the North-American traditions, one who has lived, studied, and worked in four different countries. You are an intellectual who is conversant in many languages but also who writes in English—not your mother tongue, but the *lingua franca* of academia. In this context of different traditions and languages, and as an intellectual of color who is always socially constructed by others given the constrictions of race, class, and gender, what strikes you as the most powerful message in Maxine's language, in Maxine's narrative, in

Maxine's theories, in Maxine's theoretical constrictions?

CARLOS: Peter, this question is fascinating for someone like me, coming from the Third World, and for someone who has spent most of his life studying social theory as it applies to sociology, political science, economics, and political philosophy, as well as education. What is so special about Maxine's writings? I have to reply following Bakhtin's characterization of prose art.

Bakhtin (1981) argues: "If the art of poetry, as utopian philosophy of genres, gives rise to the conception of a purely poetic, extrahistorical language, a language far removed from the petty rounds of everyday life, a language of the gods—then it must be said that the art of prose is close to a conception of languages as historically concrete and living things. The prose art presumes a deliberate feeling for the historical and social concreteness of living discourse, as well as its relativity, a feeling its participation in historical becoming and in social struggle; it deals with discourse that is still fraught with hostile intentions and accents; prose art finds discourse in this state and subjects it to the dynamic unity of its own style"(p. 331).

Prose art defines Maxine's overall theoretical and practical project, her utopian philosophy of genres, and the way she goes about developing it, linking prose, narrative, and poetry with philosophy, social theory, and art. Maxine has lived in a symbolic world that she is continuously reconstructing with her feelings about historical concreteness. Her concerns with "otherness" are well expressed in her idea that "the more continuous and authentic the personal encounters, the less likely that categorizing and distancing will take place" (1992b, p. 250).

Her prose art is an invitation to dialogue: "Life [she quotes Bakhtin] by its very nature is dialogic. To live means to participate in dialogue: to ask questions, to heed, to respond, to agree, and so forth. In this dialogue a person participates wholly and throughout his whole life: with his eyes, lips, hands, soul, spirit, with his whole body and deeds" (1991, p. 543).

Perhaps Maxine, unconsciously, defined for us her whole theoretical and practical endeavor in her struggle to create new symbolisms to overcome sexism, racism, and classism. In the opening page of her article that I like so much, "The Passions of Pluralism" (1992b), she quotes Ozick, but I think Maxine, unconsciously, is also talking about her own endeavor and achievements, commanding the metaphors, art, and imagination for a better world: "Through metaphor, the past has the capacity to imagine us, and we it. Through metaphorical concentration, doctors can imagine what it is to be their patients. Those who have no pain can imagine those who suffer. Those at the center can imagine what it is to be outside. The strong can imagine the weak. Illuminated lives can imagine the dark. Poets in their twilight can imagine the borders of stellar fire. We strangers can imagine the familiar hearts of strangers" (p. 250).

Yes, through metaphors, the past has the capacity to imagine us, and we it. Maxine has made of metaphors a reality, and of reality a metaphor in her tireless work for achieving human compassion, community, dialogue, and human solidarity while accepting, with humility, that truth is always disputed, uncertainty always predominate over certainty, and fiction not only guides the understanding of reality but could very well be reality itself.

PETER: It is, I think, important for Maxine's readers to understand that language and metaphor are fundamental for Maxine in her quest to construct robust alternative landscapes of imagination, for reimagining and reenchanting the world, for creating dynamic public spheres where democratic praxis can flourish. Her work could, I think, be described as linguacentric in this regard. As such, she is a critically situated inquirer in the sense of locating herself securely within a feminist standpoint epistemology; hers is also not a strident or militant standpoint in the sense that it excludes a ludic or playful poetics of knowing grounded in a praxis of telling. It is, rather, a tough-skinned probing of contemporary issues. Maxine (1988) describes her work in the following passage:

My hope is to reawaken concern for a belief in a humane framework for the kinds of education required in a technological society. It is to recall those who read to some lost spontaneity, some forgotten hunger for becoming different, becoming new. My hope is to remind people of what it means to be alive among others, to achieve freedom in dialogue with others for the sake of personal fulfillment and the emergence of a democracy dedicated to life and decency. (p. xii)

CARLOS: Creativity and fiction are instruments for healing and empowerment in Maxine's lifework. Her invitation continues to resonate in the halls of our universities. Let us listen to the multiple voices. Let us accept a sense of compassion as an inextricable companion for moral action. A single metaphor—argued Miguel de Unamuno, the great rector of the University of Salamanca deposed by the Fascist takeover in Spain and a noted existentialist philosopher and writer— is worth a thousand concepts.

Through the use of metaphors, Maxine is speaking of uncertainty, incompleteness, and disunity rather than system. She speaks of the need to be reinvigorated by dialogue rather than uncompromising universalism. She, indeed, creates a rationale that in a way highlights her wholesale agenda for reform. This agenda is marked by consciousness, openness to change, directiveness, but in the context of flexibility and creativity, in a world inhabited by human agencies, and in a culture reinvigorated by dialogue, empowerment, cultural and spiritual renewal. Very powerful words, very powerful concepts, extremely sharp and timely agenda.

PETER: Yes, Carlos, I don't disagree, but I think that at times Maxine seems to forget about the historical and institutional specificity of group solidarity brought about by social antagonisms related to class struggle. The problem that I have with humanism in general is that it creates rigid ontological boundaries or enclaves premised upon the notion that some people are more human than others—and so we have the Western valorization of the white Christian heterosexual male. So while I admire Maxine's work deeply, I am not sure to what extent it helps us to face current post-humanist political challenges. There is a certain humanism, I think, in her emphasis on self-fashioning through critical reflexivity that works on a kind of humanistic repression—a fetishistic disavowal perhaps is too strong a description—but a certain avoidance of the fact that the signifying field is located in the economic scarcity of class exploitation. There is a sense of hope in her work that to me points to a notion of the possibility of fully realized subjectivity even if she formally recognizes this as an impossibility. Perhaps this is just a type of modernist yearning—and at times, of course, I see it in my own work. But when subjectivity is fully realized then social antagonism ceases to exist—and identity turns into substance—a kind of Kantian "thing" as Zizek would point out to us. And when democracy is fully realized we have perhaps just empty forms that ossify into fascism. So I think in some ways Maxine's work reinstates or reinvests with validity its own limitations.

CARLOS: I think there is a powerful insight in Maxine's work, and that is that the process of work, or the labor-value nature of human exchanges, may not reach in contemporary industrial societies the same dimension in explaining human dynamics and particularly social struggles they had at the turn of the century or even until the fifties or sixties. This is not so say, however, that the dynamics of class or class formation should be ignored. Quite the contrary. I think that her attempt to launch into a discussion of aesthetics and art is also an attempt to move beyond class, or gender, or race, as discrete analytical categories, linking them together in a more integrative approach.

PETER: Carlos, your analysis brings to mind a comment Maxine made in a recent book of mine. In the foreword that Maxine wrote for *Critical Literacy: Politics, Praxis, and the Postmodern* (1993), which Colin Lankshear and I co-edited, she writes: "Not only is it considered important to identify the intersections of aesthetic codes with economic and political ones; it is important as well to discover a pedagogy that will in time become transformative" (p. x).

Maxine's work does integrate race, class, and gender,—that is quite true, Carlos. And for this reason her work is invaluable for those of us working in the area of critical pedagogy. She has helped to move pedagogy from a rather impoverished analytical framework and elementary syntax in order to expand the discursive terrain for critical reasoning so that praxis always moves forward as a living force of social change and liberation.

CARLOS: Through metaphors, art, aesthetics, poetry, history, and literature, we may do what Maxine has invited us to do: Let the past imagine us so we, in our concreteness, with our limitations, but in the company of others, in solidarity of multiple struggles, can imagine it. Perhaps Maxine will add, by imagining the past we can reinvent a better, more compassionate, dialogical future. By imagining the past, we may be able to restore the notion of the collective imagination and the collective memory in education. You and I agree that this is a most powerful message in Maxine's lifework.

REFERENCES

Bakhtin, M. (1981). *The dialogical imagination* (M. Holquist, Ed.; C. Emerson& M. Holquist, Trans.). Austin: University of Texas Press.

Gardner, H. (1995). Creativity: New views from psychology and education. *RSA Journal, CXLIII*(5459).

Greene, M. (1988). *The dialectic of freedom.* New York: Teachers College Press.

Greene, M. (1989). Foreword. In C. Schea, E. Kahane, & P. Sola (Eds.), *The new servants of power: A critique of the 1980s school reform movement* (pp. ix–x). New York: Greenwood Press.

Greene, M. (1991, Summer). Achieving the language of compassion: The education professor in search of community, *Teachers College Record, 92*(4), 541–555.

Greene, M. (1992a). Foreword. In A. G. Rud Jr. & W. P. Oldendorf (Eds.), *A place for teacher renewal* (pp. vii–ix). New York: Teachers College Press.

Greene, M. (1992b). The passions of pluralism: Multiculturalism and the expanding community. *Journal of Negro Education, 61*(3), 250–261.

Greene, M. (1993). Foreword. In C. Lankshear & P. McLaren (Eds.), *Critical literacy: Politics, praxis, and the postmodern* (pp. ix–xi). Albany: State University of New York.

Greene, M. (1994). Epistemology and educational research: The influence of recent approaches to knowledge. *Review of Research in Education, 20*, 423–464.

Marx, K. (1970/1981). *A contribution to the critique of political economy*. New York: International Publishers.

V

LIVED WORLDS

If we are seriously interested in education for freedom as well as for the opening of cognitive perspectives, it is also important to find a way of developing a praxis of educational consequence that opens the spaces necessary for the remaking of a democratic community. For this to happen, there must of course be a new commitment to intelligence, a new fidelity in communication, a new regard for imagination. It would mean fresh and sometimes startling winds blowing through the classrooms of the nation. It would mean the granting of audibility to numerous voices seldom heard before, and, at once, an involvement with all sorts of young people being provoked to make their own the multilinguality needed for structuring of contemporary experience and thematizing lived worlds.

Maxine Greene
The Dialectic of Freedom

More and more school researchers, reformers, administrators, and parents are realizing the power of "granting audibility to numerous voices seldom heard before" in quests to open the "spaces necessary for the remaking of a democratic community." Often, these voices are those of young people, students who are willing and able to draw attention to the discrepancies, inadequacies, inequalities, and sometimes terrors of their lived worlds. And teachers' voices, too, are being granted an audibility by those who, in earlier times, might have ignored or discounted them in the rush to reform and restructure schools.

The trick in "granting audibility" to heretofore muted voices, however, is both to recognize the power relations inherent in the very act of deciding who gets to speak and whose voices count, and to do something in response to those voices.

We now have numerous examples in education research and literature of "voices seldom heard before." Exactly what policies, practices, and ways of thinking would have to change, and how, in order to respond to issues, questions, situations, paradoxes raised by such voices? What might it mean to respond to Alejandro's voice in Chris Carger's *Of Borders and Dreams: A Mexican-American Experience of Urban Education* (1996), who asks,

> Right, a teacher shouldn't shove kids? Right, she shouldn't make fun of the way you talk? . . . She made a kid cry today. . . . I don't think it's right to make fun of somebody 'cause he doesn't know English. That's what she does sometimes. . . . Right, that's not good for a teacher to do? (p. 42)

Or what might it mean to respond to Haven Henderson's educator voice, grappling, in Mike Rose's *Possible Lives: The Promise of Public Education in America* (1995), with what multiple perspectives might mean for a teacher and for changing the structure of school so that all students have the opportunity to learn as best they can:

> I'm going to be in a roomful of kids who think in lots of different ways about the world, and so do their parents. To think there's not that range of beliefs is ignorant. So is it fair for me to teach them only from the lens of my perspective? Or should I introduce many lenses? I think that's more powerful. . . . To have a well-educated American population to challenge, to make democracy real, to teach kids that they can make change happen, that they can be decision-makers, that they can make their communities better. That's our hope. (p. 235)

Or what might it mean to respond to Jonathan Kozol's devastating critique, in *Savage Inequalities* (1991), of the ways in which public schools are funded in the United States, and to the voice of Israel, a Puerto Rican boy at Morris High School in the South Bronx, who articulates the insidious effects of such inequalities:

> If you threw us all into some different place, some ugly land, and put white children in this building in our place, this school would start to shine. No question. The parents would say: 'This building sucks. It's ugly. Fix it up.' They'd fix it fast—no question. People on the outside . . . may think that we don't know what it is like for other students, but we visit other schools and we have eyes and we have brains. You cannot hide the differences. You see it and compare. (p. 104)

In hearing these voices and others too long muted by dominant paradigms and those who would maintain their dominance, Maxine Greene, in *The Dialectic of Freedom* (1988), calls on us all to respond—to dare to give up old ways of thinking and acting, and to awaken, or reawaken, the consciousness of possibility. She dares us to respond in order to seek a vision of education that brings together the need for wide-awakeness with the hunger for community, the desire to know with the wish to understand, the desire to feel with the passion to see. I am aware of the pluralism in this country, the problem of special interests, the dissonances and enmities. I am aware of my ambivalence with respect to equality and with respect to justice as well. Fundamentally, perhaps, I am conscious of the tragic dimension in every human life. Tragedy, however, discloses and challenges; often, it provides images of men and women on the verge. We may have reached a moment in our history when teaching and learning, if they are to happen meaningfully, must happen on the verge. Confronting a void, confronting nothingness, we may be able to empower the young to create and re-create a common world—and, in cherishing it, in renewing it, discover what it signifies to be free. (p. 23)

REFERENCES

Carger, C. L. (1996). *Of borders and dreams: A Mexican-American experience of urban education.* New York: Teachers College Press.

Greene, M. (1988). *The dialectic of freedom.* New York: Teachers College Press.

Kozol, J. (1991). *Savage inequalities.* New York: Crown.

Rose, M. (1995). *Possible lives: The promise of pubic education in America.* New York: Penguin Books.

19

Greener Pastures

Michelle Fine

In the shadow of the brim of her dark black hat, out of lips painted a bright red, Maxine Greene fashions a world "not yet." If you've never had a cup of coffee with Maxine, you've missed a feast of ideas, literary quotes, apologies, confessions, and sparkling eyes. Maxine is a gift to us all, particularly those of us who yearn for a world that has not yet been invented, and who struggle with the one we have inherited.

In the wake of the civil rights, feminism, and gay/lesbian social movements, there is a "diaspora" of young women and men living the lives, shouting the shouts, insisting on Greene pastures just like the ones Maxine has imagined. Alone, however, with little knowledge of or connection to Maxine or the social movements from which they inherit entitlement, these young women and men demand "what could be." Right now. The gutsy legacy of "our" social movements, they look at their social institutions, their families, schools, and communities, and know they deserve better. Shouting with indignation, pain, and passion, they voice what Maxine, as if from an existential godmother, has written, imagined, struggled to portray in her writings and through the arts. But alone, lonely, they scream. Maxine writes:

> This is a time of suddenly acknowledged multiplicity and diversity. Voices long ignored or long repressed are making themselves heard, many of them demanding that we look at things from their perspectives and recognize how numerous are the ways of defining what is "real." (1993a, p. 241)

In this legacy I hear Shannon Faulkner, the vibrant young woman from South Carolina who grew up longing to attend a "good" public college. She looked at the Citadel, an all-male, public, military college of enormous prestige and fat-cat alumni networks, and asked "why not?" So she applied, using her real full name—Shannon Richie Faulkner—and got accepted, only to be rejected once the institution learned her real genital status. A *New York Times* feature story recounts:

When, in the course of the trial, college officials indicated that they would insist that her head be shaved the moment she became a full cadet, something all new students undergo, she shrugged and said, "It's just hair." When the college proposed that she sleep in the infirmary if she became a cadet, she ran, laughing, to her mother. "Mom!" she said exuberantly, "they think I'm a germ!" [Shannon explains] . . . "I've tried to open the door," Faulkner says. "My knock isn't that big a sound. But it's like the knock in 'The Wizard of Oz' [*sic*]. It set up this echo through the halls until it was heard by everyone." (Manegold, 1994)

Shannon has, in Maxine's words, "refused the normal." Daily she fought white women and men on the street and on the campus who forced her back into the box of normalcy. One black cadet at The Citadel, Von Mickel, alone defended her stance. Amidst the chaos, Shannon smiled and wore proudly a tee shirt that read, "2000 Bulldogs [Citadel football Team] and a Bitch."

In this same legacy I've watched Heidi Leiter and Missy Peters, two young women who went to the prom in Manassas, Virginia, together, arm in arm, a lesbian couple who just wanted to dance, in public, with one another, just like we were supposed to do at the prom. *Glamour* magazine tells us:

Seventeen-year-old Heidi Leiter scrutinizes herself in the mirror on the back of the closet door, one minute pleased with her appearance, the next minute totally discontent. She's so nervous about attending Osbourn High School's senior prom tonight that she hasn't been able to eat. "I feel like I'm getting ready to play the biggest district-tournament game *of my life,*" she says.

"*I* feel like I'm drunk or something, in these shoes!" says her 20-year-old friend Missy Peters, walking unsteadily around the bedroom in the two-inch-high pumps she borrowed.

"Missy in heels," says Candi Schleig, a friend who has come to watch the preparations. "I never thought I'd see the day."

"You guys look great," another friend, Tammy Stephens, says supportively. . . . Later at the prom . . .

"Smile when you stare at people!" Heidi whispered to Missy as she watched her survey the crowd.

"Heidi," Missy said, feeling gleeful. *"We're making history sitting right here on our butts."*" (Cunningham, 1992)

In this legacy I place Rovanda Bowen, a young biracial woman, a senior in high school in Weedowee, Alabama, who listened, in 1994, to her principal ask the senior class, "Who here is taking someone of the other race to the prom?" When he saw many hands go up, he canceled the prom. Gorgeous and gutsy, Rovanda politely asked, "And who would you like me to take to the prom?" To which Principal Humphries allegedly responded, "You were a mistake. I want to make sure no more mistakes happen." Her lawsuit, a civil suit for damages and college tuition, has been settled, but the case against Humphries—to remove him as principal—lingered on as he engendered wide-ranging community support. By 1997, Humphries has been elected Superintendent of Schools.

And in this legacy I can taste the bittersweet "victory" of Lin Walker, a Vietnamese-American woman, a track star, a pre-med junior in college, who in the early 1990s sued her Vietnam-veteran father for years of child sexual abuse. In 1993 he was taken out of the courtroom in "cuffs." Lin watched, "I guess I won. My father is going to prison. My mother testified that I hallucinated it all. And my sister was asked, 'Did your father rape you?' and answered, 'It's not rape if I consented.' I lost my family. I won the case."

These young women all looked at the world around them and said, No. Gutsy, rebellious, pained, and courageous, they imagined a world of justice, and they demanded no less. These are the granddaughters, in tee shirts, tuxedos, heels, mascara and sneakers, of Maxine Greene, who voice a powerful "resistance to the taken-for-granted, a desire, a way of seeing, the awareness of what is not yet . . . a critical consciousness of what is ordinarily obscured" (Greene, 1992, pp. 205, 213). They live for Greener pastures. Like tea kettles whistling across the nation, alone they fight for worlds not yet imagined. They struggle with words not yet invented. They ask for justice never envisioned. They work to right that which is wrong. They can't fathom what justice would look like. They can't name who will take care of them. But they are alone, fighting for personal rights—not always for transformation.

For these young women, public institutions, schools, families, and communities have refused to be sites of support, comfort, scenes from which to draw strength. For these young women, schools, families, and communities have instead been scenes of torture, denial, exclusion. Yet there is nothing victim-like about them. With the passion of Hester Prynne, the strength born of exclusion, and the convictions of Maxine Greene, they aim to save the world from itself:

> Again, I wonder at my own hubris, writing as I have, speaking as I have on ethical issues, feminist issues, curriculum, youth problems, literature and literary theory, civil rights, pluralism and multiculturalism, the arts and aesthetics, postmodernism, the new epistemologies, existentialism and phenomenology. Much of this has been due, strangely enough, to my experiences of exclusion: were it not for my being excluded from the inner circles of philosophy, or even from the department of Teachers College, I would not have had to reach out on my own (Greene, 1997, p. 14).

In each of their home contexts, these women have become martyrs of public opinion, peer and adult. And where are the grownups? Are we creating safe spaces? Are we interrupting the silences, taking on the violence, laying blankets for them to stretch out their identities? Or are we watching, awed and scared?

CREATING SPACES

Maxine paints spaces of strength, a collective and deliberate "not yet" in a recent essay:

> I can only say once more that situations have to be deliberately created in order for students to break free in this way. Coming together in their pluralities and their differences, they may finally articulate how they are choosing themselves and what the projects are by means of which they can identify themselves. We all need to recognize each other in our striving, our becoming, our invention of the possible. And, yes, it is a question of acting in the light of a vision of what might be a vision that enables people to perceive the voids, take heed of the violations and move (if they can) to repair. Such a vision, we have found, can be enlarged and enriched by those on the margins, whoever they are. (Greene, 1993b, pp. 219–220)

Contrast Maxine's dream for space, for places to explore, undress, roll around and be comforted with Nikki Richardson's poem, "There Is No Place Left to Go" (1993), written at age 16 by a young African American student who attends a high school in Brooklyn:

THERE IS NO PLACE LEFT TO GO

There was no place left to go.
She ran away from home.
She went everywhere.
She went to her boyfriend's house,
He told her to leave.
He couldn't keep her.
She went to family members' houses,
But there was no one home.
She's walking up and down the street.
She was scared and nervous.
A man came to her, he was talking to her
and trying to rub up against her.
She ran away from him.

There was no place to go.
She heard voices,
there was no place to go.
She walked to the nearest park,
She saw a bench.
She laid down,
and went to sleep,
and when she awakened,
she was home,
because there was no place left to go.[1]

Nikki asks, Where are the safe spaces?

In the late 1980s, I thought maybe schools could be these safe spaces. In a study of school dropouts in the late 1980s, I was appalled to learn that among urban students those youngsters *most* clever at deciphering the raced, gendered, and classed lettering on the stop signs of life, teenagers like Nikki, leave schools feeling marginal, alienated, and unsafe. I was knocked out of my naivete when I recognized that in acts of defiance, young women and men drop out. Smart and critical, they withdraw before the schools force them out. Soon thereafter, they pay an enormous price for their insight (Fine, 1991). With a bold exit, they almost certainly assure their own academic and economic dead end. Defiant acts of resistance, perhaps necessary to breathe, yield harsh economic and social consequences. But as Nikki would say, there was no place left to go.

Now it's the 1990s. Not a few, but *most,* urban students can and do narrate raw critique of economic and racial arrangements. Rap, videos, and walking the streets provide daily testimony of structural dead ends, institutional stop signs, and the destruction that has infected their homes and communities. Where does their critique live? What does it prompt? Social psychologist Jennifer Pastor recently sat in on a Girls Talk session at a middle school on the Upper West Side. The room was filled with sixteen girls, white, African American and Latina, ages eleven through thirteen, poor and working class. It was early in the year, and a few wanted to talk about "rape." In a talk filled with pain, passion, and critique, there was a sense of helplessness, futility, destiny. One girl said that she didn't want to talk about it. Pressed, gently, by her peers, she eventually mumbled that it was just too close. Jennifer reports, "The most amazing thing happened. Within the 45 minutes of the group, they went around and 9 of the 16 girls said they had been raped. They cried, held each other, and vowed not to let go. The school stopped. Classes couldn't come in. They didn't want to be broken apart" (Pastor, McCormick, & Fine, 1996). Individual pain, critique, and scars define young women and men.

Passionate survivors and resisters, they have no illusions of schools, families, or communities as a place to "make sense," to see the unseeable or speak the unspeakable. So now we ask, how does social critique—so vibrant, so embodied, and so dispersed—affect a sense of *possibility* in today's young adolescents? (Pastor, McCormick, & Fine, 1996).

Pastor set out to study that question (1993). Eager to know how young people's keen sense of racism, gender abuse, and economic injustice affects their sense of "what's possible for me," she surveyed 136 early adolescents, African American and Latino, asking about their perceptions of racism and their sense of personal possibilities. In the crisp language of social science, Pastor wrote:

> Students' perceived likelihood of achieving certain high status occupations, such as medical doctor and lawyer, drop significantly when students believe that racism negatively impacts their racial or ethnic group. The results also show that students' perceptions of fewer opportunities in the society correlated significantly with their reporting a greater likelihood of achieving the low status occupation of truck driver. If inner-city students perceive that the dominant society imposes restrictions upon what they can achieve due to racism or a limited opportunity structure, then students may not engage in the academic behaviors that would allow them to achieve high prestige possible self images in their futures. By undervaluing academic behaviors, the inner-city student is protected from feeling the threat of failure in a society that tends to limit their opportunities. (pp. 27–28)

Pastor's data, like Faynesse Miller's and Howard Stevenson's, are devastating. All of these researchers are finding that young people who are most astute about race relations and economic relations can envision only the most diminished sense of "what's possible" for me. For these young women and men, critique does not provoke possibility (see also Fine & Weis, 1997). They have been decoupled. Like Maxine's writings, they are awake, critical, and conscious. And yet they are despairing.

Young people today, alienated from social movements and unaware or cynical about ideologies for social change, can't quite imagine that much of anything is going to change, for the better, in their lifetimes. They can't quite grasp collective mobilization amidst so much distrust. Children of the Reagan-Bush era, they certainly can't envision a public sphere serving their needs or passions. Surrounding the bright and still vibrant young women noted earlier in this essay swells an adolescent sea of distrust, despair, but a yearning—looking for safe spaces.

So now the burden is on us, on adults, to carve out "spaces," to inspire a sense of the "not yet," to reinvent schools and communities that are engaging for young people who have seen more devastation, felt more pain, and witnessed more violence than anyone should. Can we create contexts, schools in particular, in which social critique can be braided with a sense of social possibilities? Maxine, that sweet light in dark times, dreams on:

> Then, as now, I was obsessive about connecting the domains of imagi-
> nation, the arts, social commitment and cultural transformation. I
> wanted (I still want) to play some part in breaking through the rigid
> structures, the exclusions, the constraints that prevent people from look-
> ing at things as if they could be others. I wanted (and I still want) peo-
> ple to become "wide awake" in Virginia Woolf's sense and Henry Davis
> Thoreau's and Albert Camus' and Alfred Schutz's and John Dewey's—
> to refuse passivity, to refuse to be mere functionaries. (1997, p. 16)

Come with me to Williamsburg, New York.

BIENVENIDOS EL PUENTE

In the shadow of the Brooklyn Bridge grows a community of fifteen- to forty-five-year-old scholars, activists, and political kin tied to a common mission—El Puente Academy for Peace and Justice. Enter the massive, gorgeous once-church, once-opera house, and you'll find a small high school grown up from the soil of pain, struggle, and passion that defines Williamsburg, Brooklyn. The school is one of the New Visions schools— public, small, and carved out of community life. El Puente sets as its mission the education of smart, critical activists, white, Black, and Latino students propelled toward collective redress of social injustice.

Students of all colors with many styles, languages, and dialects fill the main room, which is decorated with posters, billboards and murals in English and Spanish, demanding peace, justice, and struggle. Adults and adolescents circle as they construct common work, organize the Toxic Avengers, plan the women's group, arrange for Family Night, and design tomorrow's curriculum on the relation between asthma and local envi-ronmental conditions. Conversations among and between students and adults, called "facilitators," target social injustices, dissecting them as if we were in a traditional biology class surrounding a frog. Then they organize, on Fridays, their community action projects. Working the ques-tion, "How do we seek justice?" they respond, "Are we going to sit back or are we going to make our voices heard?"

This is a school—indeed, it teaches everyone all the time. It captures at once a commitment to individual knowledge, social critique, and col-lective mobilizing. The school grew up out of an after-school program, successful, community-based, engaged, and trustworthy. Striving for "excellence in body, mind, spirit, and community," the youth learn to "talk, turning their anger into productive work, into community building," says one of the facilitators.

Jessica, a young Latina ninth grader, explains that her community action project involves the Wellness Clinic, vaccinating and educating neighborhood children about health, wellness, and healing. Lamar, a young African American, explains that his project crosses the borders into the Hasidic community, serving as an ethnographer, asking questions of culture and tradition, eager to meet with the rabbi, to ask questions of cultural sameness and difference.

As Lamar described his project in a church basement to an audience of "out-of-towners," members of Urban Boards of Education, you could hear a pin drop. He was about to annotate the questions he would ask the "Great Rabbi." He reported only the first question, "Why do your people have so many station wagons?" Much to our giggling relief. Then he whispered to some of the adults, "The other question is how can they leave their babies, in carriages, unattended as they shop?" Questions of connection, humanity, and safety bridge communities in which adults barely speak and more often spar.

On the early fall day when I visited, with Naomi Barber from the New Visions staff at Fund for the City of New York, we toured the academy with the magnificent co-director, Frances Lucerna: Once dancer, always activist, spiritual leader, teacher, and, now, politician. We were mesmerized by the English/Art class, in which ninth graders were designing their personal autobiographies in their *Who Am I?* books. We were breathless as we entered José's biology class, in which the links between the first, third, and fourth worlds were articulated all over the board, through global analyses of health, environmentalism, and NAFTA. José and the other students were planning to rent a Geiger counter so they could track and document radioactivity throughout their communities.

We watched students engage the passions, politics, and very technical smarts of their lives, even as they resisted, sometimes, the intricate interdisciplinary links that their facilitator, a recent Ivy League graduate who has come home to Williamsburg, was trying to make. And we heard about Benny, a new student who "missed many days last year" and decided to transfer to a school where "someone might care." Benny had just testified at public hearings in Harlem on human rights violations in the United States. After an eloquent analysis of the health care crisis in New York City, dotted with statistics and updated figures about the incidence of asthma and the ranking of Williamsburg and Bushwick in pollution-related diseases, Benny testified:

> I believe that turning people away is very insensitive and inhuman. I
> know how it feels to call an ambulance and to have it not come. When
> I got shot defending my mother from a robber in East New York
> Brooklyn, ambulatory services were requested but never obtained. I was
> driven in a police car over 10 minutes later. This is a human rights vio-
> lation which is inflicted upon us by the insensitive, the careless and the
> racist policies. I come to you today to not only inform you but to see
> if we can find a solution to these problems in our community because
> no matter how much we deny it, we're all one race, the human race, WE
> ALL BLEED RED!

Maybe that's what the gorgeous red lips of Maxine Greene have been
trying to tell us for so long.

Benny, like Shannon and the young women and men struggling across
the country, is trying to create a world "not yet." But at El Puente, students are never alone—never tea kettles whistling on silent nights. Nurtured
by Frances Lucerna, Luis Garden Acosta, and many adults and young people in the community, these young men and women feel the arms and
hear the words, take seriously the embrace and the spirit of a community born to make the impossible possible. El Puente springs from the
reservoir of hope and passion that nourishes the community of
Williamsburg, and it gives back even more.

In this spirit, in that context, the words and dreams of Maxine Greene
carry:

> a kind of tradition, which is still alive, although a lot of people reject it.
> It is very largely a social existentialist tradition—focused on breaking
> out of anchorage, on wide-awakeness, on the risks of freedom. It is in
> my writing because I wanted so much to bring it out of German lec-
> ture halls into public schools, into teacher lounges, into my own
> classes, into the Center.

The tradition voiced by Maxine fills the air, supporting like wings so many
of us in our daily work of flying just above "reality." The 1990s are pierced
with individual young scholars and activists screaming for better; our
schools, like the New Vision schools inside the burning hearts of El Puente,
are bringing to life communities of justice and vision, flickering, fragile
and lighting our way in ever darkening times. Maxine, who has always
refused the darkness and the silence, demands—and enables—no less.

NOTE

1. This poem was written in the context of a project done in Nikki Richardson's high school, which was a collaborative program between The Poetry Exchange and The School Partnership Program of New York University.

REFERENCES

Cunningham, A. (1992, June). Not just another prom night: M. Peters and H. Leiter attend prom as a same sex couple in Manassas, VA. *Glamour, 90,* 222–262.

Fine, M. (1991). *Framing dropouts: Notes on the politics of an urban public high school.* Albany: State University of New York Press.

Fine, M., & Weis, L. (Eds.). (1997). *As the century closes: Urban America speaks.* Boston: Beacon.

Greene, M. (1992). The art of being present. In K. Weiler & C. Mitchell (Eds.), *What schools can do* (pp. 203–216). Albany, NY: SUNY.

Greene, M. (1993a). Gender, multiplicity and voice. In S. Biklen & D. Pollard (Eds.), *Gender and education* (pp. 241–256). Chicago, IL: NSSE.

Greene, M. (1993b). Diversity and inclusion. *Teachers College Record, 2,* 211–221.

Greene, M. (1997). Exclusions and awakenings. In A. Neumann, & P. Peterson (Eds.), *Learning from our lives: Women, research, and autobiography.* New York: Teachers College Press.

Manegold, C. (1994, September 11). Shannon Faulkner, one of the boys. *New York Times Magazine,* 56–59.

Pastor, J. (1993). *Possible selves and academic achievement.* Second-Year Project, CUNY Graduate Center, New York.

Pastor, J., McCormick, J., & Fine, M. (1996). Makin' homes: An urban girl thing. In B. J. Ross Leadbeater, & N. Way (Eds.), *Urban girls: Resisting stereotypes, creating identities* (pp. 15–34). New York: New York University Press.

Richardson, N. (1993). There is no place left to go. The Poetry Exchange.

20

The Social Context of Educational Reform

Jean Anyon

The most important aspect of Maxine Greene's work for me is her insistence that to understand education we must consider the various contexts that affect it. Maxine often uses the arts as a lens through which to view the social forces impinging on schools and students. In *The Dialectic of Freedom* (1988), for example, she reveals, through literature, ways that social phenomena and patterns affect varieties of schooling. Thus, she relates that when Huck Finn and Jim's river raft is torn asunder by a steam boat, we can see on-rushing technology tearing apart stable communities. School had not prepared Huck for the society to come, but for the pieties of a slave society.

For Maxine, the social context is never far away from schools, students, and learning, and it and its history can be clearly viewed through authorial and other artistic lenses. In this chapter, I also will discuss a social context that affects education: the current poverty and racial marginalization in America's inner cities. I will summarize ways in which the brutal urban milieu can eviscerate educational reform efforts, and will summarize twentieth century political and economic trends and patterns that have created this milieu. I choose as a case an inner-city school that I have been studying in a large urban district in the Northeastern United States (Newark, New Jersey). This school recently experienced a massive—and by all accounts unsuccessful—attempt at reform (Newark Board of Education, 1992; Anyon, 1994, 1995a, 1995b, 1997). I believe an understanding of the social context in which the school is embedded can provide a deeper understanding of what transpires in failed reform attempts than can an explanation based purely on "educational" factors, such as a lack of staff development, district and school organization, or onerous state educational regulations, as important as these may obviously be (see, for example, Lieberman, 1995; Sarason, 1990).

THE SOCIAL CONTEXT

The K-8 school to be discussed here is located in an inner-city minority ghetto (Wilson, 1987, 1991). Census data from 1990 show that, in the census tract in which the school is located, 45% of all persons have incomes below the poverty level; of female-headed householder families with related children under eighteen years, 66% are below the poverty level; of female-headed householder families with related children under five years, 82% are under the poverty level. According to the 1990 census, the per capita income in the census tract in which the research site is located was $7,647. (The per capita income in 1990 in the city was $9,437. Per capita income in the state was $24,936, which was 33% higher than the national average. New Jersey, the state in which the school is located, was in 1990 the nation's second wealthiest state.) Ninety-nine percent of the students in the school and 78% of the students in the district are poor and qualify for free lunch. The student body of the school is 71% African American, 27% Hispanic, and 2% Asian and white. The social context of this school, then, is of an impoverished minority ghetto, with all the attendant problems of unemployment, underemployment, drug use, child neglect and abuse; stressful, danger-filled, often chaotic lives lived close to the bustle of the universities and the downtown business district, but far from the mainstream of American middle-class society and social power.

INSIDE THE REFORM

Preceding as well as during the period of the study, the school was the focus of a massive effort at reform, with twenty-eight improvement projects underway in the building between 1989 and 1993. Almost all of these projects were carried out in the school by white consultants or other professionals from local colleges, universities, and the state, or managerial representatives of the city's corporations. I participated in the reform between 1992 and 1993 primarily as staff developer. I carried out workshops in cooperative learning in several of the eight target schools and subsequently assisted teachers in their classrooms (see Anyon, 1994, 1997).

From 1992 to '93, 51% of the certificated full-time teachers in the city were black, and 8.5% were Hispanic. In schools (such as the research site) where African American children are the majority, there are more black teachers than at district schools where the majority of the children are Hispanic or white. In the school discussed here, of twenty-five classroom teachers, sixteen (64%) are black, six (24%) are Hispanic, and three (12%) are white. All aides in the school were community women, most from near-by housing projects, and were African American or Hispanic.

During ten months in which I worked with teachers in their class-rooms as one of the "reformers," I observed that reform activity in the school was characterized by the following four phenomena (see Anyon, 1995b, for substantiating data):

1. Sociocultural differences/distances between white, professional, or executive reformers and the teachers and parents. These differences led to miscommunication and mistrust, and only minimal success on joint efforts at reform. For example, a series of meetings between two retired white executives (who had volunteered to assist the parent group improve their efforts to get more parents involved) and the school's parent group came to naught. The leader of the parent group said, "They're just white men tellin' us what to do," and one of the executives said, "these parents don't want to do anything."

2. Sociocultural differences between a white, middle-class curriculum presented in textbooks written in standard English—a dialect not spoken by the students (marginalized from the mainstream in a ghetto neighborhood) or by many of the teachers (themselves reared in working-poor or poor minority neighborhoods of this or other cities). This disjunction between the languages spoken in the school and the language in the texts had the potential to cause mathematical and scientific confusion on the part of the children (and some teachers) and, in reading, alienation on the part of students from much of the textual material. Such confusion and alienation would reduce student comprehension and therefore academic performance as well (see Orr, 1987; Baratz, 1970; and Delpit, 1996, among others).

3. An abusive school environment in which teachers' and administrators' interactions with students were often characterized by degrading comments and outright psychological (and sometimes physical) abuse—a degradation of which the parents did not have the social power to prevent. Abuse of students in the school district is apparently not confined to the school I observed. Last year the district as a whole—with only 4% of the state's students—reported over 40% of all incidents of abuse by school employees reported by school systems to the state.

    The abusive school environment created an oppositional student culture and a refusal to cooperate during class—and often, during standardized testing. This opposition to instruction and evaluation led to diminished academic accomplishment on the part of the students (see New Jersey State Department of Education, 1993; Kohl, 1994).

4. An almost universal feeling of resignation on the part of school personnel to failure of the reforms because of (as staff stated in interviews) the overwhelming nature of the students' social problems, and because of the history of failure of reform in the district in the last thirty years. The expectations of failure were accompanied by teacher explanations expressing the belief that even if the students did learn to read and write, or even if the reforms did work, it would not be enough to "do any good," and "there would be no jobs" available for the students later anyway, so what was the use? The misery of the students' lives and the lack of a receptive economy impinged on reform by producing a profound antipathy to the effort needed to make curricular and other educational changes.

I have argued that these four characteristics of the school can be attributed in large part to the social context of poverty and racial marginalization in which the school is embedded. This social environment impinged on educational reform attempts and made the successful implementation of reform extremely difficult. How did such poverty and racial isolation in this (and other U.S. cities) come about?

HISTORY, SOCIAL CONTEXT, AND THE PROBLEMS OF SCHOOL REFORM

As the above summary suggests, I believe that concomitants of poverty and racial isolation vitiated educational improvement efforts in this inner-city school. If we understand what economic and social trends have caused the ravishment of the environment in which the inner-city ghetto school is located, we can accurately identify action that would remove these powerful impediments to school reform. To this end, in the following section, I sketch a brief, preliminary analysis of this history. I will take the four characteristics of reform activity and show—historically—how each problem has resulted in important ways from "noneducational" economic, political, or other social (e.g., cultural) phenomena and trends.

1. The cultural distance between participants in the reform results in large part from the separation and alienation in our society between blacks and whites, and between poor people of color and whites from professional and corporate backgrounds (Hacker, 1992). There are his-

torical reasons why this great gap in experience, language, and beliefs exists. In the city I am studying, for example, as in most other older American cities, important history includes the following: During the middle decades of the nineteenth century, wealthy industrialists and owners of businesses lived nearby their factories and shops, in the downtown areas of developing cities. Close nearby lived their workers—immigrants from Ireland, Germany, and the British Isles.

Between 1890 and 1920, many of the elite moved to the surrounding countryside, and with the installation of a network of trolleys connecting the city and the surrounding countryside by 1900, the middle classes began to follow. European immigrants continued to pour into the cities and moved into the older wooden houses already in disrepair. Beginning in the 1930s and accelerating after World War II, business and manufacturing firms left the inner city for the developing suburbs, and large numbers of white, skilled workers and middle-class families abandoned the cities to work and live in these suburbs. During the same years, hundreds of thousands of rural impoverished southern blacks—most of whom were agricultural workers idled by the mechanization of agriculture—arrived in the Northern and Midwestern cities. The only housing that owners would rent to them were deteriorated dwellings in the central cities abandoned by the last wave of white immigrants.

In 1937 and continuing until the middle 1960s, housing rehabilitation (urban renewal) and the creation of high-rise ghetto housing (which was typically segregated), combined with redlining practices of the banks and real estate companies, resulted in extreme residential segregation in the older Northern and Midwestern cities.

When combined with the history of job segregation in the American economy (to be discussed below), housing segregation has resulted in blacks and whites living in geographically distinct areas and having little if any familiarity with each other. The minority inner-city resident (usually poor) is completely alien to the white resident of suburbs (in which nationally under ten% of residents are African American).

Because of the unfamiliarity, the media can instill fear in suburban whites and resentment in city blacks when they report black crime but not white-collar crime, which is most often executed by middle-class and upper-middle-class whites. Suburban whites fear the inner-city minority residents, and the inner-city minority residents resent and are suspicious of whites for their alleged and real privileges. This suspicion and mistrust is expressed in educational improvement projects in the conflict and mistrust between retired executives and parents, or when white "preppy-looking" psychologists from an affluent suburb try to tell black teachers (most of whom are from working-class or working-poor families) how to "cooperate" with each other—and the teachers resent and ignore the advice.

2. The sociocultural differences between curricular reforms and students' language and experience arises from the same distances discussed above, with the additional feature that these curricular disjunctions are also a manifestation of the fact that (as I and others have shown) white, upper- and middle-class experience is represented, catalogued, and transmitted in the texts, because that is the culture and experience of the dominant group (Anyon, 1979). That this story of world wars, the expansion of the railroads, industrialization, and the Carnegies and Rockefellers does not reverberate with the experience of children and youth in the ghetto does not need elaboration. Ghetto youth—for all their alleged bravado and showmanship—have often never been outside of the neighborhood; some have never been in an elevator, never been on a train, or in a car, or to a doctor's office.

Similarly, the texts are written in white standard English. However, inner-city dialect (practically synonymous with black dialect) is spoken by almost all the children in the inner-city school I studied—by blacks, Hispanics, and the few poor whites. It is also spoken much of the day by many of the city's black teachers. There are cultural attitudes of difference and pride involved in speaking black dialect (as when one is fluent in a standard dialect, too), but a good deal of the use of inner-city dialect by the students results from their marginalization from the mainstream.

3. The abusive classroom and school environment, in which both white and black teachers and administrators often degrade and otherwise psychologically abuse the students, also arises from complicated causes and can have various meanings. However, it is my view that the systematic degradation of the impoverished minority ghetto students, wherein they are treated as if they were of little or no worth—as if they were dispensable—arises as a consequence of ghettoization and their low social status. Perceiving low-status persons as if they are barely human has roots not only in the social and economic facts of having little social power, but also in characteristics of colonial-type relationships. Albert Memmi, Franz Fanon, and Paulo Freire have demonstrated how, in colonial societies, the white colonists generally view natives (colonized people of color) as subhuman or substandard in an unconscious way of keeping them the 'other' and separate from the colonial self. This view of the native permeates social interchange among the groups. It serves to maintain the white colonialists' sense of superiority, and the natives' belief in the validity of their own situation of oppression (Memmi, 1965/1991; Fanon, 1967; Said, 1978).

Memmi, Fanon, and Freire have also pointed out that in many cases natives who have climbed from the bottom of the class or caste structure into the lower-middle or middle classes view other natives still on the bottom as subhuman or degraded, or of very little worth—this also serves to separate the black middle-class self from those still on the bottom. This phenomenon, it seems to me, operates in ghetto schools like the one discussed here where black teachers systematically abuse the "natives"—the impoverished minority students. When white teachers abuse minority students, it is the dominant social view they express—the black poor are difficult, not good at school, and of little potential social value.

4. Teachers' and administrators' expectations that the reform will fail arise in part from past experience in the school system. The district has been attempting to upgrade the achievement of students in its inner-city schools since 1970. School personnel are cynical about the efforts of the Board of Education, which they state is "chaotic," "full of corruption," and "doesn't really care about the kids." The history of the city is, as with other older U.S. cities, one of extensive patronage from old ward-based machines and "patronage mills" (in operation since the late nineteenth century). Because of this history of patronage (begun before the turn of the century by Germans, whose dominance gave way to the Irish machine, then to Jewish organized crime in the 1930s, the Italian machine aided by the Italian mafia in the 1960s, and the African American's domination of the patronage and graft at the Board of Education since the late 1970s (Anyon, 1997). There are a large number of political appointees and unqualified workers at all levels of the system, as there were in 1900. Critical observers of the district throughout the last hundred years have argued that extensive patronage has led to incompetence and lack of qualification rife at all levels of the school system (see, e.g., Strayer, 1942; New Jersey State Department of Education, 1993).

There is a further dimension of the expectations of failure of reform. And that is—as many teachers and students state in interviews—even if the reform were to succeed, it would not positively affect the students' futures because the students have overwhelming life problems that the reforms "don't touch." A pervasive attitude expressed by both students and staff is summed up in the following quote: "Even if they [the students] do learn to read and write, there aren't any jobs for them." As a ten year old told me, "There aren't no jobs. That's why kids drop out [of school]." The economic reality of no future jobs for the students is painfully apparent to both students and adults. Why try? Why work hard? There will be no reward for such effort.

The economic history of the development, decline, and recent isolation of America's cities is the root cause here. Between 1880 and World

War II the American economy was primarily an industrial economy in which a factory worker could leave poverty behind on his hard-earned "family wage." The industrial wages for skilled workers helped white working-class families move into the middle class, and into the burgeoning suburbs during the 1940s and '50s. When rural blacks moved to the Northern and Midwestern cities en mass after World War II, most of the industry—and most of the skilled jobs—had already left for the surrounding areas. Most of the rest were closed to blacks by employer and labor union discrimination.

During the last several decades, the economy has changed fundamentally in other ways. Deindustrialized, heavily based not on manufacturing but on service, and newly financial, technical, and global, the economy has yielded a bifurcated wage structure that reflects the bifurcated structure of available jobs: Most new jobs are either very low-wage, unskilled service jobs or very high-income, financial/technical professional jobs. Moreover, the vast majority of jobs created are now low-income service jobs; thus, almost 20% of American full-time workers' wages are below the poverty line (Sassen, 1991; Koretz, 1995).

So, trends begun in the 1930s (but temporarily halted during World War II), as manufacturing and skilled jobs relocated in the suburbs, and recently to other countries, has left unskilled workers in the inner cities without well-paying jobs. Currently in the cities, there are few if any jobs for high school graduates that pay a wage above the poverty line. The students in the city schools know this, and the teachers know it, too. The knowledge of what kind of economic future the inner-city students are highly likely to face produces a culture of resignation that overpowers good intentions, good deeds, and educational improvement projects.

CONCLUSION

It seems to me that placing city schools and recent urban school reform in the social context reveals that the quality of a city school (and the success or failure of reform efforts) reflects the economic health of the city and the neighborhood, the perceived potential economic value of the students, and the perceived social clout of the parent population. When you trace the history of a school system such as the one I have studied, you can see that during the period of industrialization (1850–1917) when the city was producing substantial profits for its financial classes, and when the students were perceived as having a potential contribution to that profit as (factory) workers, even though the population was poor and immigrant, the schools were bristling with nationally renowned administrators and innovations.

This city, and most others in our country, is now economically moribund; many neighborhoods are crumbling ghettos. The student population is perceived as having no potential profitable economic role to play. The schools reflect this perception and these conditions. The fact that the parent and student population is perceived as deficient, as impoverished, as dysfunctional minorities, lends a racially based "legitimacy" to the condition of the schools and the failure of reform to reverse the educational decline.

I am suggesting that the structural basis for failure in inner-city schools—and the failure of educational reform there—is political, economic, and cultural. These deep structures must be changed before meaningful school improvement projects can be successfully implemented. Educational reforms cannot compensate for the ravages of society. Thus, I think (and I believe Maxine Greene would agree with me) the most promising solution to educational resignation and failure in the inner city is the ultimate elimination of poverty and racial degradation. Thus— whether we want to admit (and deal with it) or not—educational success in the inner city requires the ultimate elimination of the debilitating social context in which these schools are located.

REFERENCES

Anyon, J. (1979). Ideology and U.S. history textbooks. *Harvard Educational Review, 49*(3), 361–386.

Anyon, J. (1994). Teacher development and reform in an inner-city school. *Teachers College Record, 96*(1), 14–31.

Anyon, J. (1995a). Inner city school reform: Toward useful theory. *Urban Education, 30*(1), 56–70.

Anyon, J. (1995b). Race, social class, and reform in an inner city school. *Teachers College Record, 97*(1), 69–94.

Anyon, J. (1997). *Ghetto schooling: A political economy of urban educational reform.* New York: Teachers College Press.

Baratz, J. (1970). Beginning readers for speakers of divergent dialects. In J. A. Figurel (Ed.), *Reading goals for the disadvantaged* (pp. 77–83). Newark, DE: International Reading Association.

Delpit, L. (1996). *Other people's children.* New York: The New Press.

Fanon, F. (1967). *Black skin, white masks.* New York: Grove Press.

Freire, P. (1970). *Pedagogy of the oppressed.* New York: Herder & Herder.

Greene, M. (1988). *The dialectic of freedom.* New York: Teachers College Press.

Hacker, A. (1992). *Two nations: Black and white, separate, hostile, unequal.* New York: Charles Scribner's Sons.

Kohl, H. (1994). *'I won't learn from you' and other thoughts on creative malad-justment.* New York: The New Press.

Koretz, G. (1995, March 20). Why incomes grew less equal. *Business Week,* p. 24.

Lieberman, A. (1995). *The work of restructuring schools: Building from the ground up.* New York: Teachers College Press.

Memmi, A. (1991). *The colonizer and the colonized* Boston: Beacon Press. (Original work published 1965)

New Jersey State Department of Education. (1993). *Level III evaluation of the Newark School System.* Trenton, NJ: Author.

Newark Board of Education. (1992). *Restructuring urban schools in Newark, NJ: An evaluation of the cluster program.* Newark, NJ: Author.

Orr, E. W. (1987). *Twice as less: Black English and the performance of black students in mathematics and science,* New York: W. W. Norton.

Said, E. (1978). *Orientalism.* New York: Pantheon.

Sarason, S. (1990). *Predictable failure of educational reform: Can we change course before it's too late?* San Francisco, CA: Jossey Bass.

Sassen, S. (1991). *Global city: New York, London, Tokyo.* Princeton, NJ: Princeton University Press.

Strayer, G. D. (1942). *The report of a survey of the public schools of Newark, New Jersey.* New York: Teachers College Bureau of Publications.

Wilson, W. J. (1987). *The truly disadvantaged: The inner city, the underclass, and public policy.* Chicago, IL: University of Chicago Press.

Wilson, W. J. (1991). Public policy research and the truly disadvantaged. In C. Jencks and P. E. Peterson (Eds.), *The urban underclass* (pp. 460–482). Washington, DC: The Brookings Institution.

21

Pursuing Public Space: Maxine Greene and Sameness in Utter Diversity

Norm Fruchter

I first met Maxine Greene in the spring of 1982, when I was a Revson Fellow at Columbia University taking courses at Teachers College. Maxine's classes were obligatory, friends assured me, for anyone trying to understand how American society could simultaneously affirm public education as the key to democratic participation while systematically destroying schooling's capacity, at least in urban areas, to develop future citizens. The course I took was a large lecture class that Maxine conducted as a stand-up philosopher, creating an expanding dialogue by provoking those of us who weren't too awed to respond. Since our session was an evening class, Maxine came to us straight from the six o'clock news, which, during those dyspeptic days of the early Reagan administration, spurred her into opening monologues punctuated by outrage, her hoarse voice sometimes breaking into plaintiveness but never into resignation.

Maxine introduced us to the notion of public space as the terrain on which citizens could come together to discuss and debate how to advance the common good. Through her discussion and the readings she assigned, Maxine focused us on how past societies had provided such public spaces, as well as how contemporary societies had dissolved them. Obsessed with how the media contributed to the collapse of public space by substituting spectacle for dialogue, Maxine invited us to imagine how plain speech and considerations of the common good might replace the endless media celebration of private consumption.

So we read Hannah Arendt's *The Human Condition* (1958) to understand how Arendt had conceptualized the existence of public space in both the Greek city-states and the Roman republic, as well as how she saw its displacement and colonization by the housekeeping functions of

229

modernizing societies. (Arendt was similarly concerned with the disappearance of *private* space, its transformation into privacy and its replacement by intimacy, but that is another matter.) Arendt's view of the worldly reality we share "relies on the simultaneous presence of innumerable perspectives and aspects in which the common world presents itself. . . . Only where things can be seen by many in a variety of aspects without changing their identity, so that those who are gathered around them know that they see sameness in utter diversity, can worldly reality truly and reliably appear" (p. 57).

For Maxine, of course, the "sameness in utter diversity" that generates the true appearance of "worldly reality" still occurs, or at least has the potential to occur, in the sphere of the arts, when we give ourselves to the particular vision of a powerful work of art. But her task, in the course I took, was to make us think about the possibility of reinventing or recapturing public space. So we also read Jürgen Habermas's *Technology and Science as Ideology* to explore his notions of how the common values and shared language of traditional societies have been displaced by supposedly value-neutral technical language. As science and technology displace the structures of class domination characteristic of liberal capitalism, Habermas argues, what results are ostensibly nonideological systems of dominance that masquerade as the common sense of state-regulated mature capitalism.

Habermas's essay is more concerned to establish the dominance of instrumental rationality, "the manipulative compulsions of technical-operational administration," over older systems of symbolic interaction that produced shared values rooted in a common language than it is to suggest the possibilities for a common space in which key issues and values can be publicly discussed. Yet Habermas does begin to explore how genuine "communicative action" might be reasserted.

A new conflict zone, in place of the virtualized class antagonism and apart from the disparity conflicts at the margins of the system, can only emerge where advanced capitalist society has to immunize itself by depoliticizing the masses of the population against the questioning of its technocratic background ideology: in the public sphere administered through the mass media. For only here is it possible to buttress the concealment of the difference between progress in systems of purposive-rational action and emancipatory transformations of the institutional framework, between technical and practical problems. And it is necessary for the system to conceal this difference. Publicly administered definitions extend to *what* we want for our lives, but not to *how* we would like to live if we could find out, with regard to attainable potentials, how we *could* live (Habermas, 1970, p. 120).

So Habermas focused us back on the mass media, Maxine's *bête noire,* and the paradox of the contradictions built into its task to conceal the possibilities for progress implicit in advanced technology by entertaining and pacifying us, instead of raising and exploring issues critical to our lives.

I had not encountered, nor thought much about, notions of public space before I took Maxine's course. But the idea of a terrain on which issues could be discussed stayed with me during the following year when I ran for and was elected to my local community school board in Brooklyn. I subsequently served for ten years and helped to build an educational and political coalition that dominated the board during my last six years. The inchoate notions I took from Maxine about the necessity for dialogue with the "utter diversity" of constituency opinion in my district, as well as why it might be important to create multiple opportunities for that dialogue, led to efforts to build varieties of public space across the years I served. What follows, in too sketchy a summary, are some reflections on those efforts to create opportunities for public space in one school district, efforts generated by the explorations Maxine invited in her course.

PUBLIC SPACE 1:
FROM CAMPAIGN COMMITTEE TO ISSUES BASE

Successful electoral strategies depend on reaching, mobilizing, and sustaining an active base. Our campaign was started by a core group of neighborhood activists who built a committed base of parents from several schools in our immediate neighborhood and organized a typical insurgent campaign against the incumbents who'd dominated district politics (and its education policies) through control of the district school board. We used traditional insurgent techniques—we attacked schools' poor academic outcomes, identified incompetent leadership appointed through political patronage as the cause, and argued that leadership committed to educational reform would produce more effective schools. But because the least successful schools in our district served poor Latino and Black students, we also charged the incumbents with racism and committed ourselves to insuring that sufficient resources and support, through, for example, fully implemented bilingual programs and effective remediation, would operate at those schools.

As insurgents, the contradictions inherent in our platform did not immediately surface—how can a group of predominantly (though not exclusively) middle-class white professionals bring about the improvement of both their own children's education *and* the education of the district's more disadvantaged children? The differences between *argu-*

ing for the needs of other people's children, as opposed to trying to build a coalition that included parents and constituencies representing those children, did not immediately become apparent. (In subsequent elections we attempted, with varying success, to build coalitions across race, class, and ethnic divides. We also helped to elect the first Latina ever to serve on our district's school board.)

Our initial effort to create new public space was the transformation of the campaign committee, after our first successful election, into a permanent, district-wide "assembly of concern," which regularly discussed issues such as the reduction of tracking, the improvement of middle schools, the use of choice mechanisms to create new schools and programs, and the reduction of overcrowding. We turned our campaign issues into a series of group meetings, exploring how best to implement the changes we were seeking, and involved our campaign committee activists in organizing those sessions.

Sometimes, when we considered specific strategies, our discussions remained internal and were limited to the campaign activists. Other times, we held open public meetings and asked successful practitioners from other districts to talk with us. (Deborah Meier made an early and inspiring presentation about how to imagine and create effective middle schools, for example.) But through a series of discussions about issues critical to the improvement of schooling in our district, we maintained, even enlarged, our core of activist parents, who not only sustained a dialogue about the necessity for school improvement, but also developed a more sophisticated and informed analysis of how the problems of poor schooling in our district might be resolved. As our dialogues expanded and enlarged our base, the issues we raised evolved into a variety of solutions proposed to, or by, the school board, which we began to examine through different utilizations of public space.

PUBLIC SPACE 2:
IMPROVING OUR BOARD'S PUBLIC MEETINGS

Once we achieved ascendancy on the school board, we shifted our public meeting site from the district office to local schools. The district office was located in one of the district's traditional white neighborhoods, difficult to reach from the southern, predominantly Latino end of the district. We created a rotation so that, across a three-year period, every school got to host a public meeting. Not only did parent and community turnout substantially increase (in part because most schools preceded our meeting with a student performance), but every neighborhood in our district now has convenient access to at least one public school board meeting.

We also introduced the use of simultaneous Spanish translation at every public meeting, using an interpreter and radio-receiver headsets.

We tried to reduce the formality of our public sessions, during which we were required to pass innumerable procedural resolutions, many concerned with receipt of funds or other technical issues. We limited the time devoted to procedure so that we could increase the time for discussion and debate of issues critical to the district's improvement efforts. We decided to put all substantive policy issues on the monthly public meeting agenda, labeled *For Discussion Only,* and listen to public comment but not vote on those issues until the following month's meeting to give the public more time to consider the issues and communicate with us.

As our meetings began to focus more on education issues, meeting attendance rose; we often drew several hundred people to a monthly session. As the local press began to cover our proceedings, our meetings began to evolve into small-scale exercises in local democracy: Meetings were called well in advance and fairly widely publicized, no one was required to sign-up in order to speak, and speakers were rarely time-limited. When critical issues were presented for discussion, it was not unusual for thirty to forty speakers to argue with the board and debate each other; many of our public meetings ended far closer to midnight than to the ten P.M. limit we strove to observe.

PUBLIC SPACE 3: BUILDING CONSENSUS THROUGH DISTRICT-WIDE TASK FORCES

Early in my board tenure, we focused on trying to improve the district's five middle schools, which consistently produced poor student outcomes while clinging to very traditional school organization and instructional practices. We authorized the formation of a district-wide task force to explore middle school improvement, advertised the Middle School Task Force widely throughout the district, and appealed for a broad spectrum of volunteer membership. The superintendent supported our effort by insuring the participation of key district staff and school-level administrators, and a broad spectrum of teachers and parents throughout the district volunteered to participate.

Our Middle School Task Force met twice monthly for almost six months. We began by reviewing the literature about successful middle schools and inviting a range of middle school practitioners and researchers to discuss the issues with us. Task force members then spent enormous amounts of time analyzing district middle school practice and outcomes, investigating successful practice in other districts, developing recommendations for improvement, and drafting the task force report setting out our findings. As a relatively new board member, I was encouraged by the capacity for collaborative exploration, group self-education, analysis, and commitment to improvement that the task force members demonstrated. A very varied group of constituents managed to reach common ground and articulate the consensus we developed into quite powerful improvement recommendations within a six-month time-period. And the consensus became, over time, the district's policy goals for our middle schools.

Unfortunately, turning policy goals into school practice proved far more difficult than developing an effective task force, though the task force members have remained staunch advocates for improvement. Although a decade has passed since the task force report was issued, the district's middle schools have still not fully implemented the recommendations. But our board went on to focus the task force process on both the district's special education and bilingual programs, with signal success in the former instance.

The Special Education Task Force, a similarly broad, district-wide representative body, went through a similar process of exploration, analysis, and developing recommendations. Its final report presented a bold, comprehensive vision and proposed sweeping policy changes, which the district accepted and set about to implement. One example: Almost all the district's students with mild and moderate disabilities are now served by programs in their home schools, as opposed to a pervasive pattern of district-wide (and sometimes out-of-district) bussing before the Special Education Task Force was convened.

Our task forces worked best when there was almost universal, district-wide opinion that the specific focus of the effort sorely needed improvement; when the nature of the improvements sought were quite broad and comprehensive; and when the directions for improvement were neither sharply disputed nor potentially polarizing. Thus the task force strategy was less effective in helping us resolve our space issues (see below). But for improving both our middle schools and our special education program, district-wide task forces proved an invaluable process.

PUBLIC SPACE 4:
PUBLIC MEETINGS TO FOCUS ISSUE DEBATES

Quite early in our majority ascendancy, our board began the practice of calling special sessions to debate thorny issues, such as our efforts to reduce the inequities of our district's gifted program. Our school board had inherited a district-wide kindergarten through sixth grade gifted program (actually a gifted track in three elementary schools) that selected participating students by using the results of the Stanford-Binet IQ test administered during the pre-kindergarten year. We suffered the predictable results of such a skewed selection process: In a district composed of 80% Latino and Black students, the three gifted tracks (approximately 500 children) were 80% white.

Our first board actions as a new majority mandated district-administered testing for program selection to limit the manipulation of the testing situation, as well as the results, through the use of privately paid testers. Next we advertised the availability of gifted program placements as widely as we could, aiming particularly at Head Start and day-care centers serving preschool students of color. When the percentages of those students who passed the test for the program did not substantially increase, we tried to jettison the Stanford-Binet, but couldn't convince a majority of our colleagues to abandon it. So we adopted, as a potential compromise, a plan offered by our new superintendent: Change the program's intake grade from kindergarten to first grade and allow kindergarten teacher recommendation as well as parental request for testing. A limited solution, I thought, but still one worth trying, so I supported my board colleagues' recommendation to schedule a special public meeting to discuss it.

Who came? Almost 300 parents; more than 95% were parents of students in the gifted program or parents who were counting on getting their children *into* the program. Overwhelmingly white, overwhelmingly advantaged, overwhelmingly incensed that we were menacing their special track. Almost no opponents of the program, who were numerous throughout the district, attended. Why? In part because the administrators, teachers, and parents who supported the gifted program were well-networked and had developed resources for quick communication. And in part because we used only the board's regular meeting notification process, deciding not to mobilize the program's opponents so that we couldn't be accused of stacking the meeting.

A politically naive and inept decision, I thought as I surveyed the group. But in spite of the overwhelmingly partisan turnout, I started the meeting hopeful that our proposals might be viewed as a useful contribution to reducing the gifted program's inequitable composition. Again, a naive assumption, because we never managed to create a reasoned debate; instead, our proposals were dismissed, our motives were questioned, our legitimacy attacked. Most speakers assumed we were out to destroy the gifted program, using our modest changes as an opening wedge, and threatened that they would pull their kids out of the district if we persisted. Though many speakers indicated their concerns for equity, they objected to an equity focus on the gifted program. "Solve the problems of public education in the district," one parent argued, "and we wouldn't need this program!"

Faced with this angry outpouring, key board members abandoned their support for our changes, and the board resolution was withdrawn.

The district's gifted program continued as a white enclave and was increasingly used by advantaged parents, among them many members of our own coalition, to insure effective education for their children.

Our board learned from this initial experience, and we subsequently used special public sessions primarily to explore and debate issues that had a diversity of strong opinion. Overcrowding, and especially the use of school space to accommodate newly organized schools and programs, became another flashpoint issue during my tenure on the board. Several of our schools were badly overcrowded, funds for new school construction (and even routine school maintenance) were extremely limited, and successful parent mobilizations (see below) had convinced the board to authorize several new schools and programs. Thus reconfiguring school space became critical and predictably controversial; the new schools and programs desperately needed adequate and appropriate space to operate, existing overcrowded schools demanded efforts to reduce *their* space pressures, and the district's (relatively) underutilized schools vehemently objected to giving up precious classroom space to the new schools and programs.

Because our board realized that solving the district's space issues, or at least reducing the pressures of overcrowding and demand for new school space, could not be accomplished easily, we used an internal board process to delineate the problems, explore potential solutions, and propose a range of specific recommendations. Though there was strong disagreement on the board about which recommendations would best resolve our space problems, we agreed to hold a series of public meetings in all the schools affected by our proposals to solicit parent, practitioner, and student opinion.

The resulting meetings were jam-packed, chaotic, often volatile; several times we had to intervene to prevent fights among partisans of different solutions. But by holding a series of public meetings across the district, we did succeed in thoroughly (if heatedly) examining the key space issues, narrowing down the proposed recommendations, and defining, through the rough democracy of what seemed endless debates, the pros, cons, and tradeoffs involved. When the board finally passed a resolution on space issues that involved several compromises, there was still plenty of anger but also a fair measure of shared understanding across the district.

PUBLIC SPACE 5:
MOBILIZING CONSTITUENCIES FOR ADVOCACY

On several issues, most prominently the development of new schools and programs, board members and activists from our district-wide coalition built very effective ad-hoc advocacy groups. One group, for example, came together to create a new, small, nontracked, learner-focused school that would recruit students from the entire district rather than from specified neighborhood zones; in essence, they were proposing our first school of choice. Proponents recruited a broad membership base, visited model schools throughout the New York City system, developed a consensus document defining the new school's organization and instructional practices, produced research demonstrating the effectiveness of the practices they advocated, sought expert support, and developed a variety of mobilizing strategies to build a strong constituency base. Once they generated significant support, the group petitioned the board to hold a public hearing to consider their request for the new school.

The resulting hearing was a model of citizen advocacy. Several hundred proponents attended, and more than forty parents and teachers made presentations about the need for the school, how it should function, and what the benefits would be for both the school's students and parents and the district as well. The board was sufficiently impressed to set in motion a process that ultimately resulted in approval of start-up funds for the new school.

Opposition, oddly, mobilized very slowly; there were no opponents at the initial presentation meeting, and few opponents at the public meeting in which the board voted to authorize the new school. Only after the new school outgrew its initial space and petitioned the board to move it into a neighboring underutilized school did opponents mobilize to attack the school as elitist in student selection (though the school had a well-crafted, equity-based lottery selection process) and thereby harmful to the rest of the district because, they alleged, it creamed successful students from neighborhood schools. The resulting debate about whether, and where, to move the new school was folded into the board's effort to address the district's severe overcrowding problems and was eventually resolved through the special public meeting process described above.

The most contentious advocacy issue during my tenure on the board was the struggle about *The Children of the Rainbow* (New York City Board of Education, 1991) multicultural curriculum guide, issued by then Chancellor Joseph Fernandez and recommended for use in first grade classes. The initial refusal, by one Queens district, to implement the curriculum exploded into a citywide battle that resulted in Chancellor Fernandez's dismissal by majority vote of the seven-member central Board of Education.

In my district, the struggle began early and lasted a good six months. We held at least five special public meetings about the curriculum guide that were attended, cumulatively, by thousands of constituents; almost five hundred people spoke, and meetings stretched on until 1:00 to 2:00 A.M. What was at stake in the almost 400-page curriculum guide were several pages that urged teachers to treat gay and lesbian families as part of the district's cultural diversity, suggested instructional strategies that would introduce and legitimate gay and lesbian families, and recommended readings that would explain and situate such families.

One of the ironies of the ensuing conflict is that the Board of Education's curriculum guides are notoriously underused; most guides are issued, disseminated, received by districts and schools, and almost universally ignored. The fight about *The Children of the Rainbow* was essentially symbolic, but the issues it raised were powerful and polarizing. Proponents argued that the increasing numbers of children from gay and lesbian families in our public schools needed to have their family realities acknowledged and legitimated to protect them from misunderstandings, slights, deliberate attacks, and traditional homophobic abuse. They argued that teachers needed to be sensitized to the realities of these new but increasing family forms in order to most appropriately understand, nurture, and support the learning and growth of their students.

Opponents argued that the Chancellor had no right to define homosexuality as a culture. Many argued that at best homosexuality was a deviant lifestyle (at worst, some insisted, it was a sin in the eyes of God), that public institutions such as schools had no right to legitimate. (Therefore part of the attack affirmed "legitimate" nonmainstream cultures and applauded their inclusion in a multicultural curriculum guide, but opposed the inclusion of homosexuality because it was *not* an alternative culture.) Opponents argued that the Chancellor had no right to mandate (many transformed the suggestive power of a curriculum *guide* to the dictum of the Chancellor) teaching strategies that legitimated homosexuality. Opponents constantly expressed fear that their first grade children's sexual development would be adversely affected by classroom exposure to the reality of same-sex families and homosexuality.

The nights of argument about the curriculum guide seemed endless and seethed with intensity, stridency, rage, and frustration. One example I still remember: A passionate young Latino father roared at us, "First you took our Bibles out of the classroom, then you took away our rights to discipline our own children, and now you take away our rights to teach them about sex in our own way!" Advocates associated with the Christian Coalition organized opponents throughout the city, distributed a wildly inaccurate videotape to parent groups throughout our district, and held constant strategy meetings to recruit participants to speak at all our meetings. Since our district was home to substantial gay and lesbian communities, varieties of groups organized significant mobilization of supporters of *The Children of the Rainbow*. The resulting debates, though often so passionate that keeping order was a harrowing task, were far from one-sided.

What I remember most is how many opponents of *The Children of the Rainbow* began their statements by acknowledging how much they respected and cared for family members, friends, and acquaintances who were gay and lesbian. Relatively few people overtly attacked homosexuality or homosexuals, though those who did were vehement, rage-choked, and venomous. Most opponents tried to affirm their respect for the individual choice of homosexuality while opposing its entry into the classroom. (Many of the proponents tried hard to get their listeners to understand that homosexuality was far less a choice than the curriculum guide opponents assumed.) I was also struck by the fragility of people's notions of child development; many opponents seemed to perceive children's sexuality as so malleable that mere references to alternative family forms could contaminate their "normal" development.

Though what seemed an endless round of meetings exhausted our board, and though responding to the rage, misrepresentations, lies, and underhanded tactics of many of the *Rainbow* curriculum's opponents drained and dispirited me, I was ultimately proud of the results. First, our board passed a resolution supporting the curriculum's use and called for school-based discussions to deal with specific implementation. Second, all the critical issues and concerns raised by the struggle about *The Children of the Rainbow* curriculum guide were repeatedly and passionately articulated, explored, and argued. Though the depths of homophobic anger, hysteria, and prejudice were repeatedly plumbed, the strengths of gay and lesbian families were also repeatedly affirmed, the supports that gay and lesbian culture provided were repeatedly defined, and the need for affirmation of sexual diversity as part of a genuine multicultural society was repeatedly argued.

Moreover, opponents confronted each other, night after night, as real people rather than as stereotypes or symbols; many people on both sides consistently helped to mute stridency or venom whenever they surfaced. We managed to maintain a rough but consistent public decorum while examining so rancorous an issue because, I believe, most people wanted to continue the debate, and even perhaps hear some of the other side, more than they wanted to obliterate the opposition—or us. (Though the anger directed against us after we voted to affirm the curriculum was so intense that, as a precaution, the police who had been summoned by the superintendent decided to escort us out of the building.) After each meeting ended, and sometimes even before we convened, we would see small groups of opponents talking with each other.

Finally, the conflict became a mobilizing issue during the subsequent school board election. The claims of the opponents that they would unseat all the supporters of *The Children of the Rainbow* proved a very hollow boast; the struggle produced an outpouring of support for our district-wide coalition and helped to elect a solid six-person majority. Moreover, although a part of our board resolution authorized school-by-school discussions to shape the actual use of *The Children of the Rainbow,* few such discussions were actually held. The issue subsided almost to invisibility, perhaps because most parents, whatever their views, trusted their children's teachers and the daily practice in their children's classrooms. But perhaps, also, the anxieties, fears, angers, and other passions tapped by the struggle about *The Children of the Rainbow* had been consummated by the intensity of the conflict.

When I retired from the board, soon after the school board elections that concluded the struggle over *The Children of the Rainbow,* the variety of ways we'd learned to use different forms of public space as stages for debate, discussion, exploration of issues and resolution of conflicts had reshaped the nature of public deliberation in our district. Many times during those ten years, I wished that Maxine could have observed the varieties of ways we'd developed to engage public debate and discussion. Would she have perceived some "common world" of shared understanding emerging from our struggles? In many public meetings, and particularly during the painful debates about *The Children of the Rainbow,* I wondered if Maxine would have concluded that we'd begun to create the "sameness in utter diversity" that, according to Arendt, generates the "worldly reality" we all hold in common and can come to perceive and share. During the worst of the *Rainbow* conflicts, I felt fairly certain that we'd tapped into the "utter diversity."

REFERENCES

Arendt, H. (1958). *The human condition.* Chicago, IL: University of Chicago Press.

Habermas, J. *Technology and science as ideology.*

Habermas, J. (1970). *Toward a rational society: Student protest, science, and politics.* Boston: Beacon Press.

New York City Board of Education (1991). *Children of the rainbow: First grade.* New York: New York City Board of Education.

22

When Safety and Joy
Are Breached

Jonathan G. Silin

Contemporary events raise havoc with our belief in freedom and possibility. The informal meetings of the early childhood reading group to which I belong are punctuated by references to the incendiary rhetoric of Newt Gingrich and Jesse Helms, the impact of welfare reform on the poor, and the latest newspaper accounts describing the spread of guns in schools, drugs on the streets, and gangs in local communities. Although circumstances differ, no one is immune from the effects of urban conflict, economic instability, and family disruptions. As educators and parents, we all wonder how to talk with our children about these issues. How do we balance our desire to protect the young and our responsibility to help them make sense of the disturbing realities of contemporary life? How do we represent a manageable world to children even as we feel powerless to influence the direction and speed of social change?

Increasingly, educational researchers and curriculum makers have assumed a narrative view of life to address these questions. The new interest in narrative has brought previously unheard voices into the field (Mclaughlin and Tierney, 1993). It has allowed scholars to examine new texts for the beliefs and intentions of their authors. As an essential mode of knowing and thinking, we appreciate the way that narrative can capture the complexity, specificity, and connectedness of seemingly discrete events. At the same time, the prominence given to story has brought the potential of its becoming a new canon, one that can be as narrowly conceived as traditional forms of positivism. Debates about interpretation, authenticity, the role of normative values and purposes flourish only when we attend to the political contexts of storytelling (Carter, 1993).

Queer theorists (Bryson, 1994; De Castell, 1994) ask us to accept greater rhetorical responsibility for our narratives and to cast aside safe stories for ones that provoke and unsettle. Too often we fail to ask how our stories will move our listeners to action. In this chapter I will argue that inviting children to tell their stories in the classroom is not an end in itself but rather the beginning of our work as educators seeking a more equitable society. The sharing of stories should foster social engagement and political commitment as well as self-expression and personal catharsis.

LEARNING TO TELL OUR OWN STORIES

I acknowledge that questions of representation have special salience for me. As a gay man growing up in the 1950s, I found my life absent from the arts and literatures in which I sought to confirm my identity. How can I forget finding, buying, and devouring my first book about homosexuality at age fifteen—Edmund Bergler's bleak study of pathological deviance? Nor, as a young teacher, could I forget the limitations imposed on me by traditional representations of gay men as emblems of moral depravity, possessed of unique powers for corrupting the young. These representations always told a contradictory story: Homosexuality is both a repugnant practice and one to which it is all too easy to succumb. Collapsing two distinct categories, homosexuality and pedophilia, child abuse panics continue to threaten everyone involved with the young.

Although I had been actively involved in the gay liberation movement since 1969, when I entered a doctoral program at Teachers College, I had not begun to relate my experiences as a gay man to my work with children. Joyfully celebrating our successful efforts to declassify homosexuality as an illness in 1973, I had not stopped to question the battery of psychological theories I was instructed to use when examining children's behavior. Participating in consciousness-raising groups where we worked to reject the social stereotypes and doctors' diagnoses embedded in our own thinking, I did not consider that childhood itself might be a socially constructed phenomenon in which I participated as a professional educator.

In retrospect, I see that my encounters at Teachers College with Maxine Greene laid the foundations upon which I would build these connections. Her commitment to multiple ways of knowing underlined the limits of psychological perspectives, and her introduction to phenomenology offered an alternative tool for interpreting experience. With a new appreciation for the existential philosophers and novelists of my adolescent years, I revisited the meaning of choice and contingency, fixity and possibility, facticity and futuring. It became increasingly difficult to deny that the same intentionality informed my private life and public identity. Maxine

Greene writes frequently about the power of metaphor and narrative to suggest coherence amidst the fragments of our daily lives:

> It is difficult for me to teach educational history or philosophy to teachers-to-be without engaging them in the domain of imagination and metaphor. How else are they to make meaning of the discrepant things they learn? How else are they to see themselves as practitioners, working to choose, working to teach in an often indecipherable world? (1995, p. 99)

In my own work with teachers, I have made the creation and interpretation of imaginative texts central to the process of coming to know children. Writing about an early separation from a caregiver, a favorite play space, a difficult moment of childhood, adults begin to tell their own stories. As we search for themes together, reading and rereading our text for new meanings, students realize that their own words have an uncanny way of getting to the heart of the matter. We expect the very specificity of our experiences to enclose us in a private world. Instead we find that they call to the Other.

I hope that the novels we read, philosophy we ponder, and history we study enable teachers to place their individual experiences in larger social context. I want them to connect their own struggles to teach against the grain with earlier progressive traditions in education, to understand that even their most mundane pedagogical acts have political ramifications, and that resistance takes many forms.

STORIES OF RESISTANCE

Patsy Stafford, a student in my graduate seminar, writes about a childhood experience of resistance, one that exemplifies the confusing messages our denials of difference send to children:

> I am six, maybe seven years old. I am at my aunt's house and the subject of getting married and having children comes up. I say something about having a child, but not getting married. My aunt, in an angry tone, responds, "You can't have a baby unless you're married."
>
> "Well, Peggy Burns up the road has a baby, and she's not married."
>
> "She must be married, you have to be married to have a baby," she insists. I know what I know and continue to insist that

Peggy has a baby and she isn't married. My aunt is equally insistent, yet trying desperately to end this conversation.

"You must be mistaken," she says.

Not to be outdone, and being a farm girl, I respond, "Well maybe the A.I. man came to her." The A.I. man is the artificial inseminator who came frequently to inseminate the cows on our farm.

My aunt bursts out laughing and quickly hurries to the garden. I later overhear her telling my mother the story. They both laugh.

Now, as a teacher, Patsy works hard to clarify and extend the social knowledge of her students. Here is an entry from her classroom log:

The children are sitting on the rug after lunch waiting for me to begin reading a chapter book. Maria asks me if I'm married. I respond that I used to be, but that I'm not anymore.

"Where are your children?" another child asks. I could say, "Okay, it's time to start reading," but I decide to see where it will go. I love this sort of spontaneous discussion.

"I don't have any children," I answer.

"Why not if you were married?"

Before I can answer another child says, "If you're married you have to have children!"

"You have to be married to have children," Maria says in an authoritative tone.

"No, my mom isn't married to my dad," replies Daniel.

"My mom and dad aren't married, but they live together," adds Josh.

"My mom isn't married to anybody and she has me," adds Adam.

Maria, who raised the issue, looks puzzled and expects me to correct them. I say, "There are lots of kinds of families, just like in this class. Families with one mom like José's and Greg's, families with one dad like Nina's, families with a mom and a dad like Maria's, and families with a mom and two dads like Daniel's, step families like Honor's, and families with aunts and grandmas like Sam's and Tony's. And some families have two moms and some have two dads, and some families have no children just like mine."

Patsy's commitment to authentic dialogue forces her to cross two traditional boundaries. First, she is willing to forgo her scheduled lesson to explore and confirm the children's complex family structures. Second, she is willing to forgo the protection of the professional to make her own life history a subject of inquiry. The risks she takes, the boundaries she crosses, articulate difference in the interest of community.

Feminists (Martin, 1994; Pagano, 1990) contrast this kind of subtle, flexible, and responsive dialogue that normally takes place in our homes with the formal, rigid, and fragmented curriculum of our schools. The endless round of meaningless activities that fills most school days alienates children and teachers from their lived experience. These are days built on the traditionally masculine ethic that stresses autonomy, differentiation, and abstract ideals of justice.

Some feminists (Grumet, 1988) draw attention to the intimate, fluid connection of child and parent. After all, we know children first through their bodies, as they know us through ours, long before language emerges. This knowing is characterized by connection and continuity rather than separation and distinction. An ethics of care cannot be built upon abstract principles and mythical ideals about communities of affinity in which everyone shares common religion, race, nationality, or ethnicity (Shabatay, 1991). Rather, they must be grounded in the particular stories our students tell and a recognition of the very real communities of difference in which they live.

In the last decade, the most heated debates regarding public education have focused on the extent to which the curriculum should explore differences of race, ethnicity, class, religion, gender, and sexual orientation. Postmodernists have also made questions of difference and our ability to know the Other central to their theorizing about the contemporary social world. But when multiple identities and participation in varied discourses is emphasized, then subjectivity is often splintered and coherence in doubt. In the postmodern canon it is difficult to find images of the adults I would see emerge from schooling—agents of social change whose actions are tied to an understanding of the structural inequities that frame our lives. Similar concerns are expressed in a growing literature (Anyon, 1994; Beyer and Liston, 1992) that asks for a more politically oriented postmodernism addressing material constraints as well as discursive analysis. Maxine Greene (1995) comments:

> I want to acknowledge the resemblance of what lies around us to a "jumbled museum" (Smithson, 1979, p. 67). Yet I also feel deeply dissatisfied with what postmodern thinkers describe as "bricolage," or "collage," that style of communicating often thought suitable for the present time, when old myths, oppositions, and hierarchies are being overthrown (Schrift, 1990, p. 110). And I have looked for a way of speaking that might begin to constitute a common world for teachers and, indeed, many others. (p. 2)

The commitment to a common world is essential to understanding current debates about difference, and one that has long permeated Greene's work. Drawing on diverse sources—the social philosophy of Hannah Arendt, the educational vision of John Dewey, the phenomenological psychology of Merleau-Ponty and Alfred Schutz—Greene has always managed to hold in tension respect for pluralism and the possibilities of public conversation, our radical otherness and potential for sympathetic imagination, the alienation that comes with modern technological and administrative processes and the creation of "in-between" spaces where individuals can seek authentic voice.

A close reading of Maxine Greene suggests that recent controversies about the representation of previously silenced minorities in schools have often been based on a false dichotomy between the individual and the community, the child and the group. For if pluralism defines the human condition, then public arenas of free and open discussion define the democratic society. The very possibility of communication and dialogue presumes that there is another who is different, one whom we aspire to understand.

THE SUN IS WEARING SUNGLASSES

Teaching that invites children's stories and recognizes the communities of difference in which we live is not without its own challenges. Again I return to Patsy's classroom record to illumine the kinds of ethical dilemmas that may arise for teachers. She writes:

> Too often we deny children's real life experiences in the classroom. We tell them it's not okay to hit, that they need to use their words. Yet the reality of their lives tells them otherwise. This was brought home to me yesterday by a kindergarten girl's comment when I said, "It's not okay to hit." She quickly replied, "Then why is it okay for my dad to hit me?" How does one respond?
>
> Although I don't agree with the use of corporal punishment, can I tell this girl that her father is wrong to hit her? And what about the messages of violence society is giving her? We go to war when other countries don't do what we think is right. We kill people to punish them. What ever happened to using words?

And what happens when the words that the children use cause us to despair? The difficulties faced by contemporary teachers was again made clear to me when the director of a substance abuse prevention project talked to a group of teacher educators about her work in East Harlem schools (Project Healthy Choices, 1995). The most affecting parts of this talk were the words and pictures of the seven-year-olds themselves. A picture of two boys, two massive trees, and a football, bears the following inscription across the top, "He haves AIDS. We play together. I am his friend." Initially the artist had written, "We have AIDS," but later crossed out the "We" and substituted "He." In classrooms where four or five children may have lost a close relative to the disease, such an error is understandable.

Seeking to grasp the connections among more visible forms of violence and the less obvious but equally devastating effects of drugs and alcohol, another child draws two stick figures pointing huge guns at one another. The figures are small in comparison to the space, and across the top two thirds of the page the teacher has recorded the artist's words:

> Drugs are terrible. Guns are bad things. Drugs are weapons. Smoking is not good for your lungs. Guns and smoke are the same thing like killing someone. They are the same like drinking beer. Someone drinks and they kill themselves one day. People drink so much when they are very disappointed.

The most unsettling picture contains no words. The upper two thirds of the paper is covered by a sky drawn with large blue marker strokes and dotted with four simple inverted-V-shaped birds. In the upper left hand corner a large, bright-yellow sun has its nose, eyes, and mouth drawn in black. The lower third of the page contains rolling green hills and two trees on either side. Scattered across the ground is a mix of objects, including clearly identifiable syringes and beer cans. The child describes the scene with the following words:

> This is the sun wearing sunglasses, and the sun is trying not to see the drugs. These are all beer can and drugs and dead birds dying, and the grass is dying and the sun is dying and trying to keep everything alive, and the trees are dying and the leave are falling down and dying.

Although each of these pictures is subject to many interpretations, it was the awed silence among the adults that drew my attention at our faculty meeting. Finally one dismayed person exclaimed, "Is there no joy in these children's lives?" I don't know the answer to this question nor the best response to my colleague's evident despair. I do know that if we turn away from the children's painful and confusing experiences, then we turn away from the possibility of relief as well. Classrooms are places in which children should feel comfortable exploring a full range of emotions, including authentic moments of distress and pleasure. We are fully engaged as learners only when the curriculum is responsive to the material contexts of our lives. It is through such engagement that we realize our freedom and our humanity.

Finally, we are all historical beings. Time and place are at the heart of every biography. As teachers we commit ourselves to the future generation because we know that hope resides in time and time can only be lived in the world, a world, unhappily, that includes too much personal suffering and social oppression.

BALLAST AGAINST AN UNCERTAIN FUTURE

A widely read book, *Children in Danger* (Garbarino, Dubrow, Kostelny, & Pardo, 1992), reflects the strengths and weaknesses of the strategies we have used in the past to shore up vulnerable young lives. Garbarino and his colleagues argue that for too many children the delicate balance between risk and resilience has been shifted by the impact of chronic violence. They maintain that the school can be a critical protective factor in children's lives.

The program they advocate, as realized in a Chicago Head Start center, emphasizes strong attachments to one teacher, orderly classroom environments, and the building of self-esteem. And what of the curriculum? "Especially in the early years the content is almost, *almost,* incidental. Children learn by internalizing the attitudes, values and ways of meaningful others. And then, whatever content you expose children to, they learn it" (quoted in Schorr & Schorr, 1988, p. 234). Defining curriculum in terms of interpersonal process, the authors claim to "see teachers not as therapists but as positive role models for children in a caregiving environment that promotes mental health" (p. 130).

In fact, it seems to me that the authors do just the opposite. That is, they disregard the educational as they promote a mental health, dare I say, therapeutic approach to classrooms. They are insightful and responsive to the emotions of the children. Yet they contend that teachers should not initiate conversations about community violence, gangs, or substance abuse, only respond to specific concerns raised by the children themselves. The knowledge valued here is knowledge of the socioemotional self, the self in relation to another, not in relation to the world outside the classroom. In other words, we are encouraged to talk with children, but it doesn't really matter what we say, for content is "almost, *almost,* incidental."

It is not that the authors are unwilling to look at the children's lives, but rather that they are unprepared to turn the harsh realities they see into curriculum. The children wounded in our urban wars require psychological first aide. They also require invitations to tell their stories. It is our responsibility then to use these stories to promote a more systematic study of the world that the children describe. Stable adult relationships, predictable environments, and positive reinforcement are necessary to all children. But as educators, we should offer something beyond emotional reassurances and "coping skills" as ballast against the future.

The something more we offer, the systematic study I refer to, is the curriculum that grows out of the dramas the children create in their play and the responses that we offer as adults. This inquiry about the social world draws children together even as it directs them beyond individual experiences. There is something to be learned, after all, from the neighborhood clinic tending to the needs of HIV-positive children, from the shelter on the corner feeding and housing the homeless, and from the community organization down the block fighting substance abuse.

Unfortunately, as I observe early childhood classrooms, and I speak here of the most progressive, I see very little play or social studies and an increasing emphasis on whole language instruction. Posters detailing the steps through textual production replace charts that describe group experiences. Meetings that were once forums for discussions of shared concerns have become arenas in which burgeoning literary critics couch their unfaltering positive comments in the now meaningless refrain, "I like the way you . . ." This intensified emphasis on self-expression cannot be equated with real communication, nor is it free of class, race, and ethnic bias (Tobin, 1995).

Learning how to structure writers' workshops, reader response groups, and editorial conferences has become an essential part of teacher education. My own graduate students prepare for job interviews by defining their commitment to education in terms of process writing and whole language instruction. Language instruction that grows out of life experience is to be valued but does not constitute a philosophy of education. It offers no larger social vision against which to evaluate our curricular choices.

Children need to study what is, reflect on what might be, and experience strategies that help them to achieve their ends. It is the dynamic social processes as much as the internal psychological coping mechanisms on which educators must focus. We have a responsibility to provide opportunities for children to know themselves as young community activists and to experience the power of a collective response to large and small social problems. We must be clear that the individual we educate is a social individual, formed in and through membership in diverse groups. Harriet Cuffaro (1995) explains this Deweyan perspective on the evolving person:

The social and the individual may be said to be "two names for the same reality." It is neither the social or the individual but the *social individual,* each element functioning within the whole, named as separate elements for the purpose of analysis but in actuality transactionally related. Such a view ensures continuity and connections. It attends to process, time, and context. (p. 23)

TAKING THE VICTIMS' SIDE

Confronted by the long-term effects of poverty and racism, we have no certainties with which to arm ourselves. We can only begin with our willingness to hear the children out.

> You cannot really make the unbearable manageable or the inexplicable understandable. But in your stance of being ready, willing, and able to help, the child can find at least temporary peace and support for his efforts to cope. If little children have a 'right' to a safe and joyous childhood, they also have a right to scream out their rage and fear and to be heard and supported when their safety and joy are breached. (Warren, 1977, p. 24)

Listening, we recognize our inability to "know" the multiple risk factors to which children are exposed, to wonder if they are commensurable with knowledge at all. Such recognition directs us to the meaning of our inability to know. How do we begin to make the unimaginable present in the curriculum? How do we manage to live with the presence of absence in our lives?

Over the last decade and a half, I have struggled to live with multiple losses inflicted by HIV/AIDS. I have learned to record my own story as a matter of survival. I have had no choice. I record the stories of friends, lovers, and colleagues because they have been entrusted to me and because they are my story, too. Bearing witness to their lives insures my survival. The way forward is through history; a commitment to telling the story is a commitment to continued life. Terrence Des Pres (1977) wisely concludes, "Surviving and bearing witness become reciprocal acts" (p. 117).

The literature of testimony that emerged during the Second World War bears witness to the events of that time. It aids us in finding a way out of the paralysis that is the legacy of an unrepresentable history. In *The Plague* (1947/1972), Albert Camus's narrator, Dr. Rieux, tells the story of a deadly epidemic ravaging Oran. His very acts of seeing and telling are acts of cognition, ones in which Dr. Rieux learns about his relationship to those whose lives he documents.

Ten years later, in a striking reassessment of our ability to bear witness, Camus wrote *The Fall* (1956). Now a nameless narrator chooses not to recognize what he has seen and heard, a woman's leap into the Seine during the small hours of the morning. Paralyzed, the failed witness neither responds to her cries nor informs others of the event. In this collapse of reliable, authoritative testimony, Camus teaches us that it is through our silences, our decisions not to know, that we make history.

Learning to tell my own stories of loss and separation confirmed for me that the aesthetic is an essential way of knowing the world. I recognize that the paintings of syringes and beer cans, adults with guns and children with HIV/AIDS are an important way that students bear witness to their own struggles to survive. As teachers, we play a critical role in children's lives when we provide the tools and materials, the time and space, the permission and encouragement for them to become subjects not objects of history.

When safety and joy are breached, literature and the arts speak to us all about experiences for which we don't have words, about moments when rational analysis fails. They allow us to see the given as constructed, to glimpse new possibilities, to foster empathetic responses to others, and to capture a sense of wholeness that is so often masked by the violence of modern life. Encounters with imaginative reconstructions of experience offer a route to social engagement as well as to naming our lived worlds. Maxine Greene quotes this passage from Sartre (1949) which highlights the similar tasks of artists and teachers:

> And if I am given this world with its injustices, it is not so I might contemplate them coldly, but that I might animate them with my indignation, that I might disclose them and create them with their nature as injustices, that is, as abuses to be suppressed. (pp. 62–63)

In my own teaching and writing (Silin, 1995), I have tried to describe how we defend against difference, the unknown—people with HIV/AIDS, gays and lesbians, children—through the ruse of scientific knowledge. For it is not certainty, but contingency; not definitive descriptions of what is, but open-ended suppositions about what might be; not our knowledge, but our ignorance that best describe the human condition. Similarly our willingness to greet the stranger in our midst, foster the growth of communities of difference, and bear witness to the suffering of others best describes the ethical foundations of our work. All our texts and talks, plans and programs are without effect unless they move us closer toward what in the Jewish tradition is called *tikun olam,* or, repair of the world.

REFERENCES

Anyon, J. (1994). The retreat of Marxism and socialist feminism: Postmodern and poststructural theories of education. *Curriculum Inquiry, 24*(2), 115–133.

Beyer, L. E., & Liston, D. P. (1992). Discourse or moral action: A critique of post-modernism. *Educational Theory 42*(4), 371–395.

Bryson, M. (1994, April). *Scheherezade's revenge: Theorizing queer narrativities.* Paper presented at the annual conference of the American Educational Research Association, New Orleans, LA.

Camus, A. (1956). *The fall* (J. O'Brien, Trans.). New York: Vintage Books.

Camus, A. (1972). *The plague* (S. Gilbert, Trans.). New York: Random House. (Original work published in 1947)

Carter, K. (1993). The place of story in the study of teaching and teacher education. *Educational Researcher, 22*(1), 5–12, 18.

Cuffaro, H. (1995). *Experimenting with the world: John Dewey and the early childhood classroom.* New York: Teachers College Press.

De Castell, S. (1994, April). The lying game and the lesbian rule. Paper presented at the annual conference of The American Educational Research Association, New Orleans, LA.

Des Pres, T. (1977). *The survivor:An anatomy of life in the death camps.* New York: Pocket Books.

Garbarino, T., Dubrow, N., Kostelny, K., & Pardo, C. (1992). *Children in danger: Coping with the consequences of community violence.* San Francisco: Jossey-Bass.

Greene, M. (1995). *Releasing the imagination: Essays on education, the arts, and social change.* San Francisco: Jossey-Bass.

Grumet, M. (1988). *Bitter milk.* Amherst: University of Massachusetts Press.

Martin, J. R. (1994). *Changing the educational landscape: Philosophy, women, and curriculum.* New York: Routledge.

McLaughlin, D., & Tierney, W. G. (1993). *Naming silenced lives: Personal narrative and the process of educational change.* New York: Routlege.

Pagano, J. (1990). *Exiles and communities: Teaching in the patriarchal wilderness.* Albany: State University of New York Press.

Project Healthy Choice. (1995). *Stories from East Harlem.* New York: Bank Street College of Education.

Sartre, J. P. (1949). *Literature and existentialism* (B. Frechtman, Trans.). Secaucus, NJ: Citadel Press.

Schorr, L., & Schorr, D. (1988). *Within our reach: Breaking the cycle of disadvantage.* New York: Doubleday.

Schrift, A. D. (1990). The becoming post-modern of philosophy. In G. Shaprio (Ed.), *After the future* (pp. 99–113). Albany: State University of New York Press.

Shabatay, V. (1991). The stranger's story: Who calls and who answers? In C. Witherell and N. Noddings (Eds.), *Stories lives tell* (pp. 136–152). New York: Teachers College Press.

Silin, J. G. (1995). *Sex, death, and the education of children: Our passion for ignorance in the age of AIDs.* New York: Teachers College Press.

Smithson, R. (1979). *The writings of Robert Smithson: Essays with illustrations* (N. Holt, Ed.). New York: New York University Press.

Tobin, J. (1995). The irony of self-expression. *American Journal of Education, 103,* 233–258.

Warren, R. (1977). *Caring: Supporting children's growth.* Washington, DC: National Association for the Education of Young Children.

23

The End of Innocence

Jo Anne Pagano

Few issues in education are more vexed than that of the relation between pedagogy and the personal because it is an issue that seems to strike to the heart of the association between education and politics. For in taking on the task of education, those of us who teach have taken on a commitment to preserving all that is best in the democratic project. We have embraced the concept of a public world, the vitality of which is sustained by enabling the development of diverse perspectives that will reinvigorate that public world.

In challenging orthodox and undemocratic beliefs regarding democracy, teachers and scholars in recent decades have helped to reinvigorate democratic discourse in schools and colleges by challenging certain undemocratic practices that presume that equal treatment means the same treatment and that equal talent means identical talents. The hidden curriculum has been unmasked and its crimes against democracy named. This is important because despite our political differences and our different subject positions, we are all agreed that an American education is an education for democracy.

While we need not all agree on the particulars that constitute a democratic society or on the features of a life in which freedom is chosen in service of democracy, we must talk about what is necessary for ourselves and our students to engage the questions. If we turn to Maxine Greene's work and to her life as a scholar and a teacher, we find a language and an attitude to teaching and learning that helps us engage in such a conversation.

During the spring of 1996, I taught a seminar in curriculum theory. Students were required to study all of the work of a prominent curriculum theorist. In addition to writing a synthetic and analytical paper on the work, students were also to present an overview and a critical synthesis of their chosen theorists' work within the context of the field as a whole. The student who chose Maxine Greene began his presentation by saying, "You know how Thoreau says the unexamined life is not worth living? Remember 'Know thyself'? Well Maxine Greene says all of these things, but she says it better. I just love her." He then went on to provide a thorough explication of Greene's work and a sensitive reading of her work as peculiarly American. He concluded his presentation by referring again to Thoreau: "To be awake is to be alive."

Maxine Greene asks us what it is to be American, and she points us to the attitudes and capacities we must possess if we are to consider such a question. She writes:

> My focal interest is in human freedom, in the capacity to surpass the given and look at things as if they could be otherwise. . . . To become different, of course, is not simply to will oneself to change. There is the question of being *able* to accomplish what one chooses to do. It is not only a matter of the capacity to choose; it is a matter of the power to act to attain one's purposes. We shall be concerned with intelligent choosing and, yes, humane choosing, as we shall be with the kinds of conditions necessary for empowering persons to act on what they choose. It is clear enough that choice and action both occur within and by means of ongoing transactions with objective conditions and with other human beings. They occur as well within the matrix of culture, its prejudgments, and its symbol systems. Whatever is chosen and acted upon must be grounded, at least to a degree, in an awareness of a world lived in common with others, a world that can be to some extent transformed. (1988, p. 4)

To many, teaching seems pretty uncomplicated. It's simply a matter of telling someone what he or she needs to know. Maxine Greene teaches us that telling is probably not the best way to teach most of the time. She teaches us that knowledge is value-laden, and that teaching has moral as well as epistemological and social consequences. In this, and in other ways, she deprives us of our innocence.

Still there remains an illusion of innocence in much pedagogical discourse, even that which disavows the transmission model of teaching. The focus in such discourse is usually on the student, and we have learned in recent decades to think differently about our students than did Dewey's "traditional" teachers. We no longer think of them as passive, empty vessels to be filled with unimpeachable knowledge. But focusing on students and curriculum alone is not enough. For Maxine Greene, and for those who have learned from her, the teacher, too, is subject to investigation.

I never meant to be a teacher. I never took a course in education until I had already been teaching for several years. My work during those years taught me that education was through and through political, and that my low-income students were the victims of an educational system that operated to disenfranchise them. Still I was an innocent. I thought of my task as not to let them fail again. I like to think that I taught imaginatively, energetically, and generously. Even so, my students were the problem, and my job was to teach them to take control of the system by teaching them to take control of their learning. About myself as a teacher, I thought infrequently.

Then I enrolled in my first education course. There Bill Pinar introduced me to Maxine Greene's work and to that of others who stripped me of my innocence. I recognized in myself and my like-minded colleagues the impulse to what Greene named "malefic beneficence."

We innocents assumed that with knowledge would come desirable attitudes and dispositions. Like Plato, we believed that to know the good is to do it, and that the good could be known. We believed that we could all become part of the solution, for the truth would set us free. We believed that we could empower our students to act freely and from a critical consciousness that would make real the democratic communities within which we would find, and out of which we would make, ourselves as public citizens, as well as members of families, as lovers, and as friends.

But these beliefs require a further recognition and a way of proceeding that has only relatively recently received our attention. Greene (1988) says, "a teacher in search of his/her own freedom may be the only kind of teacher who can arouse young persons to go in search of their own" (p. 14).

Such teachers will necessarily be teachers in search of themselves, people who discover self in the dialectic of freedom that Greene describes. Such teachers will also be, in Greene's language, strangers. The teacher as stranger is, however, no tourist. The tourist will never know a place or a culture. For Greene, knowledge is a kind of familiarity that always begins in strangeness.

It was Freud who confronted us with the most radical form of our own unknowingness. He confronted us with the knowledge that we do not even know ourselves—that our actions and our attitudes are motivated by unseen forces. We are strangers to ourselves. And if we are strangers to ourselves, how can we possibly know others? Here, of course, Freud merely confirmed what Descartes and others had already asserted—that we can never know the other. Freud declared that our ignorance of ourselves is a product of our resistance to the knowledge of our strangerness and a will to appropriate others as objects of our knowledge and desire. Through psychoanalysis, Freud demanded that we acknowledge our estrangement, even that we embrace it as the starting point of knowledge.

The teacher as stranger wills her estrangement in order to find herself and others and to build the spaces in which we may meet. It is only the stranger who can finally choose freedom because freedom entails that one finds oneself in the finding of others, but not by appropriation. Perhaps finally it is only the stranger who can come to an America that is both place and consciousness formed from a kind of ego ideal. Perhaps it is for this reason that Greene takes us on a journey through the literature and arts of America—a kind of royal road to the unconscious where meeting our strangeness makes us whole.

For Greene, literature and the arts confront us with strangeness, thereby giving us back to ourselves as we traverse the distant landscapes of art and literature. And over and over again in art and in literature, perhaps especially in American art and literature, we sound the theme of loss of innocence that coming to terms with strangeness brings us.

As North Americans, we love to mark the moments when we lost our innocence: the McCarthy Army trials, the revelation that quiz shows were wired, the assassinations of John F. Kennedy, Martin Luther King, and Robert Kennedy. The number of times we have lost our innocence as a nation might suggest to us that we never had it to begin with. Perhaps it is that that the teacher as stranger must learn. For Maxine Greene, the emphasis is on the teacher-stranger's choice of freedom once the teacher has relinquished the myth of his or her own innocence. Relinquishing our innocence we learn the ways in which the formation of our own identities as teachers is figured in the worlds we make through our teaching.

The culture wars depend on the myth of innocence. This myth enables teachers to treat their students as a kind of familiar, ignoring the imperatives of the teachers' own identities in the work they have undertaken. For we come to a world already there, familiar and familial, and we come to it and to ourselves through mimetic relationships, as Madeleine Grumet has argued. She says:

> For all of us, the process of development has required this mimetic tracing of the other's relation to the world and then the negotiation, once we have arrived, of a new itinerary that will bring us back to ourselves. Male or female, wistful, yearning, repudiating, or celebrating we repeat the histories of our own identifications and differentiations through our lives. The classroom, the class period, provide the stage for transference of the relations within which we came to form: teachers and students, the cast of characters with whom we endlessly repeat, or perhaps transform, those relations. . . . That is the paradox and fascination of presence and absence, mimesis and transformation. (1990, p. 103)

A democratic education moves us to transformations implicit in searching for our own freedoms. However, Grumet reminds us of the lure of mimesis, and in *Bitter Milk* (1988), she draws a picture of teaching that reminds us to beware of our countertransferences, as well as our transferences in the transitional spaces of the classroom.

Teaching is no innocent pastime. Its stakes are much higher than suggested by many models of teaching. At issue are fundamental questions of identity and identification, and of freedom and responsibility. They are questions of desire, not only that of the students, but the desire of teachers to affirm their own identities through the identifications their students make with them.

The Kiss of the Spiderwoman, a film I have taught several times, illuminates some of these questions of identity and identification. The movie opens with two men alone in a prison cell. When one of them, Valentin, breaks from his studies of history, of politics, of economics, of revolution, the other, Molina, takes up movie narration. He recounts principally B movies: *Catpeople, The Enchanted Cottage,* and some Nazi propaganda film. When Valentin asks Molina how he remembers so many details, Molina acknowledges that he embroiders some, saying, "I want you to see it as I do."

Valentin is imprisoned for his revolutionary activities. He is a student, a teacher, a macho fighter, and macho lover of an illiterate peasant woman, having rejected, in service to this revolutionary commitment, the bourgeois intellectual woman whom he really loves. Molina is a window-dresser, a homosexual, and a mama's boy arrested for the attempted seduction of a young man. At first Valentin is scornful of both Molina and his movies. He really doesn't know how to read them or Molina. He attributes his failure to understand to Molina's confusing way of telling stories.

The two men are together in a prison cell because someone has put them there—the Authorities. Their intention is obvious and the plot simple. They want Valentin to betray his comrades in revolution. Careless of pain and privation, Valentin maintains his integrity. The police have promised Molina that he will be released from prison and sent home to his mother if he can get Valentin's secrets. Molina, knowing only his own affections, cares only for these and his own comforts. He readily agrees to comply with the authorities. He is to win Valentin's confidence by providing him with gifts of food and other luxuries denied political prisoners.

The story follows at least two trajectories. One is the trajectory of suspense. Will Valentin become suspicious of Molina? Will he wonder how it happens that he falls ill on prison food while Molina does not? Will he wonder where Molina gets the food and supplies he uses to nurse his cellmate back to health? When Molina is released from prison, will he carry Valentin's message to his comrades? And what will happen to him and Valentin if he does?

The second trajectory is that of desire. As the narrative moves through its various moments, through its narrated movies, its political arguments, its autobiographical revelations, an agony of desire builds. The movies, the arguments, the revelations maintain an exquisite tension. From moment to moment we shift our identification from the hysterical Molina to the paranoid Valentin, responding to and appropriating the desire of each as each comes to desire the other's desire. Eventually, they become lovers.

Central to their story is Valentin's coming to anticipate the moments of Molina's movies, his desiring the telling of the movies, and Molina's coming to desire the success of Valentin's political project—a desire that will insure his death. Questions of identity and identification are central to this story. As the two men talk about the movies, their conversation comes to settle on the question of which character each identifies with. Molina always identifies with the heroine; Valentin with the rational male. In *Catpeople* the rational male is a psychiatrist whose rationalism blinds him to the horror of his sexual desire for a women who turns into a vicious big cat, a blindness that entails his death. His rational resistance to the knowledge of the heroine's strangeness and of his own estrangement from his nonrational self is his undoing, and hers.

The Kiss of the Spiderwoman is neither a metaphor for education nor a model for the pedagogical relationship. Its trajectory is the trajectory of education through landscapes of learning. As we travel these landscapes, we enact the pedagogical relationship just as Molina and Valentin do. For the motive to teaching and learning both, the web within which education is embedded, is the same as the impulse to narrative—the desire to school the other's desire, and therein to situate and realize your own. I want you to see it as I do.

"I want you to see it as I do." If we take Maxine Greene's strategic position as stranger, we acknowledge this desire and try to put it in tension with another desire—the desire that students see things as they do. In analyzing movies, we cannot avoid discussion of the dynamics of identification. In doing so, we are forced to acknowledge the complex of desire embedded in our teaching. In academic texts, we can place the text between ourselves and our students and treat it as if it were an impersonal object, ignoring ourselves and our relation to the text, ignoring the fact that we want them to see it as we see it. At most we admit that we mediate relations between students and texts in the way that, say, that anonymous force "culture" is said to mediate responses to texts in certain representations of reading. The teacher may mediate relations to the text. Or the text may mediate the teacher's relationship to the student. However we may represent reading, we conceive our relations to texts as dyadic, and power as unidirectional and asymmetrical. Either the reader writes the text or the text writes the reader, for example. And the question of my wanting you to see it as I do is left unasked.

Most students come to the texts we teach as strangers. Greene teaches us that we must also come to those same texts as strangers, even though the syllabus is ours and filled with our questions, loaded with our desires. To teach our students to read so as to choose freedom and to choose freedom of humane action, we need to open landscapes to admit their questions, to change the landscape by honoring the identities they bring to the series of identifications they will make. To do this we must suspend our desire to want them to see it as we see it, even as we acknowledge that desire. When we do not do so, our own identities are overinvested in our students' identifying with ourselves, and the dialectic of freedom is subverted by monological interpretations through which we try to control the other's desire.

The current political debates in education, the culture wars in which values and identities serve as ammunition, largely avoid the question of desire, clinging to a mythic age of innocence in which identity *is* identification, and identification is mimetic of the teacher's desire. Whether we insist on the eternal verities of some sentimentalized canon or on the virtue of a politics of difference, we repress an infantile desire for narcissistic connection, thereby betraying an adult desire for transformative communities. We cannot be different in communities identical to ourselves. Nor can we be free and equal all by ourselves.

As teachers we must claim our desire, and at the same time we must transform that desire through taking up the stranger's position. Understanding that when we come to school we do not leave ourselves at home, we understand that our students also bring themselves to school. And so do our colleagues. But we cannot make our classrooms identical to anyone's home, not even our own, if we would transform our public worlds.

In her use of literature and the arts, Maxine Greene presents to us an America that is at once strange and familiar, a landscape of learning in which we may come together with passion and compassion to learn each day a multitude of ways of seeing it, and to learn to choose each day, freedom and responsibility.

REFERENCES

Greene, M. (1988). *The dialectic of freedom.* New York: Teachers College Press.

Grumet, M. R. (1988). *Bitter milk: Women and teaching.* Amherst: University of Massachusetts Press.

Grumet, M. R. (1990). On daffodils that come before the swallows dare. In E. W. Eisner & A. Peshkin (Eds.), Qualitative inquiry in education: The continuing debate (pp. 101–120). New York: Teachers College Press.

24

Maxine Greene and the Arousal of a Passionate Public

Frank Pignatelli

"All we can do is speak with others as eloquently and passionately as
we can about justice and caring and love and trust."

Maxine Greene
"The Passions of Pluralism"

Maxine Greene wants, somehow, to carry people over the threshold of
merely disinterested, rigorous critique and into a public space where mindful caring emerges as a necessary, vital response to dangerous situations.
She wants, somehow, to move people to recognize despair, to name loss
even as she calls to what is not yet, to the construction of public persons
nourished by moral imagining and distinguished by bold deeds. In so
doing, she poses for us the challenge of leading a complex public life.

Greene's is a poetic public discourse, a discourse that takes residence
in the lived lives of people real and imagined, in their felt realities and
in their desire. The images she presents—of people, characters, events,
bits of poems—pull the reader or listener in many directions, each image
suggesting a different set of circumstances, a different perspective; each
image demanding that the reader/listener "take on" that perspective, only
to be jostled by the next image and the next. Often they possess a visual
vibrancy, a lingering resonance. They congeal to provide the reader/lis-
tener with a compelling and, at times, dazzling mix of sharply drawn,
rich description and insight; insight that leads us to ask important, hard
questions about how we act toward, and with, others. We meet people
wanting to identify, resist, and break through perceived obstacles to
their freedom. We can hear in their voices our own fragility, our own
potential. They tug in multiple ways at the reader to pose, as she says,
the queer question. The queer question tests our compliance to things

as they are presently. It asks, "Shall I allow myself to be pulled by the undertow?" And as we ask such a question we situate ourselves at the margins of what we have come to regard as reasonable and acceptable. We poise ourselves for action.

Public spaces presume a locus of collectively wrought responses to matters of more than private concern. I think what is important, here, is how we bring ourselves to participate in the construction of a public discourse that might actually arouse an unease, an unsettledness. At the least, the voices Greene calls upon suggest to us that there is more to consider, imagine, and, of course, to do; and that it is possible to compose lives that move in mindful and compassionate ways toward the common.

We might think of schools as places where such efforts might be practiced and honored and where the public use of reasoning never veers very far from particular, local, personal, and immediate exigencies. Greene calls us to name ourselves as agents in a revitalized public space; a place crisscrossed, penetrated, and informed by an array of vantage points. As educators we know we need to be concerned with more than proving points and distilling and disseminating truth, but how, though, do we continue to find ways, together, to give voice to a less than precise unease about matters that speak to fundamental, enduring issues and commonly held aspirations? So many of Greene's texts and talks exhort us to do just this. And so she writes:

> We need to explore the ways in which the local and particular can feed into what we cherish as common, what we define and redefine as common ground. We need to discover how the particular can fertilize the common, how new perspectives and new visions can enrich the familiar landscapes, how the landscapes themselves can set off and highlight the new visions, enclose them in wider and wider frames. (1992, p. 8)

Greene's contribution to ways of thinking about our work is the compelling way she moves us to be continually challenged by this diffuse but palpable condition and to mine it for its potential to ignite both critical consciousness and acts of care. She helps us understand that what we determine is a public matter and how we speak of it ought never be fixed, never foreclosed; that our public discourse is a measure of our capacity to reawaken ourselves and begin to grasp what is not yet. I read and hear in Greene of a public sphere fertilized by our capacity to imagine kinder, more just, more satisfying ways of being together.

We risk, I believe, being caught in a numbing crossfire of public debate. We risk being reduced to spectators roused on occasion to take account, weigh evidence, and be done with it. We risk losing sight of or avoiding the kind of leavened discourse Greene suggests we must cultivate and take heed of. Public discourse must be about solving problems, forging solutions. But it must also probe and touch our civic conscience. Within the folds of such a discourse we might find ourselves both disturbed and exhilarated, anxious and hopeful, restless and energized. We might come to understand our responsibility to take an action, to renew our commitments, to name ourselves as being in the service of others.

Greene's writing is a strong critique of the efficacy of either the "hard data" of statistical correlation or the grand abstraction to invigorate and renew our public selves and public life. She reminds us that we serve others in the name of some enduring and fundamental human aspiration by remaining open and responsive to what is distinct and even peculiar about persons; and further, that we need to mine our own personal landscapes/memories even as we commit ourselves to wider, more diverse publics. "Reflecting back," she says, "I attend not only to and not first to principle. I attend to my grounded self, haunted by others around" (1995, p. 82). Too, Greene suggests to me that the vitality and freshness of our public discourse is a way of courting the personal commitment and assuring the individual resolve required to contest dangers shrouded by the benevolent but detached gaze, the faceless organization. It might carry and sustain our desire to question and offer a strong response to the lean-and-mean corporate ethos working its way not only through a lot of public school reform but the larger public spaces of the neighborhood and beyond. As former governor of New Jersey (and now college president) Thomas Kean put it, explaining why he chose not to run for a soon to be vacant senate position: "People are angry at one another [in Washington, D.C.], and use language aimed at destroying one another. It's so mean-spirited down there that it makes it difficult to sit down and find compromise to get things done for the public, to bring people together" ("Kean Rejects Senate Bid," 1995, B6). What we might call a "grounded" public space, a *passionate* public space, is both acknowledging that actual human lives hang in the balance amidst the rhetoric of bottom lines and budget tightening *and* setting ourselves on an equitable course of action on how to proceed with and distribute the resources we *do* have.

Greene turns to the novel *The Plague,* by Albert Camus, and to Dr. Rieux, one who chooses to fight the plague knowing, as Greene (1978) reminds us, that "everyone has the plague within him." Tarrou, a friend, reminds the doctor that "the good man, the man who infects hardly anyone, is the man who has fewest lapses of attention. And it needs tremendous will-power, a never ending tension of mind, to avoid such lapses" (p. 31). It is lapses of attention around which Greene constructs her vision of a public sphere: the public sphere envisioned as supple and respon-

sive, alert to dangers we too easily normalize and accept. And as a teacher
she challenges us to go about the business of cultivating the "teachable
capacity" (1984, p. 296) necessary to constitute a public that allows for
variety and multiple perspectives even as it moves toward creating common ground. Differences, as Greene speaks of them, are not simply reduced
to matters of personal taste and selective consumption. This way of understanding the particular occludes critical dialogue; it mitigates against
authentic encounters; it eats away at the hope of constructing a collective, democratically informed enterprise. The teachable capacity that
Greene wants us to think about and help realize is a profoundly important project for educators to attend to. It emerges, and is realized, in the
course of trying to figure out what is a public matter and what demands
our public attention and collective regard. When Greene (1988) talks about
being "eager to reaffirm the significance of desire along with the significance of thought and understanding" (p. 8), she helps us recognize that
intimate matters and public concerns are knotted, and that their disen-
tangling pulls at the threads that constitute the very fabric of real lives.
She offers us a vision of the public nourished by a commitment to persons as embodied, desiring beings endowed with a history, varied perspectives, and unique sets of circumstances.

The challenge to participate in the seeding of a revitalized public—
what, at one point she has called "participant thinking in the midst of
life, . . . relational thinking, contextualized thinking" (1992, p. 5)—lies
at the heart of recent efforts to remake schools. So much reason for hope,
it would seem, depends upon the moral dispositions and political alertness of persons, upon their ability to be publicly passionate about what
they see as unfair, as intolerable lacks of care. In New York City, the
place I am most familiar with, we are currently witnessing an era of
public school reform and revitalization that has not been matched since
the late 1960s. The stakes are high. Few would argue with the dismal
failure and anemic potential of the current system, which tantalizes
with a few shining examples of excellence while at the same time con-
dones the "deadening consequences," as Greene recently put it, of business as usual. Large scale, factory-driven models of schooling unanchored
to notions of community and uncommitted to experientially based modes
of inquiry are increasingly looking more and more incongruous, more and
more as public embarrassments. As of February 1993, the percentage of
graduates of the total school enrollment in seventeen public high schools
in the borough of the Bronx in New York City hovered between 2.0 and
7.3% per school. We are fast approaching a relatively small but critical
mass of schools in New York City that can challenge the grinding normalcy and myopic vision of schooling designed to merely monitor bod-

ies and content with a stale repertoire of logical but, by now, unjustifiably cautious adjustments to embedded failure. The mix of outside support and the active participation of diverse constituencies in the actual work of school reform is encouraging. New schools are being born and more are planned: schools that draw upon the thinking and insights Maxine Greene has offered and are enriched by her active support. Recently, she, with the help of others, formed The Center for Social Imagination, the Arts, and Education, a place where social issues can be thought through by both children and adults and alternatives shaped through their understanding of, and participating in, the arts. Indeed, people who do this hard, complicated work of reimagining and remaking schools might well recognize what they are doing and how they are thinking about their work in a question she posed recently: "If we can link imagination to our sense of possibility and our ability to respond to other human beings, can we link it to the making of community as well?" (1995, p. 38).

The shock of insufficiency has, for some, served as a stimulus for renewed, bold, courageous actions, as Maxine Greene has repeatedly and eloquently suggested it would.

REFERENCES

Greene, M. (1978). Teaching: The question of personal reality. *Teachers College Record, 80*(1), 23–35.

Greene, M. (1984). "Excellence," meanings and multiplicity. *Teachers College Record, 86*(2), 283–297.

Greene, M. (1988). *The dialectic of freedom.* New York: Teachers College Press.

Greene, M. (1992). Perspective and diversity: Toward a commonground. In F. Pignatelli & S. Pflaum (Eds.), *Celebrating diverse voices: Progressive education and equity* (pp. 1–19). Newbury Park, CA: Corwin Press.

Greene, M. (1993). The passions of pluralism: Multiculturalism and the expanding community. *Educational Researcher, 22*(1), 13–18.

Greene, M. (1995). *Releasing the imagination: Essays on education, the arts, and social change.* San Francisco: Jossey-Bass.

Kean rejects senate bid, citing a rise in meanness. (1995, August 31). *New York Times,* p. B6.

About the Contributors

WILLIAM AYERS is a school reform activist and Professor of Education at the University of Illinois at Chicago. He is co-director of the Small Schools Workshop and co-founder of the Annenberg Challenge in Chicago. He has written extensively about the importance of creating progressive educational opportunities in urban public schools, and his articles have appeared in *Harvard Educational Review*, *The Journal of Teacher Education*, *Teachers College Record*, and *The Nation*, among others. His books include *The Good Preschool Teacher* (1989), *To Teach: The Journey of a Teacher* (1993), *To Become a Teacher: Making a Difference in Children's Lives* (1995), all published by Teachers College Press. His latest books are *City Kids/City Teachers: Reports from the Front Row*, with Pat Ford (1996), and *A Kind and Just Parent: The Children of Juvenile Court* (1997).

JEAN ANYON has been Chairperson of the Education Department at the Newark Campus of Rutgers University, the State University of New Jersey, since 1982. She has published widely, with several of her articles reprinted many times in edited collections. Her most recent writing focuses on urban education and problems of school reform in the inner city, and these articles have appeared in *Teachers College Record*, *Curriculum Inquiry*, *Urban Education*, and *Access*. Her new book, *Ghetto Schooling: A Political Economy of Urban Educational Reform* (1997), is published by Teachers College Press.

LOUISE BERMAN is Professor Emerita, University of Maryland, College Park, and Adjunct Professor, University of Maryland, Baltimore County. Her field is curriculum theory and development, having obtained her master's and doctoral degrees from Teachers College, Columbia University. Among her interests are insights from creative thought and their meanings for education. She has collaborated with a small writing group on *Toward Curriculum for Being: Voices of Educators* (1991).

LEON BOTSTEIN has been president of Bard College, where he is also the Leon Levy Professor in the Arts and Humanities, since 1975. He formerly served as president of Franconia College, lecturer in history at Boston University, and special assistant to the president of the New York City Board of Education. He has published over 100 articles and reviews in leading newspapers and journals on such topics as music, higher education, history, and culture, and has contributed to many scholarly volumes. He is the author of *Judentum und Modernität: Essays zur Rolle der Juden in der deutschen und österreichischen Kultur 1848–1938* (Vienna: Böhlau, 1991), whose English translation is forthcoming with Yale University Press; *Jefferson's Children* (New York: Doubleday, 1997); and *Music and Its Public: Habits of Listening and the Crisis of Musical Modernism in Vienna, 1870–1914* (Chicago: University of Chicago Press, forthcoming).

DEBORAH P. BRITZMAN is an Associate Professor at York University, in North York, Ontario, just outside Toronto. She is the author of *Practice Makes Practice: A Critical Study of Learning to Teach* (1991) as well as the forthcoming book, *Lost Objects, Contested Subjects: Toward a Psychoanalytic Inquiry of Learning*, both published by State University of New York Press. Her current work focuses on psychoanalysis as helpful in its theories of learning and in its curiosity toward what is not learned.

LINDA DARLING-HAMMOND is William F. Russell Professor in the Foundations of Education at Teachers College, Columbia University, where she also co-directs the National Center for Restructuring Education, Schools, and Teaching. Her research, teaching, and policy work focus on issues of school reform, teaching, and educational equity. Her recent books include *Professional Development Schools: Schools for Developing a Profession* (editor; New York: Teachers College Press, 1994), *Authentic Assessment in Action: Studies of Schools and Students at Work* (with J. A. Ancess and B. Falk; New York: Teachers College Press, 1995), and *The Right to Learn* (San Francisco: Jossey-Bass, 1997).

KAREN ERNST is a teacher and coordinates teacher research in Westport, Connecticut public schools. She has taught at the University of Maine, Sacred Heart University in Fairfield, Connecticut, and is currently part of the New Hampshire Writing Program at the University of New Hampshire. In *Picturing Learning* (Heinemann 1994) she presents a framework for the integration of art and writing. *New Entriese* (1996), edited with Ruth Shagoury Hubbard, describes the many ways classroom teachers connect the visual arts to literacy instruction. Her latest book, *A Teacher's Sketch Journal: Observations on Learning and Teaching* (1997), describes how she connects art and writing in the elementary classroom.

MICHELLE FINE is Professor of Psychology at the City University of New York, Graduate Center. Her recent publications include *Becoming Gentlemen* (with Lani Guinier and Jane Balin, 1997), *Off-White: Readings on Society, Race, and Culture* (with Linda Powell, Lois Weis, and Mun Wong, 1996), *Chartering Urban School Reform: Reflections on Public High Schools in the Midst of Change* (1994), *Beyond Silenced Voices: Class, Race and Gender in American Schools* (1992), *Disruptive Voices: The Transgressive Possibilities of Feminist Research* (1992), and *Framing Dropouts: Notes on the Politics of an Urban High School* (1991). She has provided courtroom expert testimony for a number of national cases, including Shannon Richey Faulkner and the United States of America vs. James E. Jones, et al., for The Citadel. In addition, she works nationally as a consultant to parents' groups, community groups and teacher unions on issues of school reform. She recently was awarded the Janet Helms Distinguished Scholar Award, 1994.

NORM FRUCHTER was Program Advisor for Education at the Aaron Diamond Foundation from 1987 to 1996, and helped develop the New Visions Project that produced almost twenty new, small New York City public secondary schools. With several Academy for Educational Development (AED) colleagues, he wrote *New Directions in Parent Involvement*, AED, 1993. From 1983 to 1993, he served as elected member of the Brooklyn district school board, the last four years as President. In 1996, he helped found the Institute for Education and Social Policy at New York University, where he currently serves as Director. With Institute colleagues, he wrote *Hard Lessons: Public Schools and Privatization* (1996).

MADELEINE R. GRUMET is Dean of the School of Education at Brooklyn College, City University of New York, where she and her colleagues have developed a teacher education curriculum with extensive collaboration of liberal arts and education faculties. Her scholarly writings are in the field of curriculum theory, emphasizing arts and humanities curriculum, and the use of narrative in curriculum and educational research. She is the author of *Bitter Milk: Women and Teaching* (1988), a study of the politics of gender and reproduction and their relationship to the institutions of education and the disciplines of knowledge.

SANDRA HOLLINGSWORTH is Professor at San Jose State University. Here, as well as at University of California, Berkeley, and Michigan State University, she has designed and taught coursework in the areas of women's studies, curriculum theory, interdisciplinary social studies and critical literacy. Her current research interests are urban partnerships in teacher education, the praxis of "multiple literacies," and international social studies. Using the inquiry process of action research as a unifying theme across those areas, she has published two books, co-authored many articles with teachers, spoken extensively, and organized national and international conferences. She continues to conduct research into the longitudinal effects of her own teaching.

MARY-ELLEN JACOBS is Adjunct Instructor in the Palo Alto College Department of English, San Antonio, Texas. Her research blends phenomenological and feminist theories to consider the lived experiences of women as teachers and learners. She has published in *Harvard Educational Review*, *Qualitative Inquiry*, *Teaching Education*, and *Teaching and Learning*.

HERBERT KOHL has been a teacher and writer about education for over thirty-five years. In the course of this time, he has taught every level from kindergarten to graduate school. Among his written works are *Thirty-six Children, The Open Classroom, Reading, How To, I Won't Learn From You*, and *Should We Burn Babar?* Along with his wife, Judith, co-author, he's won the National Book Award for Children's Literature and the Robert F. Kennedy Book Award. He is currently a Senior Fellow at the Open Society Institute. He also continues to teach reading and writing to young people. At the center of Kohl's work there has been an abiding concern for equity and justice.

WENDY KOHLI is Associate Professor of Curriculum at Louisiana State University. She has known Maxine Greene since 1973 when she lived and worked in Manhattan as a junior high school teacher and traveled "uptown" from Greenwich Village to take courses with Maxine at Teachers College. She is the editor of *Critical Conversations in Philosophy of Education* (1995), has published widely in philosophy of education and educational foundations journals, and is an active member of the International Network of Philosophy of Education. She also maintains a passion for travel, combining work and play while visiting such diverse sites as New Zealand, Australia, Indonesia, Hungary, Russia, South Africa, and Israel.

CRAIG KRIDEL is Professor of Curriculum and Foundations and Curator of the Museum of Education at the University of South Carolina, where he teaches courses in history of education, educational biography, and curriculum narratives. He has edited and co-edited *Curriculum History* (1989), *The American Curriculum* (1994), *Teachers and Mentors* (1996), and *Writing Educational Biography* (1997). He serves as section editor of "Hermeneutic Portraits" in *JCT: The Journal of Curriculum Theorizing*. His research interests include progressive education, and he is currently completing a history of the Eight Year Study, the Southern Study, and the Secondary School Study.

PETER MCLAREN is Professor of Education and Cultural Studies, Graduate School of Education and Information Studies, University of California, Los Angeles. He is the author of numerous books and articles on the politics of liberation and critical pedagogy. His most recent books include *Critical Pedagogy and Predatory Culture* (1995), and *Revolutionary Multiculturalism: Pedagogies of Dissent for the New Millennium* (1997). His works have been translated into Portuguese, Spanish, French, German, Catalan, Polish, Hebrew, and Japanese. A social activist, he speaks frequently in Latin America and Europe.

MAUREEN MILETTA is an Associate Professor in the Department of Curriculum and Teaching at Hofstra University. Her dissertation, "Dewey and Teaching" was done under the aegis of Maxine Greene and Lawrence Cremin. She teaches courses in the language arts and the analysis of teaching. She is the coordinator of the Masters Program in Elementary Education and in 1993 was voted Teacher of the Year at Hofstra. Her research interests center on integrated curricula and multiage schools. Her book, *A Multiage Classroom: Choice and Possibility,* was published in 1996.

JANET L. MILLER is Professor in National-Louis University's National College of Education. She has served as Managing Editor of *JCT: The Journal of Curriculum Theorizing* since its inception in 1978. She is the author of *Creating Spaces and Finding Voices: Teachers Collaborating for Empowerment* (1990), which received the 1992 James N. Britton Award for Inquiry Within the English Language Arts from the National Council of Teachers of English. Her research and writing focus on intersections of curriculum and feminist theories, collaborative teacher-research and issues of school reform, and autobiographical forms of postmodern educational inquiry. She was elected Vice President of the American Educational Research Association for Division B—Curriculum Studies for the 1997–1999 term.

SONIA NIETO is Professor of Education, University of Massachusetts, Amherst. Her research focuses on multicultural and bilingual education, the education of Latinos, and Puerto Rican children's literature. Her books include *Affirming Diversity: The Sociopolitical Context of Multicultural Education* (1996, 2nd Ed.), and *The Education of Latinos in Massachusetts: Issues, Research and Policy Implications* (1993, with Ralph Rivera). She also has published many book chapters and articles in such journals as *Harvard Educational Review, The Educational Forum*, and *Multicultural Education*, among others. She has served on local, regional, and national advisory boards that focus on educational equity and social justice, and she has received numerous awards for her community service.

NEL NODDINGS is Lee L. Jacks Professor of Child Education at Stanford University. Her area of special interest is philosophy of education and, within that, ethics, moral education, and mathematics education. She is past president of both the Philosophy of Education Society and the John Dewey Society. In addition to nine books—among them, *Caring, Women and Evil, The Challenge to Care in Schools, Educating for Intelligent Belief or Unbelief*, and *Philosophy of Education*—she is the author of more than one hundred articles and chapters on topics ranging from the ethics of caring to mathematical problem solving.

JO ANNE PAGANO is Professor of Education at Colgate University. She teaches courses in philosophy of education, curriculum theory, and cultural studies. She is the author of *Exiles and Communities: Teaching in the Patriarchal Wilderness* (1990). Her work appears in many journals and anthologies.

FRANK PIGNATELLI is Chair of the Educational Leadership Department, Bank Street College of Education, Graduate School. He has written articles and co-edited books that deal with the politics of school reform, educational leadership, and progressive education. He received a Ph.D. from Teachers College in philosophy and education. Prior to coming to Bank Street College, he held a variety of positions as an educational administrator in the New York Public Schools. In 1974, as a junior high school teacher, he co-founded a school-within-a-school, The Pace Academy, with a group of fellow teachers, an experience that continues to nourish and inform his work.

WILLIAM F. PINAR teaches curriculum theory at Louisiana State University, where he serves as the St. Bernard Parish Alumni Endowed Professor. He also has served as the Frank Talbott Professor at the University of Virginia and the A. Lindsay O'Connor Professor of American Institutions at Colgate University (both visiting appointments), and taught at the University of Rochester, 1972–1985. He is the author of *Autobiography, Politics, and Sexuality* (1994), and the senior author of *Understanding Curriculum* (1995).

KATHLEEN REILLY is a teacher researcher at Edgemont High School in Scarsdale, New York. She teaches tenth and twelfth grade English and is conducting research on critical thinking and intelligent behavior. She is involved in staff development, teaching courses in literature and criticism at the Scarsdale Teachers Institute. A 1996 New York State "Educator of Excellence" she received the Phi Beta Kappa award for outstanding teaching and was a finalist for the New York State Teacher of the Year award. She has taught in the Department of Curriculum and Teaching at Hofstra University.

JONATHAN G. SILIN is the author of *Sex, Death, and the Education of Children: Our Passion for Ignorance in the Age of AIDS* (Teachers College Press, 1995). Currently a member of the Graduate Faculty at Bank Street College, he has served as a consultant to AIDS education and policy projects across the country. His research interests include contemporary childhood, early childhood curriculum, and gay/lesbian studies.

SHEILA SLATER has been a teacher for nearly three decades. She has been working with teenagers at the James Baldwin Center, a literacy program in the South Bronx since 1984. Prior to that, she worked for ten years with Vietnam-era veterans at Bronx Community College in a high school equivalency/college prep program. Her experience includes working in community-based adult education programs—and in English as a Second Language programs for newly arrived immigrants.

CANDY SYSTRA is Coordinator of Curriculum and Instruction and a teacher at the School for the Physical City. She has been involved with professional development for a decade, working as a teacher consultant for the New York City Writing Project and with several programs in the Alternative High School Division of the New York City Board of Education, as well as working with pre-service teachers at Lehman College (CUNY). She has been teaching for more than 25 years.

CARLOS ALBERTO TORRES is Professor, Graduate School of Education and Information Studies, University of California, Los Angeles. He is a political sociologist of education, and serves as Professor and Director, the Latin American Center, and is President-Elect, the Comparative International Education Society. Widely published in Spanish, Portuguese, and English, he is the author of more than one hundred research articles and thirty-two books.

MARK WEISS is the principal of School for the Physical City: An Expeditionary Learning Center—a New Visions 6th through 12th grade school educating young people to take care of and take charge of their city. He is also the founding principal of Bronx Regional High School, about to complete its 20th year of operation as an alternative for youngsters for whom the traditional, large urban high school has not worked. He is a social studies teacher and began his career at Brooklyn Technical High School in 1967.

Index